PRAISE FOR *Tomboy Bride*

"It's hard to describe just how much of a legacy Harriet Backus left with *Tomboy Bride* and her vivid and descriptive memories of Telluride and the surrounding region. . . a great read that does much to explain the unique character of Telluride." —Kiernan Lannon, Executive Director, Telluride Historical Museum, An Affiliate of the Smithsonian Institution

"#1 on the annual bestseller list at our store for over a decade. An amazing story." —Daiva Chesonis, Co-owner, Between the Covers Bookstore, Telluride, CO

"In her book Tomboy Bride, we experience her delight when she first inspected her 6-room 'palace,' with electricity and running water. She not only entertains, but also provides useful and keenly preserved details about the well-equipped company store; the segregated housing for the Chinese, Japanese and the white crews; and the crusher house and mill." —*The Northern Miner*

". . . an interesting book that records the hardships, tragedies and triumphs of a young woman in the colorful era of the mining boom." —*Annals of Wyoming*

". . . Charming book . . . entertaining and informative." —*The New Mexican*

TOMBOY BRIDE

Harriet Fish Backus

TOMBOY BRIDE

One Woman's Personal Account of Life in the Mining Camps of the West

50TH ANNIVERSARY EDITION
With a new foreword by Pam Houston

WEST
MARGIN
PRESS®

First published by Pruett Publishing Company in 1977.

First printing of the 50th Anniversary Edition 2019.

This edition
ISBN 9781513262055 (softbound) | 9781513262062 (hardbound) | 9781513262079 (e-book)

Library of Congress Control Number is on file.

Printed in China.
23 22 21 20 19 1 2 3 4 5

West Margin Press
is an imprint of

WEST
MARGIN
PRESS®

WestMarginPress.com

Proudly distributed by Ingram Publisher Services.

WEST MARGIN PRESS
Publishing Director: Jennifer Newens
Marketing Manager: Angela Zbornik
Editor: Olivia Ngai
Design & Production: Rachel Lopez Metzger

TO MY HUSBAND,
THE GREATEST OF MANY BLESSINGS.

Sharing these experiences with him has been the
main reason for the happiness I found in them.

CONTENTS

FOREWORD by PAM HOUSTON *xi*

PART I: The San Juans *1*

PART II: Britannia Beach *125*

PART III: The Heart Of Idaho *161*

PART IV: Leadville, City In The Clouds *221*

EPILOGUE *259*

AFTERWORD by ROBERT G. WALTON *261*

TIMELINE *267*

BOOK CLUB DISCUSSION QUESTIONS *268*

FOREWORD

These vertebrae of the monster included the giants Uncompahgre,
Wetterhorn, Red Cloud, Sneffles, Wilson, Sunshine, and Lizard Head,
each one higher than fourteen thousand feet, soaring to heaven like spires,
and surrounded by peaks of eleven, twelve and thirteen thousand feet.
They held our gaze through the snow falling in large soft flakes,
fuzzing our faces, whitening the robes.

When I wrote the first foreword to Tomboy Bride, back in 1996, I was
relatively new to the San Juan Mountains. Three years prior,
I had dared myself to buy a 120-acre homestead very near the
headwaters of the Rio Grande, less than 50 miles as the crow flies,
(but more than 200 as the car drives) from the Tomboy Mine above
Telluride where Harriet Fish Backus spent the most memorable
days of her life. Memories of the mining days are all around us on
my side of the mountain too, in the ruined ore houses and caved-
in shafts, in the names of the town's businesses: Kentucky Belle
Market, Tommyknockers Tavern, and Amethyst Emporium, and
in the stories of the miners, who are descendents of other miners,
and who still worked the mines here until they closed in 1985.
In my first foreword I confessed to a fantasy that one day, while
cleaning out the barn or digging in the garden, I might uncover
a diary or a bundle of letters, some written message left from the
past that neither time nor weather nor packrats had carried away.

My ranch was homesteaded by a man named John Pinckley,
who left it to his son Bob. Bob lived on the ranch from the time
he was a young boy until his death in 1966. Bob's cabin was
in decent shape when I bought the place, but over the years it
began to rise up from its own center and eventually threatened

to split at the top like an over-baked cupcake. I traded my 1964 F100 truck to a local contractor named RJ Mann for a new foundation. When RJ pulled up the floorboards, he found the treasure trove I'd been hoping for: messages from the past in the form of an old harmonica, a pipe, a pair of scissors, a pocket watch, empty tins of tobacco, several glass marbles, each of them a different shade of green. There was a well-preserved insert from a package of Super Anahist Antihistamine Cough Syrup with Vitamin C, several yellowed card stock receipts from a company in Minneapolis where Pinckley shipped the furs from his trapping business (including one for the sale of a house cat), a label from Prince Albert Crimp Cut in a can, and two beautifully rendered drawings of belted kingfishers, one that had graced a 25-yard container of Martin's Highest Quality Enameled fishing line: (test 21 pounds), and the other a "collectable" insert from a box of Arm and Hammer Baking Soda. Objects from the past hold the energy of their owners, and finding them feels like getting a letter from a long-lost friend. Buying the ranch had always felt less like a decision and more like a calling. For as long as I can remember, belted kingfishers have been my favorite bird.

The last time I read *Tomboy Bride* I was still in the honeymoon stage of owning my ranch, in love with the star-filled nights and silent mornings, with the sun making diamonds on snow-covered pastures, with soft September days when the hills are bursting with color, with the cleanest air you have ever tasted, and the hypnotizing motion of a hundred acres of gamma grass in the wind. A couple of decades later I know the other side of the story: the 30-below-zero-not-counting-the-wind-chill mornings, frozen pipes and dead batteries, soul-crushing drought years with no pasture to speak of, sick horses in the middle of the night, a bear who came for my lambs and then came again, the ashes of a few good dogs scattered across the pasture. I also know that the ranch has sunk so much deeper under my skin, not in spite of but because of how hard it can be to live here. As the list of challenges and heartaches lengthen, I grow even more committed to the place.

This must have been how it was for Harriet Fish Backus, whose love of her time living at the Tomboy Mine borders on the ecstatic, even though the delivery mule showed up only once a month and then without any fruits or vegetables, and the fire went out more often than not leaving the food to freeze to ice blocks, and there was something called the Elephant Slide between her and town, between her pregnant self and her doctor, and each time she passed under it, it could have buried her in tons of snow in the blink of an eye. Couple those adventures with the satisfaction of putting a Thanksgiving meal on the table for a gang of hungry miners, with the stupefying beauty of the morning after a storm when the world is all azure and sun-spangled snow, with the deep pleasure of a cup of good tea on a rare becalmed afternoon, with the good company of a husband she loved and a pack of robust girlfriends who, among other things, started the world's highest branch of the YMCA. It wouldn't have been the right life for everyone, but it was exactly the right life for Harriet Fish Backus.

Of the 203 homesteaders who staked claims in my valley—the Upper Rio Grande—in the late 1800s, 25 were women. John Pinckley may have filled out the paperwork to stake the claim on my ranch, but since he was often distracted by alcohol and women, it was his daughter Myrtle, Bob's big sister, who did the hard physical labor of proving up on the place enough to secure the deed. The fact that her father's name remained on the title makes a person question the accuracy of that number 25. I'll never meet Myrtle, and there is no one left alive who even knew her, but I can feel her winking at me from between the pages of *Tomboy Bride*.

Living the joys and challenges on my own homestead for 26 years has left me more in awe of Harriet Fish Backus than ever. She stood strong and optimistic in relentlessly dire circumstances, and was driven by love for her husband and her compassion for others in all things. I hope I am not merely projecting when I say I believe it was her love of the land, her love of the Rocky Mountains in general and the high San Juans in particular, where she found strength and solace and, maybe above all, a constant and ever-expanding wonder. I understand now, on a cellular level, how the tragedies that befell her in her perilous perch on the side of that mountain only served to intensify her love for it. I share with her an unending love for these most magnificent mountains, and understand that I am lucky beyond all reason to call them my long-term home.

PAM HOUSTON

FOREWORD TO THE 1996 EDITION

*But on the warmest days of summer, against the blue of the
illimitable sky, and eternal white coronet crowned the pinnacles
stretched toward the southwest. Long snow banners,
woven by winds waved farewell as they disappeared.*

When you live, as I do, at 9,000 feet in southwestern Colorado just
outside what once was one of the world's most famous silver mining
towns, history is all around you. I can't go into Creede to pick up
my mail without passing half a dozen crumbling shacks, mills,
and ore houses—many of them built in the 1890s and decaying
slowly in the high, dry air until they are once again part of the
earth. I can't enter a shop in town whose name doesn't remind
me of the mines that made my town famous: the Kentucky Belle,
the Holy Moses, the Amethyst, the Happy Thought. I can't even
take my dogs for a walk across my property without passing the
homesteaders' grave site and sending them a word of thanks for
claiming this land and clearing it, long before my mother's mother
was a gleam in her mother's eye.

I've often had a fantasy that one day, while cleaning out the
barn or digging in the garden, I might uncover a diary or a pack of
letters, some written message left from the past that neither time
nor weather nor pack rats have carried away. Then I would learn
what life was like for the woman who lived on this land a hundred
years before me, a woman who was the wife of a rancher or a
miner, somebody who believed a good life and untold riches were
to be found in this valley tucked under the Continental Divide.

Discovering Tomboy Bride was like finding that diary. And
though Harriet Fish Backus lived with her husband two valleys

to the west of where I make my home (about 35 miles away as the crow flies, about 200 miles by the paved road), we share the magic of the high San Juan Mountains—in my biased opinion, the grandest and most awe-inspiring mountains in all the Lower Forty-eight.

The largest part of the book takes place in that 11,800-foot valley that hangs above Telluride, where the Tomboy Mine operated successfully until 1925. The chapters that take place at the Tomboy are full of the kinds of stories you'd expect from a mining town: mules and horses plummeting to their death over rocky precipices; gunfights and explosions; bunkhouse pranks and barroom brawls; the rugged lawman who after being brought to trial and acquitted in a double murder asked, "What did Kammer mean in his testimony when he said I used my 'prerogative' as a deputy? Hell, man, I used my gun!"

What makes this book unique is that it tells the much less often told tales of a woman's life in a mining town. Tales of the difficulties of feeding your family when the delivery mule only shows up once a month, and even then there's not a single fresh fruit or vegetable to be had; and of when the fire goes out all the food freezes to ice blocks; and of baking at that altitude, which is always hit or miss. Tales of small children with fragile lungs and low immunities, of being pregnant and scared in a town without a doctor and something called the Elephant Slide between you and the hospital, and of the danger that any time you passed under it you could be buried in snow in a blink of an eye. Tales of falling head first into eight feet of snow when you stepped just too far to the right out your front door and of the pie you were taking to your neighbor that went sailing. Tales of the woman who sent her dog to the bunkhouse to carry home her mail in his mouth; of candlelit canned food dinners inside shacks that the wind was threatening to blow over; of how in spite of the winds and the snow and the isolation, one woman opened a Sunday School.

From Telluride we follow Harriet and her husband George to the rugged coast of British Columbia, where life revolved around the steamer Britannia that brought the mail and the food once a day; and from there to Elk City, Idaho, and a cabin forty miles from the end of the road; and from there back to Colorado, to Leadville, this time, where the cast of shady characters in town were more priceless than the minerals left in the mines. Harriet faces every challenge, change, and hardship with a practical determination and an unending optimism that even the most spirited modern adventuress would have to stand in awe of.

Harriet Fish Backus's life took her many places, but her heart never quite left the rugged mountain trails of the high San Juans. I know just how she feels. I am writing this foreword in a lovely house in California, where I'm teaching for a semester. It's a sunny March day. I can see a bunch of water birds on the small bay out my window. The beach is only a half a block away, and any reasonable person might call where I am paradise. At home right now it's most likely snowing sideways, delaying the start of mud season for another two weeks, and the March wind is howling the way it likes to do until neither man nor animal can hear himself think. And none of that information is keeping me from being so homesick that I can tell you without even getting out the calculator that I have 10 weeks, or 72 days, or 1,728 hours, or 41,472 minutes until I get to go home to the high San Juans. The people in my valley call it the Creede Curse, that once you live in that country it'll never let go of you. But if Harriet Fish Backus were alive, I think she'd call it a blessing.

PAM HOUSTON

PART I
THE SAN JUANS

Harriet Fish Backus, 1907.

George Backus, 1904.

CHAPTER 1

I was late for my wedding—so late that the date on three hundred engraved announcements had to be forever wrong. When my sweetheart of high school days telegraphed from Telluride, Colorado, saying he had found a position as assayer at the Japan Flora Mine, he asked me to meet him in Denver to be married. This caused considerable consternation in my family.

"Hattie, I don't think you should go alone," said my father with a worried look. "Young girls like you don't travel by themselves."

"I'm not afraid of her traveling alone," said my mother, "but it wouldn't be proper for her to be unchaperoned in Denver."

Working for the Telegraph Company after the San Francisco earthquake, preceded by two years of teaching school, had not conditioned me for "wild adventuring." But since George could not leave a new position for the trip to California, I must go to him.

A graduate from the University of California School of Mines, George had been on guard duty in San Francisco after the earthquake and fire of 1906 which closed the schools. Released from that, he went to Colorado looking for work. Now he was ready to take a wife, and, since his uncle had arrived in Denver, my parents finally consented to our marriage away from home.

"Will arrive November twentieth. Arrange for marriage that day," I telegraphed, for that was the twenty-ninth anniversary of my mother's and father's marriage.

As he had suggested, I packed warm clothing, heavy blankets, linens, and a red and white tablecloth which, according to all the mining stories I had read, was indispensable, the flat silver that had been a wedding gift from my parents, and a few of my precious books. The railroad official assured me that by leaving Oakland

3

on the eighteenth I would arrive in Denver at eleven o'clock on the morning of the twentieth.

"You're sure there'll be no delay?" I asked, as though he could foresee the future.

"There won't be any heavy storms this time of year. Don't worry. You'll be there on time," he assured me good naturedly.

It was a day of blue and gold, typical of Oakland in November, when my farewells were said and my big adventure began. There were few passengers and I was the only woman in the coach. The elderly conductor, seeing me alone, seemed solicitous. Late that evening we pulled into Nevada where a gold strike had aroused excitement. At the Reno depot we heard loud shouts of greetings and farewells. Into the coach swaggered a tall, bronzed miner with the air of a man who had "struck it rich." The collar of his heavy coat was turned up to his hat brim. He stood and surveyed the passengers as if to make certain they were aware of his importance, and I turned my head to avoid his too prolonged stare.

In the morning he presented me with a rose taken from the dining car. I said, "Thank you," and turned away. At noon I refused his invitation to be his guest at dinner. After several more rebuffs he snarled, "You and I would get along like a cat and dog."

"Not as well," I snapped, thinking of reporting him to the conductor.

In more amiable mood he began to coax me. "I have a sister in Denver who is meeting me at the train. Will you let us drive you around the city?"

"No. I am being met there by a gentleman," I snapped again.

Our voices carried and a young man seated across the aisle rose and strolled to where I was and sat down beside me.

"Nevada's an interesting state, isn't it," he began as if we were long acquainted.

"It certainly is," I replied, and as we continued a conversation casually, the miner left abruptly.

"My name is Pinkerton," said my rescuer pleasantly. "I am on my way to Ohio to be married. I saw that you were being annoyed and decided to interfere."

"Thank you very much. Tomorrow I am to be married." I took the card he offered and tucked it into my purse. It remains among my cherished souvenirs.

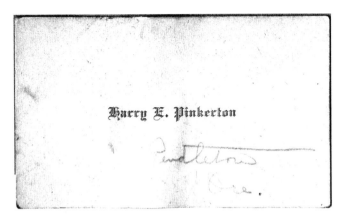

Harry Pinkerton's calling card.

At Ogden, Utah, everything was covered with lovely, downy white as I stepped off the train for a short walk.

"My goodness," I remarked to the conductor, "what a heavy frost."

"That," he replied with a superior tone, "is snow!" I had encountered the beautiful stuff in which I was to wallow for many years.

We reached Green River, Wyoming, in the evening and I was early asleep. Waking in the morning, I was aware of an ominous quiet, no chugchug of the locomotive, no clacketyclack of the coach wheels, no lonely "whoooo" of the whistle, no anything. Perhaps we had reached Cheyenne. We were due there this morning. Surely, very soon I would be in George's arms. Yet something seemed very wrong even to my inexperienced perceptions. Dressing hurriedly I called out, "Porter, where are we?"

Unconcernedly he answered, "Green River, Ma'am. Just where we were last night, waiting for the mail from a branch line that was delayed."

Like marbles spilled on a polished floor my plans scattered in all directions. At that moment we should have been in Cheyenne leaving for Denver. We still had four hundred miles to cover in thirteen hours, and that would have been really speeding.

Tears stung my eyes but before I dried them came faintly the call "All aboard!" and the wheels began to grind and roll. I turned to the window to hide my tear-stained face. Then I became aware that my name was being called . . . "Miss Harriet Fish." The conductor handed me a telegram which I feverishly tore open. Already George was aware of the delay.

"Under the circumstances are you willing to go directly to the minister?" he had wired. I wrote my reply on a telegram blank, "Yes, it must be tonight." I begged the conductor to send my message as soon as he possibly could.

That day I received three telegrams from George. The Reverend Dr. Coyle would wait for us and perform the ceremony. At seven we reached Cheyenne and boarded a special two-coach train waiting to run us to Denver. Barring another delay we would be there in four hours. But after a steady run of thirty minutes, we pulled on to a siding and stopped! I hunted for a conductor and abruptly asked, "What now?"

"We are waiting to give the right of way to the regular northbound train due through here any minute," he explained.

One hour later it whizzed by. That delay determined the date of our wedding. At one in the morning I stepped off the train for George's eager greeting. Together at last, our hearts pounding with happiness, we hugged each other tightly, the strain of the unpredictable trip momentarily forgotten. From the depot we drove to the Hotel Savoy where the bridal suite had been reserved. To this I retired a very exhausted and lonely bride-to-be, while George joined his friend, and best-man-to-be for the night.

Next morning he hurried to the jeweler to have the date corrected in the wedding ring, arrange for the ceremony, and order dinner sent up to our suite. Meanwhile, I spent the time laying out my wedding clothes.

My new corsets were too tight and the lacings had to be loosened. The silk feather-stitching of my long flannel petticoat recalled to mind my mother's patient needlework on my simple trousseau, consisting of three of everything. The white petticoat had three ruffles and I made certain the button on the waistband was secure. A white corset cover with eyelet embroidery and white drawers with ruffles were carefully smoothed free of suitcase wrinkles. Black lisle stockings were more expensive than the customary cotton ones, but recklessly I had purchased three pairs to wear with my shiny patent leather shoes accented by pearl gray buttons.

Mr. and Mrs. A. L. Fish

announce the marriage of their daughter

Harriet Anna

to

Mr. George Stitzel Backus

on Tuesday, November the twentieth
nineteen hundred and six
Denver, Colorado

The engraved marriage announcement card.
Because of a train delay, the announcement has the wrong date.

Mother had packed my wedding suit with tissue paper, and
while unfolding it my hands trembled. It had cost such a big share
of money saved from my school teacher wages of sixty dollars a
month. I smoothed the satin-like reseda broadcloth, and the lovely
jacket trimmed with gold and green passementerie that, once
glimpsed, had become irresistible.

By my watch, time was flying, so I began dressing. Three
times I coiled my hair and pinned it on the top of my head before

being satisfied. George had often said it was my two long braids of hair that first won his heart on a well-remembered day in high school. The blouse of ecru net fluffed out of the front of my jacket. Petticoats and skirt were ankle length and correct according to Armand Calleau of the exclusive San Francisco shop where I bought my suit.

From a hat box came my crowning glory. Oh, that hat! White felt with a turned-up brim faced with black velvet and topped with a curving white ostrich plume, the ultimate in style. No bride, ever before, was so proud of her bridal outfit.

Smoothing on the fingers of my gloves I gazed into the mirror hoping George would be pleased. And so he was when he arrived with the ring and a velvet box containing a gorgeous sunburst of diamonds and pearls. With shaking hands I pinned it at my breast.

"The carriage and my uncle are here," he said.

In the manse of one of Denver's splendid churches, George placed on my finger the wide gold band which never has been taken off, and Dr. Coyle said, "I now pronounce you man and wife."

We stayed in Denver until Saturday night. I was so conscious now of being Mrs. George Backus that I felt as if all who saw me must be aware of it. George bought me a pair of pretty russet-colored, high-button shoes, and it was a long time before I became reconciled to his extravagance; five dollars for a pair of shoes!

"I'm not going to tell you anything about how and where we will live," he said. "I'll let you find out for yourself." He smiled, as if picturing the somersault my life was to take. "But I think you should buy a cookbook for high altitudes."

He was so right. I needed a cookbook, any kind, because I was unable to cook a meal at sea level in Oakland. For the first time he handed me some money. Into my mind marched Grandmother Fish with her stern admonitions about propriety. I had to remind myself that now I was a wife, thereby permitted to do so shocking a thing as to accept money from a man. *The Rocky Mountain Cookbook* became my guide, philosopher, and daily companion.

George insisted that I buy warm gloves, long tights, and "arctics." I strenuously objected to the latter—heavy overshoes with thick rubber soles and high cloth tops fastened with buckles.

"I wouldn't want to be seen in such things!" I protested.

"Without them your feet and shoes would be soaking wet. All

the ladies wear them. Look." Certainly I could see several well-dressed women with them on. So, reluctantly I bought a pair of the hideous things and suffered whenever I looked down at my feet, which looked gigantic to me in the arctics.

On Saturday night we left Denver, arriving the following morning in Salida where we changed to a narrow-gauge railway. There had been no dining car on either train and no time to eat at a depot restaurant. George dashed to a store and returned with a can of sardines and some stale soda crackers for our honeymoon breakfast.

Now we were rolling through the Black Canyon of the Gunnison River that opened into its lovely valley and on to Montrose. There we changed to another narrow-gauge railway. When we reached Ridgway Junction it was dark and cold. *The Stub*, a small dingy train, was to carry us to Telluride and proved to be a mere foretaste of what was ahead. The engine, baggage car, and dismal passenger car were relics of a past generation. We mounted two steps from the small station platform and with three additional passengers stumbled along the aisle. At each end of the car dirty oil lamps shed a smoky light on adjacent seats.

With great effort the small locomotive shuddered and jerked into motion on a narrow, shaky roadbed. Puffing and straining it climbed higher into the piedmont of the lofty San Juan mountains. The cold increased rapidly and we were thankful for a potbellied stove at one end of the car. Also, I began to appreciate my warm gloves and the arctics. Such cold was new to me.

Night had fallen when we reached Telluride, named for the ore *tellurium*, a silver-white metal having properties like sulphur found near gold or silver-bearing ore. Telluride was the terminus of the miniature line which entered the gulch through the only break in the surrounding mountains. We were on the floor of the canyon but walking in the darkness along the path to the only hotel we could feel the precipitous walls closing us in. The Sheridan, a plain brick structure which had seen turbulence and mob violence, was quiet. A lonely clerk sat behind a desk in the bare lobby, dismal and dimly lighted. As I climbed the stairs a tugging sensation in my chest was a reminder that we had risen in the world 8,765 feet.

Our cheerless hotel room contained a double bed, a dresser, one chair, and the usual stand with a water pitcher and basin. Wearily falling into bed, we found the sheets cold and damp.

Next morning, in his quiet way, George said he would have to make arrangements for our trip to the mine.

"I'll show you the stores and you can buy some food, not very much, because we'll have a big order sent up to us," he admonished.

Order food! I had not the faintest idea about what brands to choose, what cuts of meat, what quantity of anything we would need, but I had to make a start and began at Mr. McAdams's meat market.

"A steak, a slice of ham, and some lamb chops," I requested.

"Sorry. All I have is mutton," said Mr. McAdams. Spotting me as a newcomer he asked my name.

"Miss Fish," I stated glibly and in quick confusion changed it to "Mrs. Backus." At his knowing smile I felt my cheeks grow hot with embarrassment, turned and promptly left his store. At Kracow's I bought what seemed adequate supplies for a few days.

It was still early so I walked on to view Telluride and its surroundings. The streets appeared strangely deserted and silent. Then I saw a hearse approaching slowly followed by two lines of men marching sedately. A funeral, undoubtedly of a prominent member of the community. At store fronts the proprietors stood watching as the cortege wound its solemn way to the small cemetery on the hillside. Thus the men of Telluride paid homage and said farewell to the leading madam of their underworld, in her way the town's best known citizen.

I continued my walk toward the end of town, half a mile away. The road ran past the mill of the Liberty Bell Mine and a short distance farther to the Smuggler Union, then the little settlement of Pandora where it abruptly ended at the back wall of the canyon.

Partway up the slope, sturdy pines and firs stood proudly in spite of their precarious root-hold in crevices of rock.

Above Pandora, in a rift between the peaks, the deep snows fed a ribbon of icy cold water which, falling to a rocky ledge, leaped headlong into the cascade of Bridal Veil Falls. Now the bordering trees, sprayed by wind-carried mists, were shrouded with tiny glittering icicles while high above soared the majestic spires of Mt. Telluride and Mt. Ajax, magnificent and austere.

The waters of Bridal Veil and nearby Ingram Falls fed the San Miguel River flowing through the gorge it had grooved past Telluride and the plateau to the west, an area containing vanadium ore—rich in radium.

On the trail approaching Smuggler Union Mine.

So high were the walls on the three sides of the valley and so narrow the floor between them that in winter the sunlight reached the little town only a few hours of the day. By mid-afternoon the purple shadows of cliffs dropped a pall over the rugged settlement. Its citizens included respectable miners and their wives, as well as the lawless ne'er-do-wells and their ilk. Near the main street huddled the houses of prostitutes. All night carousing in the saloons and gambling dens was evident from the raucous shouting and cursing. Telluride was only shortly past its wildest days.

Two years previous terror had reigned. Unruly mobs had gathered and rumors had spread that the miners on strike threatened to poison the water supply and blow up the town. A bomb had been thrown at the home of Buckley Wells, manager of the Smuggler. Fortunately, being wrapped in furs and sleeping on his porch, he escaped with no worse injuries than a ruptured ear drum. Although the town seemed quiet now, there remained an uneasy feeling of watchful waiting for further violence. I returned, this morning, to the hotel as though I had been on an exploring trip.

CHAPTER 2

"The sled will be here at ten o'clock," George informed me. "Wear your warmest clothes. It's a long, cold ride. And let's eat again because we may not reach the mine until late afternoon."

Bundled in a dark-blue wool dress with red piping on the collar and cuffs, a full ankle-length skirt, two petticoats and tights to keep my legs warm underneath, fleece-lined gloves, a soft, black sealskin cap with earflaps, surely I would never feel cold. George was equally bundled in his woolens, and under his hat a stocking cap covered his ears.

It was snowing when the sled arrived. Bill Langley, the driver for Rodgers Brothers' Stable, tall and rugged, looking huge in a long, heavy mackinaw, greeted us.

"Good mornin', folks. Sure hope you're dressed warm. Ever been in the mount'ns before?"

"I haven't," I said, "and I'm overwhelmed by the grandeur."

"Wonderful country, this here," he agreed and tucked a heavy fur robe around George and me as we snuggled close together in the back seat of the sled. Wrapping himself in a fur robe, Bill gathered the reins, slapped the horses on the rump and soon I was to enjoy my first sleigh ride.

We turned off the main road at an easy trot and glided straight toward the foot of the mountain only a few hundred yards distant. The road clung to the rock wall, zigzagging back and forth around ravines and overhanging rocks. I grew tense. The horses slowed to a walk as the increasing altitude made breathing more difficult. Steeper and ever steeper we ascended, and deeper plunged the gorge beside us. An occasional glimpse was all I dared take. Only a few inches separated the sled from the menacing drop below. I

The Tomboy in the basin with twenty feet of perpetual snow on the peaks.

kept my gaze on the peaks beyond the canyon and the wall of rock we skirted within arm's length. George explained the clicketyclack that we heard was the sound of ore-laden buckets passing over supports on the tram towers that carried the cables.

Biting cold began to penetrate our wrappings. My toes and fingers were getting stiff, and there was a long pull ahead with no turning back.

"We're near'n a spring where I water the horses," Bill drawled. The poor things were panting, their nostrils puffing in and out like a bellows. As if understanding that word "water," the animals swung the sled so sharply that it grazed the edge of the abyss. In the bend of a hairpin turn they stopped, aware that this was their last chance for a drink on the long pull. The road was covered with ice as was the spring.

Unfastening an axe from the side of the sled, Bill cautiously inched his way across the sheeted ice and began chopping the mouth of the spring.

"This is the most treacherous spot on the road," he told us, " 'cause ye see, when ya get down to the water there, some of it always spills over and freezes. Gets mighty slippery for the horses."

With their heads lowered, the jaded animals patiently waited for their refreshing drink. When again we were moving, I clutched George's hand tightly for reassurance.

"We'll soon be at the tunnel," Bill assured us. He knew intimately every quirk of every bend along this ledge that had been hacked from the mountain walls. Just where it jutted out on a shelf overhanging the canyon, we swerved into a tunnel, cut through solid rock. It was a curved archway, thirty feet long, barely high enough to miss the heads of the horses or loaded pack mules.

As we emerged, the awesome grandeur burst full force upon us and almost took my precious breath away. Far across the gulch, the jagged heads of giants pierced the leaden sky. Pointing with his whip toward the mighty pinnacles, Bill asked, "Ma'am, can ya see that basin a little ways down the slope of the farthest peak, up high there, near the top? Well, there's a little settlement there where you're goin' to live."

George let Bill do the talking because this was his home. These were his beloved mountains and pride in them glowed in his eyes and warmed his voice. More traveled men than Bill Langley had been spellbound by their magnificence. H. H. Bancroft, great historian of the West, had written in the phrases of yesteryear about the spell cast by mountains upon nature lovers.

"Nothing interests many of us like the mountains which will always draw men from the ends of the earth that they may climb as near to Heaven as may be, by their rocky stairs." Of these San Juans he wrote, "It is the wildest and most inaccessible region in Colorado, if not in North America. It is as if the great spinal column of the continent had bent upon itself in some spasm of earth, until the vertebrae overlapped each other, the effect being unparalleled ruggedness and sublimity, more awful than beautiful."

These vertebrae of the monster included the giants Uncompahgre, Wetterhorn, Red Cloud, Sneffles, Wilson, Sunshine, Lizard Head, each one higher than fourteen thousand feet, soaring to heaven like spires, and surrounded by peaks of eleven, twelve, and thirteen thousand feet. They held our gaze through snow falling in large soft flakes, fuzzing our faces, whitening the robes. Trees were sparse and scrawny. Shrubless expanses prevailed. We had climbed to ten thousand feet but the

Part of the surrounding range, including the Big Elephant slide.

grade was less steep, a great relief to the horses and to me because I suffered, hearing them panting for breath and seeing their flanks heaving with each step. Entering the Big Bend, as it was called, they picked up speed as though anxious to reach journey's end.

But the relief of this half-mile curve ended as we entered Marshall Basin where the only settlement was Smuggler, a cluster of shacks that boasted the "highest Post Office in the world." It was housed in a tiny store which, with a blacksmith shop and the upper terminal of the tram, perched precariously on a ledge overhanging a chasm that formed the outlet of the Smuggler Union Mine. Just above the boardinghouse was the tunnel through which ore from the mine was loaded into the tram-buckets. As the sled glided silently past, we heard the rattle of buckets starting their downward journey over the depths from which we had just climbed.

Snow fell heavily from the darkening sky. The horses tugged and strained to break through the soft encumbering fluff into which they sank deeper and deeper. Patient until now, Bill began urging them on through the blinding white drapery of snow. We could sense his foreboding of trouble ahead. The team made little headway and presently stopped. Leaving the sled, Bill forged ahead and after a long time, returned, plodding waist-deep through the snow.

"A stroke of luck for us, folks," he said, scooping snow from his face with a heavily gloved hand. "If we had got here a little sooner it would've been the end of us. Part of that damned Elephant has slid. That's the Big Elephant just ahead. Worst thing in the San Juans! Look at that slope. It's steep, steep as hell! Snow piles up on the peak, gets so heavy it can't hang on then lets go all of a sudden. My God! Talk about cannons, what a roar! Nothin' worse than an avalanche. Got to watch the cussed things all winter. If any more snow had come down, we couldn't have got through tonight, fer sure."

Through chattering teeth I asked, "How *can* we get through?"

"Oh, the Tomboy's already sent a crew to shovel enough away fer the packtrain that's stalled on the other side. We'll jus' have to wait. No room to turn 'round and you can't walk back to Smuggler without snowshoes. Four years ago we had a dev'lish winter. Snow was deeper than usual and lots of horses an' mules got lost. One Feb'ry morning the snow on a peak in the Coronet Basin let go right over the Liberty Bell boardin'house. Son-of-a-gun buried everything, house and men. When the call came to Telluride, we organized a crew an' got here fast as we could. Stationed a man to watch the mountain and at the sight or sound of a crack in the snow, he was to fire a warnin' shot." He continued, "Men from all the mines was there and we dug like crazy. We dug a few fellas out alive when the lookout fired. He'd heard a crack but a damn avalanche from the other side had broke loose. I don't know how any of us got out alive—some didn't, that's fer sure. You never know jus' *when* them dern things is comin' or where they come from or what they're gonna do. I'm scared as *hell* of 'em!" With increasing vehemence he finished his story and left me also "scared as hell." I squeezed closer to George, imagining the horror of suffocation in the deathly embrace of the beautiful white fluff. Historians have told that near this very range John C. Fremont, the "Pathfinder," in 1848 lost nearly all his men and every one of

The struggle to get supplies up to the Tomboy after the trail had been partially dug out.

his mules froze to death.

A faint tinkling sound of bells penetrated my fearsome thoughts. Bill grabbed the reins and urged the horses deeper into the snowbank on the inner side of the road.

"She's open," he said, "but we better stay here. Too risky to pass mules in a storm. Too big a chance of them fallin' into each other and some being knocked over the drop. Mules always have to take the dangerous side. They learn by experience how to avoid the edge by feel of the trail."

A horse and rider, half-buried in snow, wallowed toward us within inches of the sled—*so* near that I dodged. Roped behind the horse was a huge animal, the lead mule, his head down, loaded with a pack that would have been too ponderous on a smooth road in good weather. He was followed by others, equally overburdened and linked by ropes from their halters to the saddle of the mule ahead. Lunging, pulling back, struggling forward, snorting from the effort to keep up with the mule ahead, the poor brutes inched onward until the last of a string of fifteen passed us and the tinkling of their bells was muffled in the deadening silence of the snow.

Through the path that had been shoveled for the mules the snow was still belly-deep on the horses and the Big Elephant loomed ahead of us. Fighting the uphill pull the tired horses tottered against each other, obediently lunging as Bill shouted at them, tugging valiantly until finally we had passed the danger and could see a dim but welcome light ahead.

"That's the only store," said George. "It's run by a fellow named Fyfe, known as Scotty. All he carries is supplies for miners: shirts, cords, overalls, gloves, overshoes, stamps, and a little writing paper. But everyone depends on him because he rides down to Smuggler every day he can get through to bring up the mail."

As we passed the store a dull, heavy, continuous "thud" was growing louder.

"That's the voice of sixty stamps in the Tomboy Mill," George explained. "And it's a noise mining people like to hear. It never stops unless there is trouble."

We slipped past the brilliantly lighted buildings of the mill and began the last half mile of our trip, climbing past scattered huts to stop in front of a tiny shack peeping above the surrounding white expanse without a visible path leading to it.

"Home," said George with a happy smile. I forced my stiff legs out of the sled and sank up to my waist in snow. It was a frightening surprise to step suddenly into what seemed like a bottomless hole of white down.

"You'll get use' t' that," Bill said, grinning.

George rescued me and we ponderously made our way to the door of the shack.

"It was a wonderful ride," I called to Bill Langley. "I'll never forget it."

"G'bye," came his reply. "Fer a tenderfoot you' been mighty brave." And he headed his horses toward the barn.

George opened the door of our first home. The square entry was barely large enough to get inside and manage to close the door behind us.

We entered a room ten feet square which was the living room and bedroom combined. Beyond it was the kitchen, same size. That was all!

From a woodpile in a corner of the kitchen George started a fire in the cooking range. We made toast and hot chocolate with a few cooking utensils already there. After satisfying our stomachs with this small repast, we eagerly fell into bed, utterly exhausted. Our bed consisted of a mattress supported by springs with legs attached, and our blankets were borrowed from the bunkhouse of the Japan Flora Mine. This unpretentious setting was the beginning of my housekeeping duties.

CHAPTER 3

Fifty feet from our "mansion" was the schoolhouse, closed during the long winter, in session only from May through September when the teacher occupied the house. George had been fortunate in renting it for five dollars a month through the winter with the stipulation that we vacate in time for the opening of the school. No other shack on the hill had been available.

The first morning George began what was to become his foremost daily task—to tunnel a trail to the indispensable "outhouse" which belonged to the school. It was one hundred feet from our back door. A rendezvous of winds from all directions built drifts as high as our heads. Often falling snow filled in the trail as fast as George could shovel it out. Frequently by evening the task began again. Aching with sympathy I could look out the window and tell where my husband was only by the scoops of snow flying over the banks from a source invisible as he neared his goal.

What a transformation had taken place in my dapper young college grad, impeccable in his tailored suits, modern hats, stylish ties, and polished shoes! My snowman wore cumbersome clothes, a black skullcap pulled tightly over his head under a visored felt hat, much too large and hiding his ears, a heavy jacket with turned up collar and sleeves dangling below his leather, fleece-lined gloves, his feet in awkward arctics, drops perpetually dripping from his cold red nose, shoveling a path to the privy.

While eating our first breakfast in our first home, George explained, "The companies object to people on the hill having supplies delivered often because the mules have all they can do to supply the mines with necessities to keep them running. And besides, if they deliver only a loaf of bread it costs seventy-five cents when an entire mule-load costs only a dollar-fifty. Most of the women order only once a month. You'd better make a list of everything you think we will need for a while. Then go across the trail to the stable, just a short distance away, and telephone. Fred Diener has charge of the stable and his phone is the only one on the hill except those in the mine offices. Tell the store you live in the teacher's house and they will send the order to Ed Lavender's depot. His pack trains start from there."

George left for work at the Japan Flora Mine on the slope a quarter mile away. Already longing for his return I sized up our domicile.

The floors of the two rooms were clean but bare. The front room contained a heating stove, the bed, a small table, and one straight chair. The wardrobe was a curtain stretched along one wall hiding the nails on which to hang garments. There was no door between the two rooms. The kitchen contained a cooking range, a small table, two roughly made chairs, and one shelf for dishes. On a small bench in a corner was a tin basin. This was evidently for both dishwashing and bathing. I immediately put a second basin on my list of necessities. Beneath the bench was the "slop jar," a five-gallon oil can.

One small window in front and back let in a little light in the daytime. One bare electric bulb dangled from the ceiling in each room.

The bed made and dishes washed, I hung our clothes on the wall and my housework was done.

I knew almost nothing about ordering food but we had to eat. We could have nothing fresh sent up, not even milk. That list! How I dreaded to make it! How many cans and of what foods? What sizes? Would I ever learn? My beloved husband was a glutton for meat. I must get plenty of that, and chocolate, which he enjoyed so much. I thought of what my mother used to send me to the store to buy—coffee, salt, butter, and, oh yes, a sack of sugar which came in ten pounds which was always heavy to carry. A loaf of bread was necessary. I had to learn to make my own bread. Mumbling to myself I continued writing. "That's all I can think of."

Bundled to the ears I stepped gingerly out into the snow and with mincing steps started to the barn, passing the schoolhouse and a small shack across the trail. A blond, pink-cheeked woman was slowly walking back and forth. Possibly one of the Finns of our community, I thought, and smiling, said, "Good morning." She didn't answer but drew her head deeper into the collar of her coat. I couldn't tell whether she did not understand English or was a shy newcomer. Possibly she felt I was intruding.

The barn was only a short distance away. The doors were open showing five clean horse stalls along each side. In a cubby near the door, feet propped high on the iron belt of a pot-bellied stove, a man sat nodding drowsily but, hearing me approach, jumped to his feet, smiled, and said, "Howdee do."

"How do you do? I'm Mrs. Backus. My husband works at the Japan Flora and we've just moved into the teacher's house. I was told you would let me use your telephone."

"Certainly, Mrs. Backus. Everyone uses it. I'm Fred Diener, the stableman for Rodgers Brothers. You came up with one of our drivers yesterday. He went back early this morning." He pointed to a bewildering telephone on the wall. "You ring five times to get central and," laughing, "sometimes she's slow answering."

On tiptoe I stretched to wind the knob at one side of the box and evoked a timid, tin-panny jingle. After a long wait, I gave the store number. After a longer wait the answer came and my voice sounded strange ordering all that food from my list. With that done I turned to thank Fred and instantly sensed that he was a "diamond in the rough." My first impression proved correct. He was truly a gentleman, honorable, and a sincere friend to everyone. To have known him was a privilege.

The bald crown of his head shone through a scraggly fringe of sorrel-colored hair framing ruddy cheeks and clear blue eyes of a round, happy face. A moustache, thick and drooping at both corners of his mouth, exactly matched in color his fringe.

Old shapeless clothes, dirty and food stained, reeked of the stable. This tiny room containing the huge telephone was his entire abode: parlor, bedroom, kitchen, and bathroom. In one corner stood an old chair and a small table crowded with used dishes. His meals were cooked on the pot-bellied stove which now was hot with burning coal. The ash container was chock-full and spilling on the floor. On a box in the corner was an old tin basin for washing everything, including Fred. Suspended from the wall by two heavy chains was a replica of an upper Pullman berth, but it never was entirely closed because a mess of faded, worn rags that once had been blankets continually hung down the side of this bunk. As the saying goes, "clothes don't always make the man," neither in this case did his surroundings have any bearing on the fine personality of Fred Diener. This thought I carried back with me to our "spacious" two-room hut with its high-peaked roof, a blot like all the other shacks on the limitless white purity of the world about.

The storm of yesterday was spent and the sun on the snow was dazzling. Confident now that I could keep my feet on the trail, I quickened my pace to a point where the whole, vast expanse was a natural amphitheatre. In geological terms, it is called a *cirque*, formed by the sheer walls of the San Miguel mountains, a spur of the mighty San Juan Range that I surveyed from eleven thousand five hundred feet above sea level.

Without a break in its crest, it curved like a horseshoe from southwest to northeast, two thousand feet above our settlement, an unlimited, smooth-appearing backdrop of blazing white and sparkling as if sprinkled with diamond dust.

The road leading down to Telluride was obliterated by the snow, but I could trace it by the curves of the mountain round which we had ascended. Far beyond spread the lowlands, a vista in white.

My long skirts swishing through the snow, I went slowly home and found the place cheery, the fire still burning. A few minutes later, there was a knock and I opened the door for a lady, carrying a blanket-wrapped baby in her arms.

"I am Mrs. Batcheller," she announced. Her voice, smile, and manner were charming. "I remember how I felt when we arrived here a year ago, so I came to help you in any way I can."

"Please come in," I said, eager to welcome her. "Thank you for coming. I'll be grateful for your help. I know so little about anything up here that I don't know how to start. I can't even cook. Do let me see your baby."

Only six weeks old, he still seemed very tiny and his face looked thin and pinched. She was nursing him but her abundant milk was not nourishing and she kept in constant communication, she said, with Dr. Edgar Hadley, the leading physician in Telluride

Beth Batcheller skiing on the roof of her house at Tomboy Mine.

who had attended her at Billy's birth.

My new friend's large, beautiful brown eyes and face glowed with health and happiness. She was a picture of loveliness: olive skin, pink cheeks, well-shaped nose, attractive mouth with even white teeth, dark-brown hair piled high on her head. Her capable, graceful hands were used expressively.

We talked about cooking and baking with the handicap of the high altitude, and about Billy, her great joy and concern.

"Come to see me often, won't you?" she invited. "We're just across the trail and I won't get out much until Billy gains a good deal because he must not catch cold."

I promised, delighted with finding a friendship that was to endure throughout our lives, and eager to tell George about her. He brought work home—many reports that had been neglected during our honeymoon, and since I had taken mathematics and chemistry in college and had some knowledge of chemical terminology, I helped check his figures. He wiped dishes for me. Then we sat at the table checking his reports. (This partnership arrangement lasted throughout the years.)

Suddenly my ear was cocked at the sound of tin pans rattling and banging. As the noise came nearer and louder we laid aside the papers and pencils, wondering what it was so close to our little house. Then in the middle of the ding-donging and rat-atatting came a heavy banging on the house. George opened the door. "Come right in," he said. "We're glad to see you."

It was a two-man shivaree staged with the noise of an army squad by Johnny Midwinter, the foreman of the Japan Flora, a stubby blond and genial Cornishman, and the mine carpenter, Ole Oleson. They exclaimed over the hot chocolate and toast I served, and I thoroughly enjoyed the mountain tales of these two typical men of the mines, rugged and sincere, artlessly punctuating every sentence with vehement "damns," "hells," and "Gods."

The next day again was sunny. The snow had begun to settle and frost crackled in the crisp air. Some of the chill was gone from my bones. I was working happily about the house and life was all aglow until suddenly, a loud roar shook the place. The roof must be caving in! For one terrified moment my world shattered. I fell limply on the bed, too weak to stand. Instantly the cataclysm was over and I slowly began to realize what had happened. The heavy snow pack on both sides of our steep roof, warmed by the sun and the fire within, had let go with a crash heard far beyond the trail. I understood then why Bill Langley so greatly feared an avalanche!

I was still unnerved and shaking when George came home and suggested taking a walk. I went gladly.

The teacher's house was the only one on a level area known as "The Flat," built up by tailings from a mill above that had been discarded. Across the trail, scattered hit-and-miss, were several shacks which had never known paint. Rooted to the ground by small wooden blocks they squatted like setting hens as the deepening snow, even this early in winter, mounted almost to their windows.

Two hundred feet beyond and above the tailings was a level bench on which stood four houses fifty feet apart. A tree standing near one house distinguished it from every other in the Basin.

"All this," said George, "belongs to the Tomboy. It is one of the richest gold mines in North America. The mill is on a dandy site. It's a good one and uses the latest methods. The Japan Flora is much smaller and the ore is of lower grade. I am wondering if it can continue operations much longer. The Liberty Bell and

Smuggler mines open into such steep slopes they had to build their mills down in Pandora and haul the ore over the trams that you saw as we came up."

Pointing to a long line running toward the foot of the cliffs he continued: "That long wooden box in the snow covers pipe lines for both air and water. It's filled with sand to keep the water from freezing. It's just wide enough to walk along, single file, and miners use it instead of the trail going to the upper workings."

We walked past the shaft house and I had my first glimpse of a hoist. There was the machinery operating a cage, lowering and lifting men and materials within a nearly vertical opening from the surface to the lowest level of the mine.

The only splash of color in that area was the red junction house of the Telluride Power Company through which came the high tension wires distributing power to all the mines.

We came home to a scanty dinner. We were out of food, and what would happen if our supplies did not arrive on the morrow! I couldn't imagine. I went to bed wishing there were a corner grocer nearby. At four o'clock in the morning a faint sound like the muffled pounding of a hammer filtered through to my consciousness. I woke George and drawled sleepily, "Dear, what is that noise? I heard the same thing yesterday morning. It seems to be near our house."

"I don't know," he answered. "I've heard it too. Perhaps the shifts are changing at the mine. It's about that time. Anyway, it's nothing to worry about." Reassured, I fell asleep again.

Later that morning when I had finished my dab of housework I heard a threshing sound near the door. Opening it hastily I beheld a big mule, heavily loaded, wallowing in the snow. The skinner was tugging at his rope, trying to get him nearer the door while, out on the trail, the other mules of the string stood waiting indifferently.

My supplies! Just in the well-known nick of time. The skinner began dumping boxes in the snow and I gaped in amazement. That sack of sugar which, in Oakland years ago, weighed ten pounds, changed by a misunderstanding in nomenclature to one hundred pounds! Ashamed to betray my ignorance I never mentioned it. Besides, it would cost a dollar fifty to return it. But sugar was not listed on my orders for a long time.

The Tomboy Mill, 1906.

That afternoon I crossed the trail to borrow a cake pan from Beth Batcheller. Six feet of snow covered the trail separating our shacks. As I neared the door I could hear her whistling a cheery tune. Inside that drafty hut I forgot cold, snow, and isolation, for the room glowed with warmth and hospitality. A faint odor of roses came from a potpourri on a small table in one corner. Portraits of her New England ancestors looked down from the rough walls. Old candlesticks held burning candles which brought out the shine in Beth's lovely eyes and a gleam of happiness on the cheeks of this young wife who was transplanted from a life of wealth and travel to a remote mining camp. Within minutes we were "Beth" and "Harriet" to each other, exchanging family data and events like old friends long apart. The Batchellers were both members of pioneer New England families. Jim, a graduate of Massachusetts Institute of Technology, was superintendent of the Tomboy Mill. He and Beth had been married in 1905 in Mattapoisset, Massachusetts, at the summer home of Beth's parents, Mr. and Mrs. William Deyoung Field. A special train had carried the guests from Boston. We talked until it was time for me to mix the cake I was planning for dinner. Saying farewell she added, "Come over for tea tomorrow afternoon. I want you to

In the snow surrounded by friends, with Beth Batcheller on the right.

meet Kate Botkin. She lives in that house above the tailings, the one with a tree in front. She has been suffering from rheumatism and hasn't been down for awhile. Her husband, Alex, has charge of the mine office."

"I'll be happy to meet her," I said, unaware how true that remark would prove to be.

The next day over teacups and gleaming silverware I met Kate Wanzer Botkin and later that afternoon, her husband. A graduate of Yale, Alex Botkin was the son of a former Lieutenant Governor of Montana, appointed by President McKinley as chairman of a commission to recodify the laws of the United States.

Kate, the daughter of the chief consulting engineer of the Union Pacific Railway, had lived in St. Paul where she had conducted a private school. They too were married in 1905 and immediately left for the Tomboy, two sparkling persons radiating optimism and good humor. We felt fortunate and, as George said, "we struck it rich" in finding such friends in this remote eyrie.

A few days later Beth asked me again to join her for tea. There were two other guests that day. Mrs. Rodriguez, a frail Mexican girl, had coal-black hair and olive complexion, deep brown eyes with a melancholy expression, and hands roughened by hard work. She and her husband, a miner, lived in one of the houses clustered near the tailings flat.

And there was Mrs. Matson, a chubby woman from Finland, blond, rosy cheeked, and lively. With nine mouths to feed on a miner's wages she helped lay washing and ironing for others and that morning had returned the laundry she had finished for Beth Batcheller.

The beautiful silver tea service was in use again. Beth poured tea and served cake with the grace and graciousness of a hostess in a mansion of luxury. I listened to their talk carefully for every bit of information I could glean concerning the problems of living at an altitude of 11,500 feet. Indeed there were problems and I rapidly became aware of them.

CHAPTER 4

Clustered at the mouth of the tunnel leading into the Japan Flora Mine were four shacks, the boardinghouse, change rooms, blacksmith shop, and George's assay office. From our back door I could see these small buildings and the long snowshed covering tracks leading from the tunnel to the waste dump.

Roustabouts, men who did the odd jobs other than mining or mucking, pushed cars of waste-rock to the end of the track and there, by releasing a catch, dumped the rock over the hill.

As carload followed carload the pile gradually built up to the level of the track which then was extended and again a dump began building. Throughout the mountains, below yawning mouths of deserted prospects, these piles of waste were natural monuments. Some sadly marked the graves of cherished hopes, shattered and lost; others were monuments to dreams fulfilled of vast fortunes gouged from the earth.

One clear day, looking up the slope and hoping to catch a glimpse of my husband, I noticed a roustabout pushing a car from the snowshed to the end of the track. He tripped it and the rocks rolled down the slope. The air was so clear I could plainly hear them falling, but I could see the car tilting dangerously and the roustabout struggling to hold it back.

Too far out for his cries to be heard he was frantically turning his head, looking for someone who might recognize his plight. I knew if the car broke from his grasp it would crash down the steep slope and might bring death to a rider on the trail below.

I ran to the stable and, gasping for breath lost in that short distance, telephoned to the Japan Flora office. Then Fred Diener and I watched anxiously until we saw rescuers run out of the shed and help pull the car back on its tracks. Such an emergency like this prompted action by any and all who might be near the scene. Apparently, I had done the right thing at the right time. I was learning.

It was the time of year when, even far from the glitter and excitement in the cities, the feeling of Christmas was in the air with nostalgic memories of festive gatherings and feasts. The Batchellers of "Castle Sky High", as they had named their shack, invited Ned Morris, the Tomboy assayer and Al Awkerman, the master mechanic, single men living in the boardinghouse, the Botkins, and the Backuses for Christmas dinner. And on that day it was a castle, indeed!

It was a day of blustering wind and a darkening sky that foretold a storm. But we found a fire roaring in the only fireplace on the hill, and is there anything so cheery and inviting? At the other end of the room the ugly heating stove roared like a lion challenging its foes, the icy drafts lashing in through every crack. A rich red tablecloth displayed Beth's gleaming silver and glowing candles, a perfect setting for a turkey with all the trimmings except fresh vegetables, which were not available to us.

Only a genius could have managed that feast with the few facilities available. Everything canned but the turkey. A tiny cookstove within arm's reach from the table warmed the room. One step away on a small stand was what served as the sink, a dishpan and the usual oil can of water underneath. Handicapped by the difficulty of cooking in high altitudes, plus a delicate baby to care for, Beth had spread a feast for our eyes, the inner man, and complete satisfaction.

Shortly after that Christmas day I had a new adventure. Johnny Midwinter, the foreman, suggested that he and George take me into the mine. George thought I would enjoy it.

Johnny met us at the entrance. Outfitted in a miner's long rubber coat and sou'wester I entered the tunnel where Johnny fastened a miner's candlestick in the loop on my hat and with a dramatic gesture of his pudgy hand, lighted the candle.

Possibly, because I had made the effort to send help to the roustabout which prevented an accident, Johnny decided my interest in the mine warranted a wider understanding of its ramifications. After we walked some distance along the main tunnel he turned to me with a smile and said, "We'll start up this ladder in what we call 'a vertical raise.' Just climb slowly behind me and George will follow you. When we get up to the stope, take the candle out of your hat and carry it straight up and as far from your face as you can."

What did he mean by a *stope*, and would I recognize it when I reached it?

Step by step, clinging to the rungs, we climbed straight up the three by four opening in the rock. As water dripped from above and hit my hat and face, the candle sputtered. I stepped carefully for fear of tripping on my skirt. With the strange feeling of carrying a candle on my head I stared steadily at the ladder. The flickering light shone dimly on the walls caging us in, three sides of solid rock and the fourth made of timbers for the ore chute alongside. Each rung was a little harder for me to reach and cling to. By the time fifty rungs were beneath us I began to waver, then I hesitated, but remembering that George was close below and might be thrown off balance, I plunged on. After one hundred feet of this fearsome climb we reached the top of the ladder where the rock closed in over our heads.

Even today, many years later, the memory of that moment hits hard at the pit of my stomach!

Broken ore almost completely filled the cross shaft, leaving only a crooked passage to crawl through, two feet wide, three feet high. Faintness and vertigo swept through me. But not for anything would I let George or Johnny know how desperately fear gripped me. I could hardly breathe. There must have been oxygen but I couldn't pull any of it into my lungs. To cover the sick feeling of panic I made the excuse, which was real enough, that I needed to catch my breath after the exhausting climb. Unable, in that flat space, to sit up I lay flat on my stomach, resting, doubting that I could go on.

Through the pounding of my heart I could hear myself saying, "Hattie, you must go on. You are the wife of a miner. Keep going and get it over!" But my head was swimming and my stomach churning. I lay there until terror subsided somewhat, then told Johnny I was ready.

Holding the candle safely before me I inched along, face down, clawing at the rocks with my one free hand, dragging my legs forward, my long skirts hampering every move. Only occasionally could I catch the gleam of Johnny's candle ahead. Unable to look back I could hear George calling a word of encouragement as he followed.

But what if the rock overhead should cave in? The thought was torture. I struggled to wipe it from my mind. In the darkness, broken only by a flicker of the nearby candle, I twisted, turned, writhed like a snake, stopped many times to rest and capture a mite of courage.

It was one hundred and fifty feet of pure hell! Yet I lived through it. We had crossed the awful stope and there remained the descent, straight down another hundred-foot ladder in a well, scarcely four feet square, cut in solid rock. It seemed easy. I had room to breathe. With each rung lower there was more space above my head. The tunnel at last! I hurried toward the streak of daylight at its mouth, and the great outdoors. Heaven!

I was still trying to shake off the remembered terror of that adventure, when a few days later, Johnny came to our shack.

"Now you've been through a stope, let's go down into the diggin's."

My face showed how startled I was at the prospect of suffering again as I had done before. Johnny noticed it.

"Oh, it won't be like that, this time," he assured me. "We'll ride down as soon as George finishes his work." He was doing me a favor, giving me a treat, according to his ideas. Reluctantly I consented.

That afternoon George, Johnny, and I got into the cage which ran on wheels down an inclined track and were lowered into the mine one hundred feet, two hundred feet . . . down, down to the one-thousand-foot level. All the levels were lighted by electricity and we carried candles only for an emergency. The day shift had left. The air had cleared after the blasting. We three were alone in the bowels of the mountain. Sounds of water gurgling out of crevices echoed through the vaulted caverns. Our voices resounded weirdly. I wandered around the large underground cave peering into empty stopes, drifts and storage rooms until mounting claustrophobia started my stomach to quiver.

"I'm ready to get out of this," I said to Johnny.

He walked to the shaft and with a hammer pounded three

times on the air line, the signal to the man at the top that we were ready to be hoisted. The resonant sounds carried along the pipe and we waited. And waited. No answering tap-tap came from above. Several minutes passed. Johnny and George, unperturbed, talked of assays, high-grade, waste, and tonnage. I fidgeted. The happy-go-lucky Cornishman again rapped on the pipe and the metallic sounds rang loud underground. Silence.

"Why don't they answer?" I asked, a picture of being buried alive flashing in my mind.

"They will soon. Probably the cageman has gone away from the hoist to attend to something," and Johnny sauntered away, returning with a piece of ore to show George.

"Fairly good ore," he said turning it over and over, "but so far we haven't found enough of it, or a large enough vein to make it pay." While they discussed values, my ears were straining to catch a sound from above.

It was a full fifteen minutes before the answering signal sounded, clink-clank, faint and wavering at first, then louder as the cage wheels rattled on tracks only slightly off vertical. Never was music sweeter to my ears, and as the platform settled gently on the floor, one thousand feet down, I was instantly on it. George and Johnny took their time, talking as they strolled. Men! But answering the "up" signal the cage began to climb, and I was thinking—never again! A morning stroll to the stable to pick up the mail was all the adventure I wanted for a while.

Next morning I encountered my Finnish neighbor pacing back and forth close to her shack and at my "Good Morning" she merely inclined her head, not from shyness I decided, but from some inhibition that repelled friendly advances. I had seen her husband, a tall blond Finn, several times and on each occasion he too seemed preoccupied and avoided speaking. Their reserve intrigued me. It was so unlike the attitudes of everyone else on the hill. And after weeks of hearing that strange sound of pounding in the early dark of every morning, I began to think it was coming from their house. Well, George had said it was nothing to worry about so again I dismissed it from my mind.

One noon early in March, George came home unexpectedly, a worried look on his face.

"What in the world is the matter, dear? Do you feel sick?"

Fear really struck me because of his expression.

"No, I'm not sick, but the manager told me that in a month the Japan Flora will have to close down. I don't know what I'll do."

"Oh, just get another job." I answered unconcernedly, hoping to lessen his anxiety.

"That's not so easy, Kiddy (one of his pet names for me). It will take money to leave here and hunt for work."

"Why not go to the Tomboy and apply?" I suggested.

"I couldn't get on there, they always have a full crew. Men stay on and on there, when they're lucky to get hired."

"Why not take a chance? What can you lose? We'll skimp more with money until you get something else. Don't worry, we're young and everything will work out for us." I was so confident.

My beloved husband always listened to what I had to say and we always worked things out together. He was always right when it came to the final decisions. I had hoped my cheerful attitude toward the news he brought would lend encouragement, but he returned to his office with a heavy heart. Our first problem had arisen after only three months.

Late in the afternoon he went to the Tomboy office and asked to speak with Mr. Herron, the manager.

"He's up on the pipe line but will be here later on," Alex told him.

George came home, had a hurried dinner, and returned to the Tomboy office. There he met Mr. David Herron, known as a kind, loyal, and considerate gentleman, esteemed by both his friends and his employees.

George stated his problem and asked for work. "Yes, George," Mr. Herron answered. "I'll have a job for you whenever your work at the Japan Flora terminates."

A changed husband returned to me . . . full of joy and happiness. He completed his assay work, closed the records, and lost not a single day in transferring to the Tomboy Mine, the richest gold mine in Savage Basin.

CHAPTER 5

Baby Billy Batcheller was losing weight. His beautiful brown eyes were dull and lifeless. Jim had rigged a pulley to raise the bassinet into the center of the room and there Billy lay halfway to the ceiling out of the drafts that blew frigidly through Castle Sky High. Dr. Hadley had prescribed fresh milk for him and by special permission it was brought up on the pack train. Anxiety and the troubled days and nights were beginning to show on Beth.

I was greatly concerned about the baby and every morning I went across the trail to help her, although the slightest exertion or attempt to hurry made my heart work faster.

On some mornings I did Beth's housework while she hovered over little Billy. On other days I watched him, always alert to note any change. He was never a moment unwatched or alone. But he did not improve and lay in a stupor. Beth tried canned milk. Finally, after two days of a special mixture, he showed the first signs of improvement. The bond of friendship between Beth and me grew stronger as happily we watched Billy improve. During these days the walk across the trail and helping Beth were all the extra exertion of which I was capable. I felt listless.

"Oh, it's the altitude," Beth said. "I felt the same way when we first arrived." True, at sea level the air pressure is 14.7 pounds to the square inch, or 30 inches of mercury. We lived at an elevation at which the air pressure was only 9.5 pounds or 19.4 inches of mercury, and the low pressure kept one's lungs working much faster to obtain the necessary amount of life-giving oxygen.

Yet the continued fast beat of my heart was annoying and the feeling in my chest was difficult to describe. It felt burning, yet icy cold. I had to slow down my walking pace. And my cold feet!

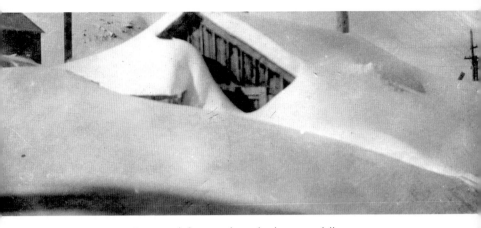

Occupants had to tunnel out after heavy snowfalls.

Nothing helped until I saw a picture in a mail order catalogue, the standby of everyone in the Basin, of felt shoes which I sent for immediately. They fitted inside my arctics and were comfortable and warm. My foot problem was solved. But I had another one as troublesome.

Due to the thin, cold, dry air my lower lip split down the middle. It was painful and bled profusely, especially during extreme cold weather. I tried every known remedy except one which old-timers assured me was the *only* cure. Ear wax! I couldn't bring myself to use it. So long as we lived up there my lip never healed and to this day a lump of thickened skin remains where the crack was.

Thirty years after we left our home in the clouds, I had occasion to be examined by a physician dwelling at an elevation of only 1,700 feet. He did not know where I had lived.

"You are in perfect condition," he assured me, "but you have an astonishing high count of red blood corpuscles. Astonishing," he repeated, "but nothing to worry about."

"What would cause that?" I asked him.

"It's hard to say, but sometimes living in very high altitudes will build up such a condition."

I soon overcame the discomfort of cold feet and high altitude, but bread making was the bane of my existence.

"It's very easy," said Mrs. Matson. "There are nine of us and I have no trouble keeping enough bread on hand."

"It's simple," said Beth. Kate Botkin agreed. Attractive Mrs.

Driscoll, wife of the chief steward of the boardinghouse, added, "Oh my, yes. It's nothing at all to make bread, and my four children keep me busy at it."

Surely I could make bread if I followed their instructions. Patiently, carefully and often they described the different steps: soaking cakes of compressed yeast in potato water, determining the proper temperature at which it must be kept, and on mixing day, adding the proper amount of fresh potato water, flour, lard, sugar, and salt. Each one had her own method of mixing but all were happy with the results.

"Thanks, I understand now. I'll get it *this* time," I replied every time.

But usually when baking day arrived, no bubbles greeted my gaze. The yeast would be dead and I would hurry to borrow a new starter, a mixture of yeast and potato water kept constantly on hand, alive but not active. All my attempts failed and my generous friends supplied the bread for George's lunch basket. I sent for a bread-making machine—a bucket equipped with a hand-cranked mixer to knead the dough. Surely this would end my troubles.

Confidently I mixed a batch in the new machine and went to bed. Next morning when I lifted the cover from the bucket the dough was no higher than it was the night before. There was no use baking it and I wept as I threw away *more* flour, lard, sugar, salt, and yeast. But on the next attempt I was delighted to find the dough near the top of the bucket. I molded it in loaves, let them stand the required time, and baked them. The bread came out golden brown, tempting, the wonderful aroma of freshly baked bread throughout the house. I couldn't resist cutting a warm slice for myself. What a disappointment! I almost cried. The loaf was nothing but a mass of holes with a webbing of dough, resembling genuine Swiss cheese. How would George ever eat the stuff, I wondered. One answer, he had to for there was no other bread for him.

I was one bride who couldn't boil an egg. Only after repeated trials were our frozen eggs boiled long enough to be palatable. It was hard for me to realize that water boiled at only 190 degrees and to determine the additional time required to boil an egg.

Salad dressing was another Waterloo. If it were a degree too cold the oil would not mix with the egg. Many messy mixtures of eggs, oil and vinegar were wasted, and I did so love mayonnaise! At home in California I had made delicious cakes and decided to use one of my mother's recipes. I mixed the batter with great care and put it in the oven for the required time to bake. The result—it remained battery!

I tried a pot roast and we eagerly anticipated dinner. It was browning beautifully and a savory odor came from the pot. George loved meat, and with his strenuous work, required much of it. But alas! No knife we possessed would cut that roast.

One day I said, "All miners eat beans. Do you like beans, George?"

"Yes, of course," he answered, always amiable about my experiments and probably hopeful of a triumph. So for two whole days I boiled beans. They neither swelled nor softened but remained as hard as marbles.

Most of my days were spent perusing the *Rocky Mountain Cookbook*, mixing recipes, washing dishes, in a desperate endeavor to set before my husband appetizing meals from our limited larder. I learned to cook the hard way, but it took time. Yet, never during all the years did George ever complain or criticize my efforts.

While I was learning my job, he was learning the different steps in milling gold ore in that sixty stamp mill of the Tomboy. His first job was assistant to the amalgamator, Osborn, who had grown old in that one position.

After the ore had been crushed it was washed over copper plates covered with amalgam, a sticky mixture of gold and quicksilver. Excess amalgam was removed from the plates and stored in the office safe until there was enough to charge the retort furnace where the quicksilver was recovered and the gold prepared for melting into bars.

Gold ore has been found running as high as $70,000 to $80,000 a ton. Though the Tomboy never reached that high in gold content, pockets had been found which assayed from $10.00 to $15.00 a pound. In such rich rock the gold shows plainly. Precautions were taken against theft in such veins, but it was difficult to watch the men and easy for them to sneak out small, valuable pieces. Reports disclosed that from one mining town alone the express companies shipped $100,000 more cash each year than was reported by the mines.

One morning, as I went to get the mail, I saw several grim-faced men standing near the Finn's shack. I wondered if an accident had befallen our taciturn neighbors. In this small community everyone was concerned about the welfare of the miners.

It wasn't many hours before the story, which the company tried hard to keep quiet, had spread from one to another and I was able to piece together several bits of it. Early that morning, Tom Sullivan, a big, good-looking Irishman with curly red hair and vivid blue eyes, was standing by the shaft house about ready to go off duty. He was the night watchman with many responsibilities. It was his duty to wander over the property with eyes and ears alert to anything out of the ordinary—theft, sabotage, fire hazards, danger of slides—and to be at the shaft house at four in the morning to notice anything suspicious among the night crew coming up from the mine. Tom had found no trouble that night and was ready for his rest. One miner after another greeted the well-liked guard. "Hi, Tom, how'r you?" "Fine, how's it below?" "Hello, Tom." "How's the ol' mule that was sick last night?" And so went the usual conversation. Then our neighbor, the Finn, stepped off the cage hoist and suddenly slipped on the icy ground. Sprawling there before Tom he frantically tried to cover the contents of his opened lunch bucket. Too late! The tell-tale pieces of ore lay evidence to all his secret activity. Needless to say the man was caught "dead in his tracks."

The Finn's shack was thoroughly searched. On the ground under a freshly nailed floorboard a cache of one thousand pounds of high-grade ore was discovered. It was taken to the mill where George amalgamated it and recovered a large amount of gold. The noise in the early morning hours that had puzzled us had been the sound of the high grader crushing the ore with a mortar and pestle to extract the gold. This is what the Finn was up to when he reached home after his shift. My curiosity about the "aloof" neighbors was finally satisfied.

Several months later a trial was held in Telluride and the entire story was told. The Finn had been employed at the Tomboy for several years and recently had been under suspicion, but there had to be proof of his crime before he could be accused. He had been working in the "lower workings" where rich pockets had been uncovered—so rich, in fact, that the management mined low-grade ore in greater quantities to average the values. The man could not resist the temptation. He took out several pieces of high-grade ore without being caught. Growing bolder, he repeated the theft time after time, only a few pieces every day but he knew how to select them and his filching continued until that fatal slip on the ice.

The judge set a high bail and his wife promptly deposited thousands of dollars in Finnish securities purchased with the stolen gold. He was convicted and sentenced to three years in prison. However, he said he didn't mind. He needed a rest and he had bought enough securities in Finland to assure independence for himself and his wife when, after his prison term ended, they would return to their homeland.

CHAPTER 6

When the storms and bitter cold of March were upon us, we learned that a shack on the bench above the tailings was to be vacated. The school teacher would need her house shortly so we thought it wise to get settled permanently.

It was customary for those leaving the hill to sell their meager furniture to the new occupants, usually a so-called bed, a table, chairs, and stoves priced from thirty-five to seventy-five dollars. We bought the outfit from our predecessors for seventy-five dollars and moved into our "furnished" home.

The view was superb. On three sides the great white range of mountains stood close like a surrounding guard of honor and we could look down the deep canyon as it sloped off into the valleys toward the horizon.

Our entrance porch was made of three rotting planks weakly supported by a six-inch-thick log on the down side. Squatted flat on the ground unpainted, like all the other shacks, it measured twenty-two feet by ten feet in size and was built of one-inch boards with battens, but no lining whatever. It was divided into three sections by partitions with doorways lacking doors. Between the front and rear sections, our parlor and kitchen each eight feet deep, a six-foot sleeping compartment was literally squeezed in. A small window on each side of the front room and one in the kitchen supplied daylight. The middle or bedroom had no window, but from the middle of its rough ceiling was a long cord and a small electric light bulb which could be carried into the front or back rooms to light the darkness. This room contained only a double couch. There was no space for a dresser—even if we had one. The only daylight came through the doorways.

In the depth of winter, our shack is faintly seen at extreme right.
The range on the left is part of the 13,000-foot cirque surrounding it.

The "parlor" consisted of a pot-bellied stove in one corner, a single mattress on legs, and two chairs, one of which was made of three twelve-inch-wide boards painted black.

The kitchen seemed larger only because there was no ceiling to hide the rafters. A large coal range, a small table, two chairs, three narrow shelves on the wall completed our kitchen equipment, except of course for the tin basin in its stand with the utilitarian five-gallon can beneath.

Yet, more accessible than at the teacher's house, the important outhouse was only fifty feet from a decrepit lean-to attached to the kitchen, less than half the distance George used to shovel snow.

The flooring of our shack was of ugly, splintering planks. Something had to be done about that! At least in the "parlor." With blue denim, brought up from Telluride by the faithful mules, we nailed our "carpet" over a padding of newspapers, then we went to work on the walls. They were rough-surfaced boards impossible to paint. George got enough blue building paper to line the entire house, tacking the paper to the boards and over the narrow ledge that ran horizontally around the walls three feet above the floor.

The snow was too deep for the mules to climb to our shack so our sacks of coal were dumped near the main packed trail, two hundred feet away. The labor George was saved digging to the privy was more than doubled carrying coal four times the distance. Every night when it was time for him to come home I watched until I could see him start up the trail with a hundred-pound sack of coal on his shoulder, propped the door open for him, and turned and dashed to the kitchen in order to avoid seeing him at this Herculean task. I couldn't bear to watch and suffered with him all the way. If one foot slipped from the icy ridge, he would sink deep into the feathery trap, sometimes able to hold fast to the sack of coal, but more often it would slip from his grasp and only with strenuous effort could he lift it from the snowy depths and start again. And that was not all!

Water was as precious as on a burning desert and in winter the mine company's most serious problem. The only available source was at the summit of the range, beautiful Lake Ptarmigan, named for that bird of high altitudes that changes its dark summer plumage to white in winter. The lake was small, its capacity limited. The amount drawn for running the mill and all other uses must not exceed sixty gallons per minute. Consequently, not a drop could be wasted. Besides the coal, George had to carry water from the shaft house four hundred feet away. A five-gallon oil can on his shoulder contained our entire daily supply. Fortunately the can had a screw-on cap because often George slipped off the trail and not a drop could be spared. We longed for the day when a frozen spring behind our shack would thaw. This natural source of supply was the only luxury our friends envied.

On about the same level, ninety feet away, was "Cloud Cap Retreat," the home of the Botkins and their pride and joy, a great Dane named Thyra. Sometimes Alex would walk three quarters of the mile uphill to have lunch at home, taking Thyra back to the office with him. A little later she would come bounding back with Kate's mail in her mouth, her beautiful head held high above the snow to protect the package for her beloved mistress.

Except for two houses at the upper workings, our shack was the highest. I could see the panorama below, miners walking the pipe lines, riderless horses returning to the stables, occasional skiers catapulting down the opposite peak, packtrains on their wearying journeys—fascinating scenes indelibly etched on my memory.

Most horses in the Telluride district were owned by Rodgers Brothers. In the town the main stable housed fifty, with a small barn at the Tomboy. Day and night, summer and winter they were ready for hire. Riders, experienced or not, distances to be traveled made no difference. On reaching his destination the rider tied the reins to the pommel of the saddle and turned the horse loose. Regardless of the distance, knowing the trails far better than most riders, the horse quietly and surely returned to the nearest stable, at the Tomboy or in Telluride. In winter they went directly to the barn. In summer they might wander awhile, seeking tufts of grass. A riderless horse was part of life in these mountains and no cause for concern.

How I loved them! Never did I lose the pleasure of knowing that with an affectionate pat I could dismiss my horse confident that he would return to his barn with the certainty of a homing pigeon.

And how my temper blazed when I saw a horse slowly approaching the end of the trail, head drooping low, flanks dripping foam, for I knew what it meant—a miner in a hurry!

We had several favorite horses. Chief, a gentle handsome chestnut with lighter tail and mane, somewhat heavy and not so fast but reliable, a woman's horse, and safe for beginners, could always be depended on to take his rider smoothly and safely anywhere; Fanny, more slender though not as handsome as Chief, a mottled, reliable roan; Bird, slender and spirited, ready to jump at anything but as comfortable to ride as a rocking chair. Poor Bird, strained by drunken riders who unsparingly ran him up miles of steep slopes, a bundle of nerves, never permitting another horse to pass, running as if to avoid the lash. And King, tallest of them all, a raw-boned rangy horse able to cover ground in long strides.

Horses were used to haul heavy machinery, lumber, and mine timbers on sleds in winter and wagons in summer, usually six to a team. Frequently in winter it took three days to cover the five and a half miles from Telluride with horses and men laboring through

Our method of moving.

the daylight hours to break through drifts on the way to the mine. A rate of a mile and two thirds a day!

Only by horses were we able to go up or down the mountains, but the daily existence of those on the hill depended upon mules.

The pitiful patient mule! Fury still burns within me when I recall the cruelty and abuse that animal endured. An interesting book, *Early Western Travels, 1778 to 1846*, edited by Rueben G. Thwaites, gives a short account and pleasant tribute to that long-suffering animal: "At that date the mule traveled hundreds of miles, carrying unwieldy burdens weighing three or four hundred pounds. Due to exposure and lack of care, the mules often suffered from swollen legs and feet and then, unable to go farther, were beaten and dragged and if still unable to move were left by the trail to die."

In 1906, in the San Juans, the mule had some care, to be sure.

His day was one of regular hours. He traveled a beaten trail. He was well fed. But with all that his condition was not much better than the author described in *Early Western Travels*.

All freight for the Tomboy was sent to sheds in Telluride. Freight included everything used in the mines, mills, boardinghouses, and shacks: bedding, towels, shoes, potatoes, sugar, beef, pipes, shovels, tools, blasting powder, and lagging. Led by a skinner on horseback, fifteen big raw-boned mules formed a string. Each skinner loaded his own string, weight, balance, and security being the paramount necessities. A large pad afforded some protection although too often the mules' backs were chafed and bleeding. Over the pad a wooden cross-saddle was held securely by a cinch around the mule's belly so tightly drawn by a ladigo that the belly was often compressed many inches and the animal shaken to his very hooves, causing great discomfort. Yet, this was necessary to prevent the heavy pack from slipping which caused more chaffing and could be very dangerous. A side load was lifted into place and firmly secured by a rope deftly thrown and tied. The mule sagged lopsidedly until counterbalanced by a load on the other side roped securely by a flip of the skinner's hand. The third load was thrown on the back, and ropes crossing from side to side lashed everything together.

The most unwieldy burdens were large crates and boxes. The total weight could not exceed three hundred pounds but bulk made the load difficult. A still more awkward load was lagging, often twelve feet long, lashed on both sides, reaching high above the mule's back, the ends dragging beyond his heels.

From our peak I could often spy a string of tiny specks, like ants coming out of the tunnel, black against the snow, disappearing in the Big Bend of the mountainside to reappear later, larger, nearer and higher.

No less rugged was the skinner, bent low over his saddle. His face was almost hidden under the wide, turned-down brim of his slouch hat.

Rhythmically he slapped his long arms against his sides to ease the numbness from a mountain blizzard. His body was a shapeless hulk under layers of heavy shirts and jackets. Long gauntlets and heavy boots were fur-lined protection from frostbite. Sheepskin chaps, leather-fringed from ankle to waist, were held in place by a wide, metal-studded belt. For emergencies an iron shovel was strapped to one mule and a long, heavy coiled rope was looped around the saddle of his horse.

Passing a string of mules a rider always took the inside of the trail, and in winter, when snow narrowed the path, he threw both legs over the saddle toward the bank lest they be crushed by a packload rubbing against them.

The load of an entire string might be destined for the mill, or storehouse, at the mouth of the Cincinnati Tunnel, or to the boardinghouse. In winter the strings could seldom get up to the "Upper Workings." Sometimes one mule was loaded with small orders for different families, a cause of annoyance and delay because often an entire load must be removed to find a single package. If it was possible to reach a cabin the skinner would detach and lead a mule from the string. But more often in winter the orders were dumped in the snow along the trail and we had to tramp down the snow or dig into it groping around to find our packages.

While the skinner made the deliveries the mules enjoyed a short, well-earned rest. Unloading was done as skillfully as loading. A twist of the rope released the top pack. The side loads were removed and the mule rose up like a ship lightered of cargo. The skinner's horse knew instinctively when to step forward to advance the string for unloading the next in line.

Immediately after the string was unloaded it was reloaded with three one-hundred-pound sacks of mill concentrates destined for the railroad station in Telluride for shipment to smelters. The afternoon trip then started. At day's end, often seven in the evening, the mules had covered more than twenty miles, ten of exhausting ascent. During storms it took all day for one round trip. At times the skinners gave up partway up the trail and returned to Telluride with their loads.

The mules! Large, gentle, patient pictures of dejection, trudging along, heads sagging, ears flapping to shake out the needle-sharp particles of ice driven in by howling winds. Packs cutting deep into their backs and irritating large running sores, forelegs and ankles swollen with rheumatism to twice normal size! Through four long winters I shuddered with indignation and pity at sight of their suffering.

"Stubborn as a mule" is a phrase of meaning to a skinner. Day after day the mules plodded through their unbroken routine, but if one fell—it was a different story. Urged by the skinner, he might try to get up, sometimes succeeding but mostly not. If he failed, the skinner had to unload him. If one mule fell, the entire string was knotted. The short, connecting rope jerked the mules in front and the fallen one behind, and the others restlessly twisted this way and that until finally there was an entangled mess of mules falling like tenpins. Quite often one rebel would lie down deliberately while the skinner wrestled with another.

But stubborn as mules are, my anger leaped to white heat whenever I saw how an obstinate or possibly helpless mule was sometimes mistreated. Then came the measure of the skinner's temper, brutality, and his command of profanity. At first he might coax, then he swore. "Swearing like a mule skinner" in the mining world means the most vehement, vile, profane, and obscene maledictions invented. When strong language brought no response from the mule, often stuck deep in the snow, the skinner kicked him with his heavy boots or lashed him brutally with a strap. The mule might lunge feebly, and settle down again calmly, perversely. Then the enraged skinner resorted to the iron shovel—banging it on the animal's head.

Though I had been warned that it only infuriated a skinner to berate him, I often rushed through the snow and in my kind of violent but less evil anger called down vengeance on his head! Pausing only to cast a withering look at me, he would turn back and the deadly "thud, thud" of the shovel on the mules would begin again. Only when he was ready would Mr. Mule struggle to his feet, if possible.

Accidents to the mule strings were bound to happen in that rugged country. During our sojourn a mule loaded with boxes of deadly blasting powder fell from the trail into the gulch. Fortunately he landed in deep, powdery snow which cushioned his impact and he was dragged safely back to the trail.

A year before four mules, loaded heavily, fell over a deep cliff. Rescue seemed impossible so no attempt was made to extricate them. This could be the fate of a mule at any time on those trails.

CHAPTER 7

In good time my ordering of supplies was systemized so one delivery would last a month helped out by a store of extras, Maryland oysters shipped frozen in cans, canned salmon, chicken, and turkey which I kept on hand. George had a ravenous appetite requiring plenty of bacon at breakfast, an abundance of meat in his lunch bucket and for dinner. My monthly order list of meat generally included two legs of mutton (I remembered not to ask for lamb), three dozen veal, pork, and mutton chops, half a ham, a slab of bacon, several beef steaks, two roasts of beef, and a beef tongue.

We hung the meat from the rafters in the woodshed where it quickly froze solid. If I required small pieces, I tackled the job armed with both a butcher's and a carpenter's saw, whacking and slashing, "geeing" off there until I was exhausted. Too often the result was a hunk of meat a quarter inch thick on one side, two inches on the other. Sometimes I had only shreds, especially when trying to slice bacon.

Our canned fruits and vegetables, the best to be obtained then would not be acceptable now. Unbelievable improvement has been achieved in canning. We bought fruit, vegetables, and milk by the case. Occasionally two or three neighbors divided a case of something special to vary the monotony without investing too much. Canned food and eggs were allowed to freeze, but never potatoes or oil.

Ice cream, such as it was, often was our dessert. I merely poured the ingredients into a can, buried it in the snow stirring it occasionally. Chocolate or caramel flavor disguised the taste of canned milk. Chocolate and leftovers from dinner were kept on the end of a kitchen shelf.

One morning I couldn't find a baked potato, left from the night before, which I wanted to fry for breakfast.

"George, did you see that baked potato I put on the shelf last night? It certainly isn't there now!"

"No," he called as he dressed for work, "I didn't see it."

"I can't understand it," I continued. "I've been missing several things lately. Yesterday I was certain that I had some Baker's chocolate left, but last night I couldn't find that either. It's mighty strange because I have no other place to put those things."

George had a strenuous day at the mill and that night we went to bed early. I was not long asleep when a noise woke me. Something was running around in the springs of our bed. Not moving a muscle I listened. Good heavens! Thump, thump, like the sound of a hammer but a hammer moving rapidly from head to foot of our bed. I grabbed George who was in a deep sleep. As he slowly woke up I whispered, "There's something in the springs of this bed. What in the world is it?" I did not know whether to jump out of bed or play possum and not alarm this thing until George investigated.

Half asleep George listened, then sat bolt upright.

"Must be the packrats the old prospector told me about."

"Rats!" I shouted. "How horrible."

George got up and turned on the light. Instantly all was silent. Then we sat in bed with the light on, waiting. Where did they come from, and how did they vanish without our seeing them?

"Thank goodness they're gone," I said.

"There were two of them at least," George said. "We must have scared them away by turning on the light. Don't be afraid, honey. The miners say they never bother people."

"But I don't like the idea of rats under the bed. It's terrible."

George turned off the light and we settled down again but only for a few minutes. Back came the uncanny invaders bustling under the mattress, busy as bees.

Again George turned on the light and again the rats scooted away before we could see them. For the rest of the night we left the light burning and heard no more from our unwelcome callers.

But in the morning we both stared in amazement at the floor. Stretching from the kitchen through the diminutive bedroom and on across the denim carpet into the parlor was a train of kindling wood from the box beside the kitchen stove and our silver spoons, knives, and forks all crisscrossed in pairs as neatly as though I had arranged them myself.

This decorative project was repeated night after night. As soon as we were asleep, having abandoned racing up and down in the bedsprings, these clever rodents busied themselves silently with a soldierly formation of kindling and cutlery on the entire length of the floor. One morning there was an extra touch. A twenty-five-cent piece that had been in a small glass dish on the table the night before, now lay like a medal in line with the rest. Through all their work we had not heard a sound.

I longed to be transformed by some good fairy into an owl and perch in a corner to watch these dexterous creatures laying our kindling and flatware so silently and neatly in a chosen design. But longing was futile. I *never* saw our visitors. To this day I wonder why they went to such an effort and how it was achieved. They gained nothing by their hard work.

Johnny Midwinter who knew considerably about them could not explain *why* the packrats did what they did, but he knew how they did it.

"They are the cleverest devils I've ever known," he said. "They're about fifteen inches long from the tips of their noses to the end of their tails. The tails are long and are very bushy and look larger than their bodies. My partner and I had a great time with packrats. One year we were prospecting beyond Imogene Basin, living in an old cabin that had a loft." He paused, as though recapturing old memories. "Yes, old Tim and I thought we had found a mine and we worked hard but it didn't pan out. But the damn packrats sure gave us a bad time. We were always looking for missing things. We stored a crate of eggs in the loft and when we were ready to use them there wasn't a single egg left in the crate. Those devils had carried every egg down that ladder and it was ten feet high."

I smiled at him, "You're just trying to make a monkey out of me."

"No, I swear it. That's the gospel truth. They can do harder things than that," he said.

"But how could they carry eggs down a ladder?" I questioned.

"Well, we didn't actually see them do it. But we'd seen them carry things over boxes. They work in pairs. One holds whatever they are stealing between its two front paws and the other drags him by the tail. And are they quick! By God, they move just like that!" He snapped his horny fingers.

It was hard to believe but all miners told the same stories, men whom we had no reason to doubt, and before it was ended we were convinced packrats are invisible and unbelievably smart. Yet we wanted to be rid of these nimble, resourceful inhabitants of the high country before they multiplied. We set traps but had no luck. We didn't want to use poison lest they'd go near the house to die.

"Next time I hear them in the woodshed I'll shoot them," George declared boldly one day. Knowing he was anything but a marksman with a gun I had my doubts. However, next night, there came a low whisper from the shed: "Shssh! Bring the gun. I can see the eyes of a rat and I don't want to lose sight of him," and George prepared for the "kill."

I had a terrific fear of guns. Nevertheless, I tiptoed to the rarely used pistol and cautiously holding it at arm's length crept back to where George stood like a statue, glaring at one spot. Fingers stuffed into my ears I backed away, waiting, watching. George raised the gun and pointed it. The pair of eyes had vanished!

He turned toward another corner where eyes were gleaming and aimed again. I waited for the "bang." Nothing happened. The beady shining eyes were gone before he could pull the trigger. George gave up.

"There's only one way to catch 'em," said Charley, the powder-monkey who each morning drove his sled to a small shed nearby to pick up blasting powder for the shifts. "If you'll do what I say you'll get rid of them damn things. Cut the top off an oil can and half fill it with water. Then balance two sticks across the top so they overlap a little. Tie the ends together loosely with a piece of cheese on top. How the devil they get up onto the sticks I don't know, but they do. When they get to the middle they'll drop in and drown, sure as hell."

George came home that night, changed his work clothes, and, as usual, set his high leather boots behind the stove ready for the next day. After dinner he painstakingly carried out Charley's instructions, placing the can in the kitchen. Thank goodness we'd now be rid of the other inhabitants of our shack. We were certain because George tested the sticks with his fingers and they flipped easily at a touch. With the trap all set, we went to bed.

I don't like to see drowned creatures, even rats, so in the morning I waited for George to dispose of the victim. Then, hearing no cry of triumph, I cautiously looked. George was standing beside the oil can with a look of amazement on his face.

"Look!" he gasped. "The sticks are balanced exactly as I fixed them but the cheese is gone and so is the rat! How could he walk along that tottering stick and not fall in? I give up, I give up!"

Dismayed and discouraged he finished dressing and reached behind the stove for his boots. He shoved a foot into one and it struck a snag. Running his hand down inside the boot to the toe, he pulled out—the missing cheese!

Some weeks after the failure of the rat trap, I invited four friends for afternoon tea, a social highlight in the Savage Basin. That afternoon as I saw Beth coming up the hill pulling her precious Billy in a box on runners, the sled Jim had made, I hurried down to help.

The baby was a picture in his bright red snowsuit with peaked cap and mittens to match, tucked in deeply with a heavy white fur robe, his shining eyes and cold-pinked cheeks framed by the fur.

We chatted about everything over the teacups: cooking, sewing, our families, etc. Everything except styles and fashions. The latest addition to the group was soft-spoken Martha Snyder, wife of the man then establishing a branch of the Y.M.C.A. that we were to boast was "the highest Y in the world."

"How is the Y getting along?" Beth asked.

"Hal thinks everything will work out nicely," Martha said. "The company is very cooperative. Mr. Herron is going to put up a small building long enough for a bowling alley. And the national Y will furnish us with a small but good organ and song books. Hal says quite a few men have signed up already."

We discussed the Y project and then the Sunday School that Grace Driscoll was starting in another month. The roster would contain the names of nine or ten children when the Frazier children returned including little Billy and the Matson baby.

"And mine," cried Edna Caplinger, laughing and proud of the child within her. "I'll be going down to the hospital in a few days. I thought I never would get up this hill today."

Kate Botkin, guarding Thyra from the reaching hands of Billy who was fascinated by the dog's eyes and nose, kept us entertained with her cheerful witticisms. When we began speaking of families and native states, I wanted to show them pictures of mine in California and George's in the state of Washington. His parents lived there long before it became a state. The pictures were under the couch on which Beth sat and she rose to let me pull out the box.

Reaching into it I touched something rubbery and jerked back my hand. Reluctantly I held the box of pictures and said nothing but handed out some, commenting on them, until I cleared away enough to see what I had touched—something very obnoxious I was certain.

"Oh, look here!" I shouted.

I had uncovered an accumulation of old baked potatoes, pieces of cheese, and some chocolate. In unison came the shout "Rats!" From experience the girls knew the culprits. It made fascinating conversation until the party broke up. I heard more incredible stories of packrat ingenuity and achievement but no one could tell why the rats hid the food instead of eating it.

The wind had risen and was blowing in strong gusts. Beth tucked Billy into his sled and set out for home, but the minute she stepped on the icy trail she lost her footing and her hold on the sled rope. Like a flash the sled sped down and before our horrified eyes landed upside-down at the foot of the hill.

"Run, Harriet, run!" Beth screamed, waving her arms wildly but her legs unable to move, petrified from fright. "Billy's been killed!"

Without snowshoes and with my long skirts entangling my legs I lunged down in huge strides through deep snow. My frigid hands pawed for the sled and turned it right side up. I feared and dreaded what I would find. There was Billy, looking up, a bewildered smile on his face, but chuckling happily.

CHAPTER 8

In the high alps of the world, winds become gales. Clouds of every shape and size scuttle overhead just out of reach and are swirled every-which-way by blasts of wind that rapidly gather force. On one such day of gathering fury our unprotected shack shook violently and creaked. I watched George coming up the hill tightly gripping our daily can of water and struggling to make headway. Slowly, planting his feet carefully, he finally reached a packing box and two planks near the house just as the can fell from his shoulder.

My greeting to him was "Do we dare stay in this rickety shack tonight?"

"Oh yes," he said mildly. "We'll be all right. It just seems worse up here than down on the flat."

When we were in bed we could not sleep. All night long in that jittering hovel we listened to the fury and howling of the wind. What kept the cracker box standing I'll never know.

Crash! What sounded like pounds of glass breaking into bits was only an old cigar box filled with nails that had fallen from a shelf. Even the rats laid low that night, at least we did not hear them. My chattering teeth kept time to the rattling of the old stove-pipe fastened by wires to the rafters. The denim "carpet" rose and fell like ocean billows and wind crackled the newspaper padding.

"Please, George, let's get out of here," I pleaded.

"Where do you want to go?" he asked me.

"Anywhere down on the flat. Beth will take us in."

"We can't wake them up at this time of night." As if anyone could sleep on such a night.

"What difference does the time make when we may be

crushed to death any minute?" I screeched to be heard above the racket. Toward daybreak, George, seeing me so exhausted, said, "Probably Beth and Jim will be up early, so we'll go down now. You can stay with Beth while Jim and I go to work."

We dressed hurriedly in the bitter cold. In the corners of the front room, blown through cracks by the screeching winds, snow was heaped halfway to the ceiling. We stepped out clinging tightly to each other. The packing box and two large planks, which George had spilled our water on the night before, had been blown far *up* the hill. Around the Basin, stovepipes and an endless variety of articles were strewn. The sheet-iron roof on Lee Galter's house had been lifted and tossed aside. George held me tighter as we braced ourselves against the lash of the wild wind.

We found that Beth and Jim were up and dressed as they had been all night, ready for any emergency. Their welcome and Beth's hot breakfast made the storm less terrifying. Jim and George then left for the mill.

By afternoon the wind had eased, the temperature rose, and snow began to fall in big blinding flakes. When George's shift was over and we climbed our hill, he set long stakes beside the path protruding three feet above the snowbank as there was every indication we were to have a heavy fall and he must outline the trail. He wired the stovepipes securely again, shoveled the snow out of the house, and made up the fires, and after the fury of the night before we settled down to enjoy the silence and beauty of softly falling snow.

By morning our world and all it contained was white; the dips and gullies filled, the trails hidden. On his way to work George pulled up every buried stake and set it higher. Miners walking the pipeline looked like ghosts in white sheets. So did Charley, the powder-monkey, as his horse broke a trail to the stone house for the morning supply of blasting powder. George took off his snowshoes (webs, as we called them) and struck them upright at the foot of the trail to use later on his way home, then followed the path opened by Charley's horse and disappeared behind a snowbank.

Kate Botkin's rheumatism had been painful lately and about noon I decided to see if I could help her. It was only a short distance from our door straight across to her woodshed. On my webs I stepped out. One web sank. The other went still deeper. I tugged and strained but like a fly on sticky flypaper, I could not budge. Burrowing in the snow I unclasped the buckles, slid my feet out of the toe clips, worked them loose from the straps, pulled up the webs, and floundered back to the house, my soggy skirts clinging to my legs. I couldn't cross the snow and only by following the stakes, my webs on again, could I make my way down to the trail and up to Kate's front door.

For three days snow fell heavily. Few women left their shacks. Like quicksand, deep snow is bottomless. We often laughed hilariously seeing somebody trip over webs and suddenly disappear, soon to emerge looking like the proverbial snowman.

After working for hours one day I finished two caramel pies, one of them intended for Martha Snyder. Rigged out completely in snow-gear, coat, scarf, cap, arctics, and snowshoes, I stepped out on the trail proudly holding the pie, too soft to cover. The golden meringue looked perfect. I started down the hill in the awkward waddle necessary on snowshoes. In a flash one web overlapped the other. The pie and I rolled over and over, my long skirts whirled in the air, and I landed upside down. The meringue flew in one direction, the gooey caramel in another, leaving only a brown spot in the snow.

Seeing my acrobatics, Kate called from her doorway, "Harriet, you and George come over tonight and eat stew with us."

It was a most welcome invitation for on the hill Kate's Tomboy stew and heavenly fresh baked bread were famous. Kate had the only piano on the hill. George took his mandolin. Alex had both a mandolin and guitar, souvenirs of his years at Yale where he shared a room with Henry Seidel Canby, who later became well known in literary fields. We had not heard music in a long time, so made up our own quartet. No instrument was in tune but Kate played the piano, a slow, mournful ditty about stars, and we labored desperately to reach the final note in unison. We never succeeded, but it was great fun.

Kate's rheumatism had been getting worse steadily, and shortly after that night she left for Denver, hoping for relief in the lower altitude. Alex moved into the boardinghouse. About this time, due to ill health, Mr. Osborne retired and George was promoted to his position taking charge of recovering gold amalgam and delivering it to the mine office. Two or three times a month it was prepared for shipment on what was called Bullion Day.

This was a day of importance on which the gold, free of quicksilver, was melted and poured into three bar-molds each approximately nine inches long, five wide and four deep, containing five hundred ounces and at that time worth ten thousand dollars. The crucible, filled with molten gold, was lifted from the furnace by a chain block and swung to a point directly above the molds in a proper position to pour. Using long tongs the superintendent tipped the crucible just enough to let the white hot liquid flow into the molds.

Bullion Day arrived and under Jim's supervision George was ready to pour the gold. The chain block slowly raised the crucible from the melting furnace and swung it to the pouring position. Grasping the tongs, George cautiously tipped the crucible. To their consternation, when the golden stream touched the first mold, a shower of gold drops spattered over the floor. Instantly George raised the tongs and stopped pouring. Unfortunately, a supporting brick from the furnace had fused to the bottom of the crucible throwing it off balance just enough for the stream to hit the edge of the mold. The brick removed, George finished pouring.

When the spattered gold cooled into solid drops there was intense sweeping until most of it was recovered, but for days the millmen still found drops and even after diligent search, two hundred dollars' worth was never found. When the gold bars had cooled, George and Jim weighed them and placed them in a special iron case with three compartments. Mr. Herron arrived at the mill on horseback leading a mule with a special saddle to carry the containers. When in place, a heavy chain was attached to one side of the box, passed under the mule's belly and padlocked to the other side. Only a key in the safe in Telluride could remove the burden. An armed guard followed the animated gold mine down the mountain to the bank in Telluride.

In 1907, a year of depression, withdrawals from banks in California were limited to seventy-five dollars. My sister, in Oakland, about to be married, could not withdraw her own savings to buy her trousseau. But as depositors in the Bank of Telluride backed by Tomboy gold, we were permitted to cash checks against our total balances, so we bought United States postal orders which she could cash anywhere.

To increase recovery values from the ore, a new concentration process designed by J. M. Callow, a nationally well-known engineer, was installed in the mill and George was moved from the amalgam plates to the tables and vanners. This made necessary the changing of his shifts every two weeks. The day shifts were from seven in the morning to three, three to eleven at night, and the graveyard shift from eleven to seven next morning. I adapted my schedule to fit his.

While installing the new process, Mr. Callow stayed at the boardinghouse. Mr. Herron's home was in Telluride so he rode the trail several times a week except during the heaviest storms when he stayed at the boardinghouse.

George's association with both men had been so pleasant that we decided to invite them to dinner, although the thought of being hostess to such important officials somewhat frightened me. They readily accepted the invitation and I looked forward to that evening with mixed feelings. I hoped, as most wives would, to make a satisfactory impression so that these successful engineers might see in my husband the great engineer that I saw in him.

Seriously I contemplated the menu. Maryland oysters from the deep freeze of our woodshed for the first course. Salad for the second course, according to the fashion of the day (no lettuce, of course, as it was almost unknown there), leg of mutton for the entree, potatoes and canned peas, pudding for dessert. With dishes limited I would have to wash a few between courses.

On the important day I bustled about trying to make our hut as attractive as possible with our few ornaments. I moved the kitchen table into the "parlor," spread our one white cloth, polished the silver, and shined the glasses. I fed the coal range all day and about four o'clock put the roast in the oven. George came home and we both dressed in our best.

When our guests arrived it was ten below zero, but with two stoves roaring we were snug and cozy. Dinner was ready.

The cocktails looked inviting in the little dishes we had, but I was disturbed to see Mr. Callow toying with the sauce while Mr. Herron was obviously enjoying it. The salad of canned fruits seemed to please and I was delighted with the ease with which our conversation fell into a friendly and interesting trend.

The salad plates removed, I set in front of George the warmed dinner plates and the carving set. Oh, it really was fun. Then, proudly, I handed him the platter with the beautifully browned mutton, so crispy looking. I was beginning to learn some of the things my lovely mother had told me about cooking and a feeling of pride went over me. Slowly dishing up the potatoes and canned peas so as to give George time to carve the meat, my greatest concern was over. But as I stepped toward the table George was looking not at the roast but straight at me with an expression of pity, embarrassment, and "what shall I do now?"

Nothing was lacking. It must be something serious.

"Dearie," he said in his gentle manner, "I am afraid this meat did not get quite done."

Not quite done! done! done! It was still frozen solid.

All three gentlemen came to my rescue and if ever diplomacy saved the day in an emergency, it was then. Mr. Herron said he preferred his mutton "rare." Strangely, so did that noted engineer J. M. Callow! By slicing browned bits from the entire surface, George was able to serve each one of us with a few morsels of skin one quarter-inch thick.

Later, when we knew the Herrons more intimately, we learned that David never ate mutton anyway, and Mr. Callow could not eat oysters.

Possibly to somewhat assuage my feeling of humiliation, as we finished pudding and coffee, Mr. Herron said, "Mrs. Backus, if there is anything you want that I can do for you, just let me know. Can we make this house a little more comfortable?"

Boldly, and probably presumptuously, I disclosed what had been on my mind. "Well, Mr. Herron, a bedroom would add a great deal to this house."

"We will put one on," he assured me, to my joy. "Of course, we'll have to wait until summer and there is always so much mine and mill work that it will probably be September before we get around to it, but I'll tend to it then."

"Thank you very much," I said. "That will be fine and a real bedroom will be a great improvement."

I had learned something. When again we invited guests for dinner, I took the meat out of the woodshed the day before to let it thaw. But that was not the last of my cooking humiliations.

Beth and Jim were coming for dinner. I planned the very best meal possible and on the day before brought the plump, tempting-looking turkey from the woodshed.

The next day I again dragged the kitchen table to the parlor. I made dressing, stuffed the well-thawed turkey, mixed ice cream and set it outdoors to freeze. The turkey was browning nicely and I anticipated the feast that night and nibbling the shreds of white meat and cold dressing the following day.

Frequently I basted the browning bird until juices spurted when a spoon touched its sides. It looked wonderful. So did everything else when we saw Beth and Jim, carrying little Billy, climb the hill.

Seated at the table, George sharpened the carving knife, which wasn't necessary, really, because the turkey was so tender it almost fell apart as he sliced it. I served vegetables and gravy and passed the plates and we all began to eat.

With the first taste of white meat I gagged! I looked at Beth and saw the effort she was making to remove a bite from her mouth politely. May I never again taste *decayed* turkey! Ugh!

"Don't touch it!" I shouted and rushed platter and turkey to the kitchen. George followed and put the bird on the roof of the shed and next day burned it in the fire box of the shaft house.

Where and how long that dead turkey had traveled before it reached our woodshed, we would never know.

For the men in the boardinghouse the only relief from the monotonous food was a dinner elsewhere. Beth, Kate, and I often invited members of the staff for dinner, rarely more than two at a time for lack of space. They loved a home-cooked meal and an opportunity to dress up.

Our guests one night were Don McKean, the mine electrician, and Ed Krammer, timekeeper and hill jokester who kept us entertained telling stories of their years in the mountains. A few nights later, Al Awkerman, the big lumbering master mechanic, whose good humor was often offset by his quick, violent temper, was our guest. He ate heartily, and when we had finished, he shoved back his chair and burst out, "Damn that Krammer! He warned me to fill up on anything you served first because you and George didn't give much to eat. Why the devil did you let me take that second big dish of soup?"

The boardinghouse, a three-story building painted gray and

white, standing on firm, level ground out of reach of snowslides, housed two hundred and fifty men. Miners have prodigious appetites and the most important room to them was the big, barnlike dining room.

On a beautiful evening, George and I, as invited visitors, were seated at a bench at the staff table at one end of the room. Suddenly came the rush of two hundred feet in heavy boots as men rushed to the benches and sprawled over the tables reaching right and left for dishes of food slid within their reach by the flunkies. Immediately came the slurping of hungry mouths sucking in soup. Before I finished my soup, they had shoveled down meat and potatoes. When they began on pie, I neglected my dinner and sat fascinated as a rabbit by a snake. What a scene!

Our life was different here. It was rugged, challenging, adventuresome, humble, and many other things to two people so much in love.

CHAPTER 9

Many of the flunkies were Scandinavians accustomed to skis in their homelands. The slopes were too steep in the Basin for ski runs, but not long after our boardinghouse dinner I stood at our front door staring in amazement. Across the gulch, halfway up the awful slope opposite the shaft house, where not even a tree could grow on that forbidding precipice, four distant figures were zigzagging down below the twenty-foot crown of snow that never melted.

Terrified, I couldn't look away. What kept them from toppling down from the peak? Suddenly one figure did plunge down, skis waving over his head and disappeared in the drifts at the foot of the mountain.

The next one stayed upright until near the bottom and then rolled over and over. The last two reckless flunkies crisscrossed the slope gracefully until near the bottom and successfully glided to the finish.

That bleak cliff became our barometer as a rise in temperature inevitably started snowsliding. I learned to recognize the peculiar crack of breaking snowbanks echoing through the Basin and by looking quickly I often saw the packs breaking away. Sometimes huge masses tumbled down. Fortunately, the houses were just out of their reach. Often small snowballs started rolling, gathering snow as they tumbled, then falling and hitting a snag, bounding high in the air, exploding into tiny powder-puffs.

One morning, while stirring ice cream packed in the snow, I heard a dull crash. Instinctively I looked up. By rare chance, my gaze bridged the wide canyon and fastened at the very peak from which a great wall of snow had broken and was toppling down the abyss. The entire facade of the mountain leaped forward and

Sitting atop horses are the night guard, day guard (Bob Meldrum), and English assayer.

dropped. I prayed that no one was in its path below.

Oh the terrors of those peaks, the menace from which there was no defense!

From time to time since 1902 a threatening undercurrent of labor trouble had made itself apparent. On three different occasions we heard rumors that the mill was to be blown up.

One morning when Charley reached the powder house he found a candle tied to the door, suggestively. And only recently a small explosion at the boardinghouse had occurred and had not yet been explained.

The daytime guard on the hill was Bob Meldrum, one of the most conspicuous figures on the side of law and order during the disturbances in Telluride. He had been a guard in the famous trial of Hayward, Moyer, and Orchard in connection with the dynamiting of the railway station in which Governor Steunenberg of Idaho lost his life. For years a deputy sheriff, Meldrum was said to have killed more than a half score of men as an officer of the law. According to the verdicts, the killings had been justifiable. Seemingly fearless, he strode boldly into union meetings fully aware that the men feared him as much as they hated him.

Of medium size, with a swarthy skin, black hair, and heavy moustache, Meldrum looked like the typical intrepid westerner. In his dark flannel shirt, leather jacket, high boots, black leather gauntlets with wide flaring cuffs, and a large, black, high-crowned hat drawn to a peak, he was easily spotted on the trails. He rarely spoke to anyone, perhaps because of extreme deafness, but what he lacked in hearing was made up in keen vision. His dark, sharp eyes seemed never to move but nothing ever escaped his notice.

He and the woman, generally accepted as his wife, lived a short way down the trail from us. Like him, she never mingled with the families in the Basin. In the saddle of her beautiful white horse, she made a romantic picture riding the trails, but her withdrawal from all contact with any of us on the hill caused some comment. Meldrum, "the law" on the hill, rode daily through the Basin watching for signs of trouble of any kind, until at night Tom Sullivan took his place. No liquor was allowed in the boardinghouse so there was no trouble from that source. The majority of the men were respectable, decent, hardworking miners.

Three o'clock was the time the millmen reported for the afternoon shifts. During the long winters I kept the pot-bellied stove going until George returned toward midnight. Then as though we had been separated for months, we relived our high school and college days together while he enjoyed the hot chocolate and toast always ready for him. We didn't miss the so-called luxuries of a city. We were together and oh, so happy! And the days flew by.

Alone on the hill I was never afraid at night and seldom turned the key in the loose lock of a door that even I could have shaken down. If there were strange noises, I walked around the shack to investigate. It is the unforeseen that causes fear. Did I say I was never afraid?

It was nearing the witching hour of twelve and, waiting for my George, I sat reading. The night was cold and crunchy, like so many winter nights in that rare atmosphere, a time when stillness reigns and sound carries far. The snow was deep, half covering our windows, but sitting near the fire I felt content and cozy. Miners were underground, millmen at their work, only the roaring of the overworked stove, fighting frigid air that charged in through unseen and invisible cracks, broke the silence.

Engrossed with a book, I suddenly heard a soft sound like a padded footfall outside the window, but I continued reading. After a moment it was repeated under the opposite window. I laid down the book to listen.

It was nothing, I assured myself. No one could come up here without making more noise than that. I picked up the book but not with my former interest in the story which read ". . . not a soul was anywhere visible. The path stretched downward." Again I stopped reading. From the nearest window came that same pat, pat. I had difficulty finding the place in the book again . . . "Far away in the vale a faint whiteness of more than usual extent showed that the rivers were high. The absence of all life clinched his intentions and he knocked at the door." I read it twice without making sense out of it.

The thing to do was investigate. But the snow was far too deep and my heart beating too fast. George was a millman. What if the troublemakers were to molest the homes of the workers! The windows had no shades and I avoided looking at them for fear I would see eyes, a face, the perpetrator of those sneaky steps and footfalls.

I slithered to the floor and crawled on hands and knees to the door—carefully turning the key. It just *might* hold. I crawled back to the couch to be out of direct line of the windows. More taps! Would George get home in time to save me? I shivered through an eternity, lying there. The fire needed coal but I dared not move.

Thank God! From far down the hill, through the crisp air, came the loud, brittle snaps of George's familiar steps, nearer, louder. He turned the knob expecting the door to open as usual, but the lock held.

"George, is that you?" My voice quavered.

"Of course. Who were you expecting?" But I could not even smile at his joke. I unlocked the door, threw my arms around his neck, half throttling him, and burst into tears.

"What happened?" he asked.

"Someone has been sneaking from one window to another. I could hear steps in the snow," I sobbed.

"Well, we'd better go out and find him," he said mildly. Company gives courage. Unmindful of the cold I wallowed behind George around the shack to the window where he stood, looked down and laughed.

"Yes, there are his footsteps." He pointed to a row of long, thick, crystal icicles which, warmed by the roaring fire, had dropped from the sheet-iron roof deep into stiff, crusty snow, one by one—pat, pat, pat, from both sides of the house.

With water so scarce we reverted to the nineteenth-century custom of the Saturday night bath. Our daily supply of five gallons was not enough for bathing so George made an extra Saturday trip to the shaft house. Leafing through the mail order catalogue, the dog-eared standby of miners' families, we saw a picture of a folding bathtub. Eureka! No more bathing in a tin hand-basin. We ordered one and waited—and waited for weeks. Finally, digging at the foot of the trail, George found the package in the snow where the mule-skinner had tossed it some time before. Cheering each other, we tore open the package.

A folding, cot-like wooden frame, the size and shape of the regulation bathtub, rested on the floor, and from it depended a tub of black rubber sheeting.

On time-hallowed Saturday nights we set up the tub near the warm kitchen stove on which snow was melting in every utensil we owned. But with all that and the extra five gallons, the water stood only two inches in the pliable tub. George, always ready with the necessary solution to a problem, shortened the tub by placing a box under one end. Up came the water.

As ladies are first, even at the mines, I bathed. George used the same water. Then came the job of bailing out the tub. We earned our luxurious baths.

One day, somewhat apologetically, I was telling Mrs. Herron about our tub. With a smile of happy recollections, that lovely lady said, "Oh, that's nothing. When we lived in Nevada where David was mining, we had to buy water by the bucket at a high price and bath night for one had to be bath night for the entire family. We had a round galvanized tub in which we washed the baby first. Then in the same water, turn by turn, went the next oldest child until all four were bathed. Afterwards, I took my turn. David came last, scrubbing the grime from his mine-soiled body with that well-used water."

Long after, we laughed about mishaps and makeshifts, but we would sigh and fall silent over tragedies. The company prepared for less serious emergencies by using two clean, well-lighted rooms in the boardinghouse as a hospital with a doctor, generally young in experience, in constant attendance. His equipment was adequate for minor accidents, burns, cuts, etc. All critical cases were sent down the hill as soon as an ambulance could work its way up from Telluride. In winter this might take hours getting the victim to the Miners' Hospital and the capable hands of Dr. Edgar Hadley.

Often men set out on foot, confident of reaching their destination safely. Many times it was at the cost of frozen hands, feet, or life itself. The benumbing cold, the fatal mistake when exhausted of stopping to rest, the sense of drowsy comfort causing a fatal delay. Whenever men were sent to an isolated place to repair wires or carry supplies, they were timed and if they did not report back in due time a searching party was dispatched to find them.

One biting cold day, two men started over the range to Lake Ptarmigan with medicine for Pete Solari, the lone attendant at the pumping plant. Dr. Caplinger, who had talked with Pete over the telephone, feared pneumonia, the most dreaded illness in high altitudes. The two men had the formidable assignment of climbing on snowshoes an almost perpendicular wall two thousand feet high over a fifteen-foot depth of wind-driven snow. When the allotted time had passed with no word from them, everyone on the hill became concerned. As night approached and clouds closed down, anxiety increased and many offered to go in search. Three men were selected and went with our prayers that they would find the climbers safe. But when at last they were found, one, with his feet frozen, was lying beside the dead body of the partner he had tried desperately to keep warm.

Heavy and prolonged snowfalls followed that cold spell. Soft flakes showering down day and night raised the surface of the Basin several feet. Walking was extremely difficult, but after the snowfall ended there came one of those breathtaking beautiful days of brilliant sunshine after the storm. The cloudless sky was deep azure; the world below was blinding with sunbeams sparkling on the glistening white. The air still. Standing at my door, bewitched by the beauty of the scene, I saw two men carrying a stretcher from the upper workings. As they passed the foot of our trail, a man with a stocking cap tight on his head raised his body from the stretcher and leaning on one elbow, gazed toward the mountains as if taking a last look. It was Nick Bertini who had gone to the lake to replace Pete Solari. Nick had fallen and struck his head so severely that Pete had called for help. At once two men started over the range. Seeing Nick's condition they improvised a stretcher and, handicapped by snowshoes, inched down the mountainside, hauling the injured man. By the time they reached the boardinghouse, Nick was delirious.

It was just four hours later when the ambulance from Telluride was able to break through the trail and reach the mine. By this time, Nick was a raving maniac and it took three men to control him. In the hospital next day he died of a badly fractured skull.

To deepen our sorrow, word came from the hospital that the baby Edna Caplinger had so hoped for was stillborn—dead a week before she had gone down the mountain.

CHAPTER 10

In a group we attended the opening services of the loftiest Y.M.C.A. in the world, in a building near the stable.

Men of all faiths attended. Robert Snyder spoke inspiringly. The small organ sounded forth real music under the fingers of Sam Neustadt, the surveyor, and we all joined in familiar hymns.

After the service we watched the miners bowling, then said our goodnights. I pulled my earflaps down tight before shoving my hands in fleece-lined mittens. The cold stung my face and I wrapped my woolen scarf up to my eyes. The sky was closely speckled with the great stars and planets and millions of tiny ones that shine only for those on mountains two miles high.

Hurrying home we met young Tom Sullivan making his cheerless rounds, his big body enveloped in a long mackinaw the high collar completely hiding his neck.

"Hello Tom," we called and I added, "I'm glad I haven't your job tonight."

"Hello, folks," he called in his genial way. "You bet it's cold. Twenty below when I passed the shaft house. But it's not so bad when I walk fast. Wish I could have been at the Y opening tonight."

"You missed a good talk from Bob Snyder," George said.

"Goodnight," we called in unison.

Tom walked briskly past the barn and down the trail to Scotty's store where he stepped in for a minute to pass the time of day with miners off shift. They often gathered in this social center, perchance to buy something, more often just to chat, especially in winter, spending an hour or two around the huge pot-bellied stove, a break in the monotony of a boardinghouse evening.

After a little talk, Tom headed again into the night, exchanging

71

quips with the men who liked this burly, popular young Irishman. "Goodnight, Tom." "Don't freeze, Sullivan, it's a damn cold night." "See you tomorrow night, Tom," came from Scotty who was putting jackets on a shelf behind the counter.

Tom opened the door and in the rush of cold air, Joe Lambert, a miner, staggered in without hat or jacket, his feet in bedroom slippers. As he reeled toward them the men stared in surprise. Drunkenness meant instant dismissal from the mine. Weaving close to a couple of men, he broke into their talk with belligerent remarks.

Sensing trouble, Tom walked back quietly, saying, "That's all right, Joe, let's go back to the boardinghouse. You're not dressed for this cold."

"God damn you, Tom. Shut your dirty mouth. You can't tell me what to do," Joe blurted.

"There's nothing to get excited about, Joe. Sit here then, until you get warm," Tom invited.

Infuriated and without warning, Lambert jerked a pistol from inside his clothing, aimed point blank at Tom and shot him in the stomach. As Tom dropped, Joe Lambert, instantly sobered, was gone. Scotty rushed to the wounded man. A miner reached the door in time to see Lambert disappear in the direction of the mill.

Bob Meldrum, "the law," was awakened by a miner, out of breath, pounding on his door.

"Bob, come quick, Tom Sullivan's been shot."

Meldrum and Dr. Caplinger, summoned by another miner, reached Scotty's store within minutes, and, as the doctor knelt beside Tom, Meldrum, the intrepid, asked, "Which way did Joe go?"

"Toward the mill," someone shouted. Without waiting to glance at or speak to Tom, Meldrum ran to the nearest door of the mill and above the roaring of the stamps shouted to a millman standing near the plates, "Did you see a man run through here?"

"Yes, a moment ago. He was mighty excited and out of breath, and what struck me queer he was yelling 'I ain't got a gun, I ain't got a gun.'" Shouting through his cupped hands into Meldrum's ear, he added, "I couldn't leave my post but I saw him head toward the change room."

It took the guard only a minute to open the door of that room.

Facing him from the opposite side stood Lambert. Calmly, but loud enough to be heard above the thunderous noise of the mill, came Meldrum's command—"Hands up."

Lambert moved his hands. Were they being raised above his head or reaching for a gun? A crack shot, lightning on the trigger, Meldrum took no chances. He fired and Joe Lambert fell dead instantly.

As soon as an ambulance could come up from Telluride on that cold, cold night, Tom Sullivan was taken to the Miners' Hospital. Only twenty-nine years old, he wanted passionately to live. In every way possible nurse Margaret Perril and her assistants fought to keep him in bed and alive.

"I must live. I must live. Let me up," the young Irishman pleaded. But his wound was deadly. Two days later all the hill mourned his tragic death.

Meldrum was brought to trial. Being a deputy sheriff and risking his life to arrest a murderer, supposedly armed, he was acquitted. Talking with Alex Botkin after the trial Meldrum asked him, "What did Kammer mean in his testimony when he said I used my 'prerogative' as a deputy? Hell, man, I used my gun!"

As the weeks passed, storms were less severe. The temperature rose gradually. We could hear an occasional drip, drip from the roof. As the glazed snow receded, dirty, uneven expanses of rock appeared. Trails in the Basin, tamped so solid that they were impervious to the early summer sun, protruded high above the soggy, sagging snowbanks. Mule trains slogged along six feet above the ground on the ice levees. It was more and more difficult to keep their footing until a road crew dug out and tossed the packed ice on either side which rose with the additional debris until the trail itself was deep in the narrow cut. As fifteen mules plodded through the ice defile with a load of lagging to line a tunnel at the mine, all that could be seen were ends of timber and thirty long, black ears bobbing along between the banks.

Days were longer. Clouds skimmed overhead and vanished. Under the welcome warmth of the sun great steep slopes melted into water running down the canyons. From the towering cliff, the ski run of the flunkies and last stronghold of winter, patches of snow broke loose and leaped joyously down the precipice.

Snowshoes, now useless, were put away. Long skirts and

petticoats dragged in the slush, spattering water over our arctics until only our long, close-fitting tights gave a degree of body warmth and dryness.

By the time school opened tiny rills trickled from every slope and cranny. Here and there small patches of shaded snow relieved the barren look of bleak rock walls. On our hill a few stubby stumps appeared, relics of timberline trees sacrificed to make way for the shacks. The ugly, dark pipeline emerged and the snap of miners' feet on the bare boards echoed through the Basin.

After their long winter hole-up, groundhogs popped out, hugging the ground to search for anything edible. But cruel scarcity of vegetation took its toll and numbers of them died of starvation on the slopes.

A few tiny chipmunks appeared from nowhere and eagerly searched for food. After much persuasion, one dared creep to my fingers which were holding a walnut meat. If our door was open he would enter timidly looking for food. We saw them only for a short time and then, like the packrats, they disappeared as suddenly as they had come.

Luckily we were too high for flies and other insects.

Many missing objects, missing and sought for, carelessly lost before the snows fell, broken dishes, even garbage thrown out by the slovenly, came to light in the Savage Basin where, "verily, every prospect pleased and only man was vile."

But on the warmest day of summer, against the blue of the illimitable sky, an eternal white coronet crowned the pinnacles stretched toward the southwest. Long snow banners, woven by the winds waved farewell as they disappeared.

In the deep canyon below, yellow pines, stately firs, and Engelmann spruce burst from their ghostly mantles, intensely green to our unaccustomed eyes. The Big Elephant, attacked by the sun, rapidly shed his heavy coat of snow and burst forth in myriad of long-stemmed purple columbines nodding gracefully. Delicate and lovely, these flowers native to the Rockies seek and cling to the crags and precipices of the heights, happily and lavishly squandering beauty in the lonely wilderness.

Mrs. Tuller, gentle, dignified, arrived from far down the valley to teach eleven scholars in the school house, where on Sunday, Grace Driscoll conducted Sunday School. Under her enthusiastic and competent leadership they were soon singing to her accompaniment on the small organ:

Jesus bids us shine with a clear pure light
Like a little candle burning in the night.
In this world of darkness we must shine,
You in your small corner and I in mine.

And they made up in volume what they lacked in numbers.

The backdrop of the amphitheatre, a solid expanse of white all winter, became bare, rocky, forbidding from the floor of the Basin to the heights. Not a shrub or blade of grass grew in the loose surface of slide-rock. The face of the mountain was unbroken except for a path ascending in sharp switchbacks about every fifty feet. Wide enough for only one horse, it zigzagged like a ragged cut, each turn ascending only a few feet There could be no passing, but no one looking from the pinnacle where vision was unobstructed would have started down unless the way was clear. Trips between the mine and the lake were few, and rarely did anyone take the trip for pleasure. Yet, somehow, the top of the world beckoned George and me and we decided to respond. We talked it over with Fred Diener.

"It's a wonderful experience, one you'll never forget, but you'll have to wait until more snow melts from the drifts near the top," he said.

"I can't go for a month anyway. I have to wait for my long day," explained George. The change from day shift to graveyard shift gave him thirty-two hours off work.

"The weather should be just right then. You must choose a fine day, with no wind or rain. There are only three horses Rodgers will rent for that trip because it's dangerous. Chief and Fanny are the best. They're reliable, surefooted and never get frightened. When the time comes I'll have them up here for you. Sometimes you can't get the horses you want unless you speak ahead," a fact we knew from experience.

"Fine, Fred. We'll figure on it in a month. I want to visit the Camp Bird Mill," said George as we left the stable.

Reaching our shack we saw Kate and Alex riding up the trail from the boardinghouse. He had gone to Telluride the day before to meet her on her return from Denver. We were happy to see her dismount easily with the old sparkle in her eyes. And once again she began inviting men from the boardinghouse to her home-cooked dinners.

We could walk straight from one shack to the other. A few weeks later she came with a book in her hand and a puzzled expression on her face.

"Harriet," she began, "Don brought me this book yesterday, in appreciation, he said, of the dinners he had with us."

"Nice of him, Kate," I smiled.

"Yes," she agreed with uncertainty. "I said I knew I would enjoy the book. Now I don't know what to say to him. He told me he hadn't read it, but it was highly recommended."

"And, is it good?" I asked eagerly. On the hill, books were scarce and I was hungry for reading.

"Well, I stopped reading it after a couple of chapters. I don't know how such an obscene book ever was printed." An expression of indignation crept into her eyes and voice.

"Obscene! How could Don give you a book of that sort?" I asked.

"He said he bought it at the drugstore in Telluride. You know, the only store that carries books and only about a dozen at that. Not being a reader, Don said he asked the druggist to choose one for a lady. I suppose the druggist didn't know one book from another."

That night Kate showed the book to Alex, he couldn't help smiling as he knew how Don would feel. So the next morning he took it to the office and gave it to Don.

At noon that day Alex climbed up the hill for lunch. Always genial and smiling, he was this day laughing as he said, "Kate, I showed the book to Don and I have never seen an angrier man in my life. I've never heard him curse before, but he burned the book with a string of cursing that rivaled the mule skinners! Poor Don." The poor druggist when next Don saw him!

We were all pleased when Beth's Aunt Fanny arrived from Boston to spend the summer. A welcome new face from far away, with fresh conversation and ideas and news from the Eastern Seaboard. Wealthy, she had traveled widely, but she loved our mountains and claimed they surpassed the Swiss Alps. She readily adapted herself to our primitive accommodations and was the inspiration for extra gatherings. The altitude limited her walking but she was happy to be with Beth, Jim, and little Billy and interested in the ride we were to take to the lake, when we pointed out to her the zigzag trail we were to follow.

Picking up the mail at the stable a few days before George's long day arrived, I saw Chief and Fanny coming up the trail, stumbling along wearily. Chief's pretty head dropped dejectedly. The flanks of both horses were lathered with foam, red with blood oozing from rowel cuts. Fred caught their bridles and patting their heads said to me, "Isn't that awful? I suppose a couple of men did the town last night and started up the hill late this morning and were trying to get to work on time. They must have run the poor beasts all the way up." He shook his head sadly.

"Fred, why don't you stop such cruelty?" I cried hotly. "Why does Rodgers rent his horses to such brutes?"

"Well, Rodgers can't tell what kind of riders they are in advance, Mrs. Backus. Most people are decent and treat horses right. But some men are devils. Sandy and Tuff are so windbroken they're no good anymore. When are you planning to go over the range?" he inquired.

"George says we can go day after tomorrow if the weather is good."

"That's fine," Fred said as he relieved the horses of their saddles and bridles. "I'll give Chief and Fanny a good rub down, and they won't be rented out tomorrow. They can have a good day's rest and be ready for you on Wednesday."

I patted the noses of Chief and Fanny, and seeing their bleeding flanks I left the stable, crying inside myself.

CHAPTER 11

Wednesday dawned clear and warm. We hurried through breakfast and I put on the skirt of my brown corduroy riding habit which was very full and reached halfway between knees and ankles. It buttoned down the front and had the look of an ordinary too-short skirt. To mount a horse I unbuttoned the front, the fullness fell on each side and a wide gore attached underneath permitted me to straddle a horse. A divided skirt would have been shocking to everyone, including me.

At eight o'clock, Fred arrived with Chief and Fanny looking newly groomed and fresh. The wounds of their vicious goadings were beginning to heal and no spurs would touch them this day. We carried flexible quirts to be used only if absolutely necessary. George mounted Fanny. Fred helped me onto Chief's deep, heavy, western saddle, adjusted the stirrups to proper length, slid my feet into the high tapaderos, and tied my jacket to the back of the saddle.

"Now, *please*," his voice was serious and impressive, "please go the way I tell you to. After you reach the top, you will come to a narrow trail cutting straight across the face of the next steep peak. *Don't take that trail!* It is extremely dangerous, especially now while there is still snow and ice on it. Go to your right, around the peak. It will take a little longer and there is one steep place, but it's not as risky as the other one. Let the horses take you. Don't try to guide them too much. They know better than you do."

With the wise warning of one who knew the trails well, we headed toward the great divide between Savage and Imogene Basins and soon were behind the upper workings and at the foot of the zigzag. I held the reins loose but firmly gripped the pommel of the saddle. Chief kept a few feet behind Fanny.

After a slight ascent the horses wheeled on a sharp turn. Back and forth on that narrow trail, mounting slowly, testing their footing with each step as small chunks of slide rock littered the trail. My hands gripped the pommel more tightly as each time, with God-given horse sense, they cautiously turned at each switchback, taking us higher and higher. I glanced down on the diminishing shacks and prayed that the horses' feet would not slip. There was no turning back; we had to go on. Two-thousand-foot rise in a mile—approximately a thirty percent grade!

I sat rigid with my eyes riveted to the trail. We were nearing the top of the slide rock formation when the trail leveled out and we could see ahead the saddle between the tawny, jagged peaks through which we were to pass. I was tingling with excitement, thinking of the challenge these formidable barriers had been to pioneers first trying to cross them.

We reached Virginia Pass and dismounted on a small level spot. The silence was awesome and absolute except for the labored breathing of the horses. Without speaking we gazed upon this masterpiece of the Great Sculptor about which Bancroft wrote, "The view begins nowhere and ends nowhere. It is infinite . . . mountains beyond mountains."

Standing more than two-and-a-half miles above the line where sky and oceans meet we could see our settlement, diminished by distance. Shacks, boardinghouse, and mill dotted the depths of that white-crested spur of the range curving like a sickle above them, the first sparse sprinkling of trees increasing in density down the slopes. The pencil line drawn around the opposite slope was the trail leading to Telluride, only the tip of it visible in the ravine almost a mile below. From where we stood the great walls of rock hiding the town seemed only hedges. The great plateau stretched across western Colorado one hundred and fifty miles into the mountains of scenic Utah.

We could see what Bancroft meant by "mountains beyond mountains." To the northeast were the peaks of the great Continental Divide, forming giant saws, every crag a tooth linked together so closely there seemed to be no intervening valleys. To the southeast, one mass of giants glowed a deep rich red, dyed by oxidation of abundant iron in the rock. The many peaks of these

Red Mountains were uniform in height and wonderful to behold among the pale colors and somber shadows of other ranges.

The tremendous upheavals by which they were upthrust in spires of majesty and grandeur, range after range, were beyond imagination to picture or understand. Awed by the solemnity of the limitless panorama we mounted the horses and turned to find the trail leading down the other side of the ridge.

On this northeastern slope of the Sneffles range in Imogene Basin was located the famous Camp Bird Mine and Mill with outlet, the town of Ouray, hidden like Telluride in a narrow canyon below. Directly ahead lay the trail that Fred had warned us not to take. It was a frightening thing, looking like a mere crack across the almost perpendicular side of the jagged, cone-shaped peak with no shelves or ledges below to break the fall of rock, snow, or living thing until the slope leveled out at the base, one thousand feet below.

Lingering patches of snow and ice added to the grim and treacherous aspect of the path which obviously was a shortcut, a beeline crossing, and siren-like, might tempt a belated rider of the mountains. Fred's warning had been necessary. We dared not take that trail. Rather than attempt it, we would have turned back. A slight touch of the reins and the horses turned to the right, stepping carefully over a bed of broken rock, weaving a pathless way among giant boulders strewn haphazardly over a gentle slope. Then, as we rounded the domed pinnacle the trail abruptly plunged headlong down to its juncture with the end of the trail we had avoided. I reined Chief to a stop and called, "Oh, dearie, we can't go down there!"

"I think we can make it," he said quietly but somewhat hesitantly. "Down below the path looks firm, and with good footing."

"Good footing below!" I protested. "Ride down that awful drop? Can't we walk and lead the horses?"

"No," he answered calmly. "That would be more dangerous than riding. The horses might fall on us and the path is too narrow to walk beside them through the rocks."

"I'm afraid to go. How can Chief hold back?"

George stopped and was looking down as if trying to decide what to do. I shuddered. But having made up his mind, he said, "You wait until I get down to where the trail is wider. Then give

Chief his head. Don't pull on the reins. Kick your feet out of the stirrups and be sure to keep your legs stretched in front of you." With that he gave Fanny the signal to start.

My heart was pounding as she took one step and seemingly aware of danger stopped. George patted her neck and spoke softly and Fanny justified Fred's confidence and praise. Drawing her hind legs under her body she inched forward as if trying to get into the right step. To prevent his weight giving any forward impetus, George leaned far back in the saddle and stretched his legs out in front. Fanny's haunches were scraping the ground.

I was silent for fear even a sound might throw Fanny off balance. Those few moments lasted an eternity! Where the two trails met, the descent leveled out enough for Fanny to straighten up. A few feet beyond, George pulled her to a stop and called to me to come on.

"Be careful to keep your feet forward." He reiterated.

Well, thank God George was down safely, but my voice was quavering as I said, "Go on, Chief. We've got to follow."

With his first step I leaned far back and pressed my legs tightly along his neck. Rocks, big and little, lined the path. With mincing steps Chief edged forward. I made ready to slide off in case he stumbled for I was only inches from the ground. My heart raced and pounded. Only vaguely could I see George watching. Then I knew we had made it when I heard him say, "Well, Kiddy, we got down that cliff all right. That is easily a forty-five-degree grade, and believe me, these horses must have had experience. No wonder Fred reserved them for us."

"Let's wait a few minutes until my heart slows down. And I want to see that trail from the bottom instead of from the top." Looking again at the narrow line across the cliff, "Surely, no one but a fool would attempt *that* path," I said.

Not a cloud sailed in the blue heavens. With the sun overhead it was noon so we quickened our pace, having a long way to go before our venture would be over.

Around a curve came two riders, one of them mounted on a beautiful white horse. So rarely did anyone cross this range that we were mutually surprised. They will soon be climbing that awful path, I thought, dreading the time when we must do the same.

Smoke from a few scattered cabins assured us that prospectors

Fred Diener, trying to get one of our horses out of the snow.

still followed the rainbow. Although it had passed its days of fabulous gold production, the Camp Bird was still operating. Relaxed now I could enjoy the easy trail and denser verdure as we went lower. Then I heard galloping and turned to see the white horse coming, his rider waving my corduroy jacket which evidently I had lost on the trail.

"Many, many thanks," I said. "I'm sorry you had to turn back with it. What a beautiful horse." I looked long at its arched neck and long, flowing mane and tail.

"Yes, I think he's beautiful," he answered proudly, patting his pet. "He means a great deal to me. He's reliable, and he's carried me over these ranges a long time." We exchanged goodbyes and the stranger turned his horse and galloped up the trail. An easy mile of riding brought us to the Camp Bird Mill and lunch at the boardinghouse.

The company had recovered enormous values from the mine located on an adjoining slope. This bonanza was discovered by Thomas Walsh, a prospector who, during the early days of Leadville, had run a hotel in that historic town. Moving his family to Ouray, he roamed the heights surrounding the pioneer town searching for gold. Claims in Imogene Basin were being worked for silver and lead ores, but Walsh recognized the gold content. Buying up nearby claims, he developed one of the richest gold mines in the world. Eventually it brought him over twenty-five million dollars.

He moved his family to Washington, D.C., where in good esteem in the Government, he cut a wide swath. Redhaired, freckle-faced, little Maggie Walsh blossomed into "the beautiful Miss Walsh of Washington, D.C.!" She married Edward McLean, son of a newspaper publisher and their combined fortunes earned their son the title of the "richest baby in the world." Mrs. McLean acquired the Hope Diamond, and it was she who paid Gaston Means one hundred thousand dollars to aid the Lindbergs in the search for their kidnapped baby.

I rested while George spent some time in the mill, his main interest, until it was time to start home. Fed and rested, the horses began the return journey with vigor. Curving away from the last human habitation and few trees at timberline, we reached the bare, menacing cliffs separating us from our Tomboy home.

To me the climb looked steeper than the descent.

"Can we walk and lead the horses?" I asked George.

"Oh no. You go ahead. I'll be right behind you." This time I leaned forward. My head close to Chief's neck, feet out of the stirrups and legs stretched backward.

Chief did not hesitate. Slowly and carefully he struggled, breathing hard, his pretty head low as I coaxed, "Go on, Chief. Good Chief, go on." I patted his neck and he strained harder until, finally, we reached the top.

Fanny and George followed and when we were together, resting a minute and saying, "I'm glad that's over." The horses nodded as if in agreement.

"Coming up wasn't nearly as scary as going down, George," I said.

"No, it wasn't, Kiddy, and you were a fine sport," he encouraged.

Threading our way between boulders we soon were in the pass, looking down at the settlement. The sun was setting and the slopes opposite our shack were already purple shadowed. Almost as slowly as we had climbed, we zigzagged lower and lower and reached the upper workings a half mile from home.

"Let's go to the barn," I said. "I want to tell Fred about our trip and how wonderful the horses were."

At the stable Fred was stirring stew on the top of his rusty stove. He knew I was stiff and hurried to help me down from Chief.

"God, I'm glad to see you folks back. Did you pass two riders on the trail?" He seemed concerned.

"Why, yes," George replied. "We passed them on the other side of the range just as we were going into Imogene Basin. One of them, on a fine white horse, turned back to bring Harriet's jacket she had dropped. Who were they?"

"That one is Tom Eckley. He has a very responsible job with the power company and rides the range often. That horse was his pride and pet. Summer and winter he has ridden him all over the mountains. He loved that horse."

"What do you mean, 'That horse *was?*' Fred, did anything happen?" I broke in.

"Well, those men were in a hurry and took the shortcut across the cliff. Thank God they walked and led the horses. Tom's horse stepped on one of those damned icy spots and plunged all the way to the bottom. You saw that peak. You know there was nothing to stop him for a thousand feet. Tom ran back over the trail and it's a wonder he didn't go down, himself. Then he ran down the side of the mountain and crawled out over the boulders to where the horse lay. The poor thing was still breathing but his neck was broken. Tom ran on down to a prospector's cabin and borrowed a gun. His friend couldn't turn back on the trail so he went across, then took the longer way, the way I told you to take. He met Tom just after he'd shot his horse. They walked the rest of the way down and came here to get another horse, to ride to Telluride. He was pretty hard hit, poor Tom. I tell you, you can't take chances in these mountains."

CHAPTER 12

Summer remained delightful. Never hot, because of the height and snow above us, most of the days were sunny and bright. We had few electric storms, none close or severe. Thunderheads were quickly blown away but often we could see lightning in the valley below, and heat-lightning far, far away.

One summer blessing was a vendor who ventured up the trail three times a week, bringing fresh vegetables and willingly fetching meat we had ordered from Telluride. His prices were as steep as our high shacks, but we cleaned out his stock and wailed for more.

About this time of year, up to the Basin came groups of sure-footed little burros, diminutive alongside the tall, big-boned mules. These "Rocky Mountain Canaries," as they were known, were not roped in strings. A skinner on horseback, assisted by his invaluable dog, drove them from the rear. Their little legs looked too small and delicate to support the loads which, though lighter and less unwieldy than those carried by mules, consisted of heavy boxes of powder, caps, fuses and such things.

Occasionally the burros went to the upper workings but generally they were unloaded at the mouth of the Cincinnati Tunnel, the main level of the mine which extended a mile from the portal to the base of the cliff, under the upper workings.

This well-developed mine had been a rich producer for years and with the combined tunneling of the upper, main and lower levels, contained more than three miles of trackage underground.

Passing by one day I heard the clang of the gong, a signal from below for the engineer to raise the cage. I stopped to look as the hiss of the exhaust indicated that the cables were hauling up a load. Two minutes later a miner led from the platform a giant, raw-boned, feeble, bedraggled, and blindfolded mule.

"What's the matter with that mule? Why is he blindfolded?" I was always asking questions.

"This is Old Tony," replied Ed Tower, the hoistman. "He's sick and can't work anymore. And when a mule is brought up he is always blindfolded for a couple of days to gradually accustom his eyes to daylight."

And, as I knew, when he was lowered into the mine it meant goodbye to sunshine and God's out of doors. He would remain below hauling ore cars from the underground spurs to the main track until he was too sick or feeble to work. And always without sunlight. Yet I thought he would be more humanely treated than his brothers on the trails.

As Tony was led away, the clang clang of the gong sounded again. It was time for the day shift to stop work. The cage was lowered. Again came the signal and cables began coiling around the half bare drum fetching up the first load of men, lunch buckets in their hands, rigged out in motley assortment of woolen shirts, shapeless trousers, old coats, jumpers, overalls worn over high leather boots to prevent small rocks dropping into them, wide-brimmed, slouchy old hats soggy from dripping water. Although there were swarthy-skinned men from Austria and Italy, blond giants from Norway and Finland, western Americans, begrimed from a day's work, scraggly haired, they all looked alike—typical hard-rock miners. But air drills and electric haulage at the Tomboy made their work seem child's play after years of single-jacking and hand-trimming in less equipped mines.

With the thawing of snow and ice our "spring" had arrived. We had copious water nearby instead of George hauling it from the shaft house. I could carry all I needed from the spring, although slowly for it still was an effort for me to lift any weight in this altitude.

It was August but resembled that feeling of "rare as a day in June." The bowl of blue sky over the cirque, sun glitter sparkling on the snow crowning the rocky heights, the velvet-green of trees in the canyon, and far below the mesas of the San Miguel reaching for the lost horizon.

Resting my bucket one day, I saw Thyra leaping along the

Thyra carrying Kate's mail home from the boardinghouse nearly half a mile away.

tailings her head held high, Kate's mail in her mouth. And coming from the shaft house was a tall woman, unusually tall until I discerned the water pail balanced on her head, the Old Country custom of a newly arrived wife of an Austrian miner wearing her foreign village dress.

Kate was hurrying over and I drew her attention to the newcomer. Then I noticed she was wearing her kitchen apron and seemed greatly excited.

"Harriet, what do you think?" Tears were shining in her eyes. "Thyra, bless her heart, just brought me a letter from my cousin Lavine in St. Paul and when I opened it this fell out." Her trembling fingers held a check for five thousand dollars, a fabulous sum for any one of us on the hill.

Cousin Lavine had been concerned about Kate's health, and having heard her wish to go farming in the West, had sent the means to help it come true.

So we were losing Kate and Alex who immediately prepared

to leave the land of long, cold winters, deep snow and howling gales. Kate was to leave in October. Alex would follow later. How we would miss them!

Winter was coming. A chill in the air and light snowfall warned of coming storms. David Herron had not forgotten his promise on the night of the frozen mutton dinner. One morning two carpenters arrived. Without drawings or blue print, in a short time they attached to our shack an extension of the six-by-ten-foot cubby-hole. Two small windows lighted the new room by day. For nighttime the usual small electric globe allotted by the company dangled from the ceiling. It brightened the middle of the room but left the corners dark.

Hanging clothes on the walls, I felt we were living in real luxury. An adequate bedroom, a dresser which was a denim-covered packing-box. And when George put two shelves in it, I was delighted. I didn't dream how cold that room would be in winter without heat.

The days grew shorter. Snow blanched color from the sky. The first frosts nipped our hands and feet. Working in the kitchen one night when George was on the afternoon shift, I heard the door rattling. It was no polite knocking but a firm attack. Walking through the dark front room, I opened the door, unable to distinguish the face of the man standing there.

"I'll bet you don't know who I am," a happy voice said. His accent stirred something in my memory.

"Wait until I get a light and I bet I'll know you." I brought the central hanging bulb trailing the long cord and shone the light on his face.

"Jack Arnold!" I exclaimed with glee. We had danced at my sorority parties and strolled on the college campus. "Where in the world did you come from?"

"I've been working down at the Smuggler for three months. I didn't know George was up here. This is the first time I've had the chance to come up and see the Tomboy Mill. I was certainly surprised and glad to see George. He told me to come and surprise you."

I hooked the light in the front room, stoked the fire, and we chatted gaily about his arrival at college from his native New Zealand, mining courses he and George had taken, and the earthquake which had shaken them both out of college.

"You must have dinner with us as soon as George is on day shift," I said as he was leaving.

"You bet I will. I don't see how I can stand boardinghouse cooking much longer without a break. A home-cooked meal might tide me over for a while."

"Do you happen to know Matt Slaughter, the electrician at the Smuggler?" I asked.

"Yes, from the Missouri School of Mines. A nice fellow," Jack said.

"Then you and Matt come to dinner together. What about on Thanksgiving Day?" I suggested.

"Fine, I'll tell Matt." Turning his coat collar high about his neck and shoving his hands in heavy gloves, he started down the mountain to Marshall Basin.

The middle compartment of our shack now was a so-called dining room and we increased the number of guests by inviting Hall and Bob Evans, two brothers from the Colorado School of Mines, working at the Tomboy. That made six, all of us recently college students interested in the football games played on this day at our alma maters. I wrote to California for small footballs, blue and gold pennants and ribbons, and glory be, they arrived in time to add a festive touch around the shack. As the poet Joaquin Miller had said to me one day long ago, "Youth, youth, how beautiful is youth."

On the day before I really worked baking bread and pumpkin pies, making cranberry jelly from the real berries kept with difficulty from freezing, stuffing a big turkey, making gelatin salad and ice cream to serve with candies. From the potato sack I took twenty-two potatoes. I shall always remember that preposterous number because next morning there was not a tablespoon of mashed potatoes left.

I was the happiest hostess ever. The appetites of those fine young miners were prodigious. Jack insisted on waiting on the table, filling and refilling serving dishes. George was kept busy carving turkey until only the bones remained.

"The Tomboy Company charges a dollar a day for room and board," George said, chuckling. "And they put on a swell meal on holidays, everything from soup to nuts. I have a young fellow just over from Austria, working for me. Today he had his first American turkey dinner. You should have seen him when he came back to work half an hour later. He came to me groaning and rubbing his stomach, yelling 'By God, like that every day, I pay a quarter more.' " Four young men began rubbing their stomachs.

Years later in New York, George met Jack Arnold by chance and Jack's first remark was, "Do you remember that Tomboy dinner? I'd go to hell to eat a dinner Hattie cooked."

Had he been among his former comforts instead of on a bleak and remote mountain peak, daily eating miners' boardinghouse food, he would not have walked far to eat my dinner, let alone go to "hell" for it!

Between Thanksgiving and Christmas, in some unexplainable way, whooping cough broke out among the children in Savage Basin. They seldom came in contact with other youngsters except those in the family. How do such viruses reach such incredible heights and isolated victims? Nobody knows. But nine-month-old Nicky Tumer, eight-month-old Nancy Matson, and two of Grace Driscoll's children were stricken with that dreaded and distressing disease. It was frightening to see and hear the small victims coughing, fighting for breath in the rarified atmosphere where mere breathing was difficult.

Trying to be neighborly, I visited the wife of an Austrian miner who in her late forties had given birth to her first child. She was unable to speak a word of English, was short, stout, and very lame. I shall never forget her rocking back and forth in an old chair, nursing a baby that at birth weighed only three pounds, nor the look of pride and joy glowing in her eyes, nor her breast that was almost as large as the infant itself.

Silently, continuously, the legendary "old woman plucked her geese" in the sky and the white down piled higher and higher. Our bedroom windows were half hidden but through a space thawed by my breath among the frost flowers of the front window I watched the big soft flakes falling gently, wrapping our house in silence and privacy. Only the roof of Sam Farraday's shanty down on the flat was visible, and I saw him crawling from the opening of his snow tunnel to the trail.

And I could see Fred Diener riding from the stable and leading a second horse to the Matson cabin near the foot of the trail and knocking on the door.

Strange, I thought, that they should need a horse on a day like this. Olga Matson was taking care of her sick children. Anyway, she never left the hill.

But Anton Matson came out and swung himself on one of the horses. Bundled in a heavy coat and with a wool fascinator almost covering her face, his wife Olga followed him, in her arms a little form wrapped in blankets.

Gently handing their dead baby to her husband, she turned to Fred who helped her onto the other horse, and slowly they started down the long mountain trail, the snow softly enfolding the small bundle and veiling their sadness.

CHAPTER 13

Christmas Day dawned clear and cold, with sapphire skies, a bright sun, sparkling diamonds from the surface of ten-foot-deep snow. The Spirit of Christmas, wearing snowshoes, a fleece-lined leather jacket over her riding habit, perky fur hat, a sack stuffed with toys slung over her back, was abroad in Savage Basin. Beth Batcheller was making her annual visit from shack to shack making certain no child was forgotten.

Warm-hearted, generous Beth. She loved her fellow man whether rich or poor, learned or otherwise. Her enthusiasm for life was not lessened by her surroundings, though her roots were deep in aristocratic New England.

How happy George and I were together opening the many Christmas packages from our loving families and friends. Over our dinner we reviewed the years since we met in Oakland High School when a blond, pink-cheeked boy from a small town in Washington walked into my English class saying to the teacher, "I want to sign up for this course." That was the day! He came, he saw, he conquered. From that moment on our thoughts were for each other.

Christmas over, George and I rode down to Telluride to enjoy a few days in the lower altitude, do some shopping, renew acquaintances, and eat meals I had not prepared. George's shift began early on the morning of New Year's Day so we had to start for home on the last day of the old year.

By noon of that day Rodgers had tied three horses to the hitching post in front of the hotel, rangy King for George, easy-riding Bird for me, and Pudgy for Alex who had been in Telluride closing his books before leaving for Oregon.

Unfortunately for us the wind, steadily increasing in force, blew snow viciously in all directions. We were in for a rugged ride. Single file, their heads lowered, the horses struggled against the blasts and at times were forced to a stop to steady themselves. In the lead, Bird, who never permitted another horse to pass him, was followed by King, then Pudgy.

The cold bit into my hands for carelessly I had not worn my warmest gloves. Large flakes of snow falling from the skies and whirling up from the chasm constantly covered our fast reddening faces. In the hairpin turn the little spring so charming in summer was again a block of ice and we had no axe to break it open. Directly ahead a deep drift blocked the trail. Before I could tighten the reins, Bird, high-stepping nervously to avoid the drift, swerved to the outer edge of the snowpack which overhung the rock like eaves of a house. For one heart-rending instant Bird's hind foot pawed the air above the thousand-foot drop. Only his God-given instinct and sharp reaction saved us both. He thrust forward full weight and strength with his forefeet and miraculously pulled himself away from the edge.

I screamed above the screech of the wind, "George, *make King take that drift!*" He did.

Emerging from the tunnel my heart was still hammering. Suppose we should meet someone coming down the trail. I could not have seen a horse until it crashed into me because of the blinding white veil covering my face as the force of the blizzard increased. I shuddered, wishing I could talk with George, but it was impossible to make myself heard. Frequently I dropped the reins on the pommel to restore some feeling in my hands and drew my feet from the stirrups to swing my legs back and forth to warm them.

From Telluride to Savage Basin was a five-mile trip. After three hours riding we had reached only the cabin that hung over the brink below. Bird stopped. Blocking the road were three heavily loaded sleds and twelve dejected horses standing by. From the cabin came a grizzled teamster wrapped to his ears. Looking at us in amazement, he yelled, "What the hell are you folks doing out in this storm?"

"Trying to get to the Tomboy," shouted George wearily.

"You'd better come in and thaw out." And the teamster came

to help me dismount. I could hardly move my feet, and my hands were completely numb.

Near a roaring fire in the cabin sat two other teamsters who quickly drew up boxes for us to sit on.

"Your hands are almost frozen, Ma'am," said one as I slowly pulled off my gloves. "Don't get them near the fire." And taking an old tin basin from a wall peg he filled it with cold water and set it on a box in front of me. "Now, keep your hands in that until they begin to warm up."

Looking at Alex he added, "Surely you're not going on tonight, are you? It would be damned foolish."

"We have to," Alex said. "We both have to be at work early in the morning."

A tingling feeling, more painful than the cold, began to run through my fingers as I listened to the teamsters all talking at once.

"We won't go on, and we've been driving this trail for years," said one of those hardened teamsters.

"Ever since we left at six this morning, this storm has been growing worse," joined in the third man. "We're leaving the sleds right where they are. We won't take the chance of passing the Big Elephant. We've been expecting it to slide for weeks. This storm is liable to bring it down any minute. Any jar, even a sudden noise, could do it."

Even at the Smuggler there was no place for a woman to stay, so George said, "But my wife can't stay here, and we can't take that ride back to Telluride."

"Well," said one called Nels, shaking his head forebodingly. "It's up to you fellows, but if that damned Elephant slides while you're passing, you're goners for sure. And they won't locate you till spring."

George and Alex discussed the dangers and decided the only thing we could do was to push on. The word "slide" terrified me, but I knew we had to take the risk. As we passed through Smuggler, no living thing was to be seen. Except for the howling of the storm in which even the mountains seemed to shudder there was no sound.

When my hands thawed out we left the teamsters and, nervously I am sure, climbed onto the horses.

"Alex," I screamed to make my voice heard, "promise you'll

tell me when we start across the slide area." If half a mountainside were to dash us down the chasm I wanted to know so as to brace myself and gather my courage.

"I'll tell you when we're near it," Alex shouted back. He forced Pudgy into the lead. George followed me closely. The drooping horses, staggering from the force of the gale, plodded on, faltering only when breaking through heaps of drifted snow churned up by the whirling winds.

"Haven't we reached it yet?" I hollered again.

"Not yet. Just a little ways more," came indistinctly back to me. The menacing monster was invisible but I could feel it near, making ready to hurl down a wall of snow upon us. A sudden violent attack of wind slammed Bird against the bank. I gasped and shuddered, every nerve strained to its limit.

"A minute more and we'll be at the edge of it," came faintly from Alex.

"George, are you near me?" I shouted, turning in the saddle, trying to see him.

"Very close, Kiddy."

Suddenly I remembered that even a loud shout could jar loose that ready wall of snow and ice. "Shut up," I told myself. I dared not hurry Bird because quickened footfalls might create enough vibration to start the avalanche.

The strain had become unendurable when I heard Alex's triumphant assurance, "It's all over now. We've just passed the Big Elephant." I relaxed.

Another half mile and exhausted we dismounted at the foot of our own trail just as a furious blast struck. I saved myself by hanging on to Bird and cowering beside him. Then we turned the horses loose and they headed eagerly for the stable.

Without snowshoes it was difficult for our feet to find the trail. The stakes had been obliterated. Plunk. Down went George waist deep. My turn next. I regained my footing just as another attack came roaring in upon us. This time I threw myself flat on my face in the snow.

Two very thankful, storm-battered persons were home safe. By morning there was reasonable calm in the Savage Basin and I went to the stable to see if Bird, King, and Pudgy were all right. Fred had just returned from Scotty's with the mail.

"Oh, they were fine. They're probably halfway to Telluride by now. Three of the miners went down."

Fred also had picked up news of a terrible tragedy over the range, during the storm. Four teams of horses, six horses in each team, were hauling heavily loaded sleds from the Camp Bird Mine down the nine-mile trail to Ouray. An avalanche almost as wide as the Big Elephant came roaring from overhead and swept horses, sleds, and men into the yawning chasm below. No one saw it happen and only the vast scar down the slope revealed to those searching, the snowy graveyard of men and animals.

CHAPTER 14

In the following spring George was put in charge of the lead and zinc mill where pulverized concentrates, containing these ores, were roasted and sacked.

In a few months he developed lead poisoning and for several weeks suffered excruciating pain and was unable to work. When he was well again he went back to the stamp mill, but on the day shift only, which was more convenient and acceptable to us both.

Summer passed all too quickly. The solitude of our mountain cabin, the splendor of azure skies kissing mountain peaks, the vista of winding roads clinging to precipices, faraway valleys disappearing into the distance, all mingled in nature's harmony, lulled me into daytime reveries—the wonders of this paradise of magnificence and dreams of happy years ahead.

Life was indeed easy in that season of the year. We drifted along, needing no enjoyment except that of living and being with each other. We were resting, preparing ourselves for the inevitable winter ahead.

Improvements and signs of prosperity were intruding on our wilderness. The company was now building four new houses on the tailings. By comparison with the shacks, they were mansions: square-built of used lumber, partitioned into four rooms, walls lined with building paper, roofs of sheet iron. Attached to the kitchen was a shed four feet wide, eighteen feet long with the supreme luxury at the far end—an "in house" instead of an "out house."

Dr. Caplinger moved into the first house finished. The telephone which was installed made this house unique.

Early in September snow began to fall. We ordered coal before it was too deep for the mules to reach our shack. Our shed was stocked with food and kindling, so there was room for only one ton.

We had badly missed Kate and Alex and now Beth and Billy were to leave for Massachusetts to spend the winter. The school teacher, Letta Tuller, after five months cramming small heads with the lore of the alphabet and three R's, was getting ready to leave for her home in Naturita. The children loved her and adults had been thrilled when Fred Diener dressed up in his suit of long ago, his shirt yellowed by age, a bow tie, unanchored and rising halfway up his shirt collar, crossed the trail ostensibly to carry in Mrs. Tuller's coal. It made us happy when he was invited in to sit and chat and probably take tea and cake. Could there be a budding romance? Alas, there was not, to our disappointment.

The Snyders with their two boys were leaving and the Y.M.C.A., successfully launched, had a new director, Mr. Morrison.

By November we again wallowed in five feet of snow or else waddled on snowshoes. Returning one day with the mail, I saw flames inside the window of the Wynn shack. Slowed by the effort of keeping one snowshoe from overlapping the other, I hurried to the door, opened it, and saw Mrs. Wynn trying desperately to tear down curtains ablaze at her kitchen window.

Fire on the hill was dreaded. There was no water for such a catastrophe as might follow. Fortunately, the shaft house was directly across the trail. Turning toward it I shouted in my always too loud voice, "Fire, fire! Mrs. Wynn's house!" The hoist men lost not a second in responding and, leaping to the house, tore down the curtains and threw them into the snow. This damage was the only loss.

Considerably shaken, I reached the bottom of our own trail to find Syd Riley, one of the more patient mule skinners, with his string tangled in a knot. One of the seven mules carrying more coal for us had fallen in a deep drift. The skinner had detached him from the rest of the string and was tugging furiously on the halter, trying to make the animal get up. The poor thing, loaded with three hundred pounds of coal, had no firm footing. Knowing this, he merely raised his head, shook his long ears, and settled down again. I wanted to run away. I had seen what was to happen many times. Syd pulled, jerked, then cursing with every blow, his heavily booted foot kicked again and again the animal's head, the only part sticking out of the snow. A shake of the mule's ears showed his disdain for the skinner.

All this time the horse was standing sleepily on the trail, his head sagging, unconcerned with his master's troubles except when the restless mule behind him pulled back too hard. Bellowing at the other mules, knotting together and threatening to bump each other off the trail, Syd removed the top load and again tried to force the mule to rise. Finally, in utter disgust, he removed the remaining sacks and the mule struggled to his feet. The sacks on the other six mules were dumped at the foot of our trail. Poor George! He had a task ahead of him.

Our third Tomboy Thanksgiving came and went. Toward the end of the month our food supply was low. The meat was gone and I had not put in a new order when on the last day of the month, Dino Cerini, a millman, brought a message from George asking if I could have a guest at dinner.

"Dino, please tell George I'll be glad to have anyone willing to take potluck with us," I said, wondering who the guest would be and what to serve. We still had bacon and canned beans, all too common a meal in mining country. Beth had left the key to her shack with me, "just in case." She must have left cans of food that I could borrow and replace later. I strapped on my snowshoes, hurried down the hill, and returned with a can of turkey from her cold, cold "igloo."

I popped potatoes in the oven to bake, opened a can of tomatoes, gave the can of ice cream in the snowbank another stir, creamed the turkey, and dinner was ready when George and our young guest, a stranger to me, arrived.

He was Lionel Lindsay from London, England. He and George had been friends at the University of California. Occasionally mine experts, and those hoping to become expert, journeyed to the Tomboy for one or another reason.

In college little was known of Lionel Lindsay's background He was friendly but reticent. After graduation he had gone home to England. Now he was in the United States on a mining mission which brought him to the San Juans. All that day he had traipsed through the mountains, and upon reaching the Tomboy he and George had been pleasantly and mutually surprised at meeting again.

He was a charming and appreciative guest at our frugal table. I well remember his appetite. He ate three large baked potatoes, three servings of turkey, an equal amount of tomatoes, several slices of my home-made bread, and topped all with dishes of ice cream and many cups of tea.

It was several years before I learned that our guest at that simple meal was the son of the Earl of Crawford and first cousin of Prince Gelasio Caetani, later one-time ambassador to the United States.

In World War One as an officer in the King's Own Regiment, Sir Lionel Lindsay's name was honored throughout England as one of its many heroes.

That was a winter of heavy snow. By Christmas, slipping off the trail meant sinking eight feet. Twenty feet of the white cottony stuff filled the canyons. Only on tightly packed trails could we walk without snowshoes. Paths leading to our shacks were steep and slippery and often we landed wrong-side up. Each morning men shoveled their way out because an all-night fall had blocked the doors.

The bedroom in our shack was completely buried. Not a ray of light came from the window. Though it was icy cold I began sleeping more than usual, afflicted by an awful stupor. Only with great effort could I waken in the mornings long enough to help George off to work. Then a strange nausea overcame me. The ubiquitous oil can had a new use and I returned to bed. I slept till noon and by evening again was eager to snuggle down.

"George, something's the matter with me," I said. "I've never felt like this before. I have to fight to keep this lethargy from overpowering me."

We both were worried, but it was George who took a day off and rode to Telluride to consult Dr. Hadley. That day dragged. I was always worried when he rode the trail, and he seldom did except when very necessary. I was anxious, too, to know if there was anything serious the matter with me.

At the end of that long day, there he was, coming along on old Pudgy. Turning the horse loose, he walked up the hill a little faster than usual although careful to follow the trail. Shaking the snow from his clothes, George came in smiling broadly.

"Dr. Hadley says to let you sleep all you want to. It's all

right. You'll get over it soon—and the baby will probably come in August." Needless to say this diagnosis of my condition was gratifying to both.

During the next months one snowfall followed another. Several times the Tomboy was cut off for days from the outside. The mules simply could not get up, much less horses.

One particularly stormy day Paul Stuparich of Telluride started up the hill on his own horse. Coming to a heavy and dangerous drift, he dismounted when suddenly the horse stumbled, struggled a moment, then went over the mountainside falling two hundred feet in the soft snow where he lay buried up to his neck.

Unable to go down to the horse, Paul made his way back to Telluride and returned on another horse, carrying blankets and snowshoes. On the webs, he ventured down the snow-filled canyon. The only thing to be done was to force the horse to go all the way down, an additional thousand feet. By coaxing or using a lash, he got the animal to lunge forward. It sank, then lunged again until both the horse and Paul were exhausted. Night was falling fast. He wrapped the blanket over his horse and left. In the morning the struggle began again and continued all day. It was late when they finally reached the floor of the canyon. Paul's horse was unhurt and after a good rest was ready to ride again.

All winter, walking was difficult but I managed to waddle over the snow as usual. Often one snowshoe would "step" on the edge of the other. Then I would go headfirst into the snow, the whole top of me buried in the stuff, only afloat because of the life-saving snowshoes into which my feet were toe-clipped and tightly strapped. I would flounder and squirm helplessly until someone pulled me out and "dusted" me off.

If there had been any books on the "do's and don'ts" during pregnancy and prenatal care I knew nothing of them. I got along with plain common-sense care and as nature intended for me.

In April Dr. Caplinger decided to shake the top-of-the-world snows off his feet and return to Indiana. His house would be vacated, and we were lucky enough to rent it, telephone and all. We would miss the magnificent view from our "nest" but it would be much more convenient after the baby came.

To move our worldly goods down to the Flat, George made a long sled of two twelve-foot planks with a piece of sheet-iron curved gracefully in front. With the help of two millmen we were soon settled in our new house.

Jim Batcheller had gone east to bring back Beth, Billy, and an Airedale puppy they named Jackie. Billy was now a beautiful, sturdy boy of two and a half years, pink-cheeked, bright-eyed, and with winning ways and smiles. Once again only the trail separated us. The snow was settling and Billy played with his devoted dog which looked like a crossbred porcupine and canine, every whisker and his beetling eyebrows glistening with snow. All was well and everyone was happy until one day in May Billy developed a sore throat. It cleared up quickly, but a few days later after only a short romp in the snow, he gave up. "Mommy, I'm so tired," Billy said.

It was the same the next day and several more. His eyes looked dull. Beth began to show the strain of anxiety after night and day watching and care. The new mine physician, Dr. Carter, could find no definite symptoms; yet, obviously Billy was a very sick child.

The day Billy said, "Mommy, I can't walk!" we were all frightened. Dr. Carter telephoned Dr. Hadley who ordered Jim to take Billy down at once. The snow for three miles out of Telluride was not deep enough for a sled, so a carriage was sent up, struggling through the last part of the trail. Beth, Jim, and Billy were ready when it arrived.

Three hours after Billy was put to bed in the hospital he went into convulsions. The beginning of a desperate struggle to save his life was underway. Day and night Beth and Jim were with Billy, holding his little hands as feeling, sight, and hearing gradually dimmed. He no longer suffered, but their agony mounted.

By telephone I begged Beth to let me go down to them if I could be of any help, but she refused saying, "No, Harriet, you must not come. You must not run any risks now."

"I'd like the advice of another doctor, a specialist, Jim," said Dr. Hadley. "There are several excellent ones in Denver."

"Get one," said Jim. "Don't spare expense. Billy must be saved."

"Jim, don't hope too much," Dr. Hadley said gently.

Telephoning, Dr. Hadley got the noted Dr. Hall to make the twenty-four-hour trip. The only daily train had gone, but a "special," a locomotive and one car, was quickly made ready.

Beth Batcheller, her son Billy, and Jackie the dog.
(Photo courtesy of Telluride Historical Museum, all rights reserved.)

With white "right-of-way" flags flying on the locomotive, it sped from Denver to Salida where a narrow gauge "special" waited in readiness. Through the lovely Gunnison Valley without stopping, up to the foothills, around the mountains, white flags and warning whistles, throttle wide open, the smaller "special" rushed in answer to Jim's plea.

Immediately on arrival Dr. Hall carefully considered all the information to be obtained from Billy's hospital chart and Dr. Hadley's meticulous care and sound opinions. He shook his head. A short visit at Billy's bedside was enough. Nothing now could combat the deadly meningitis. The following morning Dr. Hall returned to Denver.

On Saturday night the spirit of little Billy slipped away. In a few days his heartbroken parents returned to their desolated shack. Brave as they were, there were no distractions or interests to help them bear their loss. Two months later Jim resigned his job to leave as soon as a man was found to replace him.

"You *are* wonderful," I told Beth one day. "Never have you uttered one word of complaint."

"Why, Harriet, I wouldn't dare complain. I would be afraid that God would not send me another baby. I love them so very much and desperately want babies. I hope and pray you will have your baby before we leave, I do *so* wish to see it."

CHAPTER 15

As August came nearer, George went to Telluride to find a temporary home for me to be near the hospital. The owner of a four-room house was leaving Telluride for a few months, so George rented one of the bedrooms, made arrangements for my meals at the hospital one block away, and engaged Nurse Margaret Perril.

The small, neat square brick hospital had been built for miners only. Throughout the mountains accidents occurred almost daily. As there were no other facilities for the needs and emergencies of families, a few outpatients were admitted; so far no babies.

I was uncomfortable and found it difficult to walk on our rough paths. My long, brown maternity dress had a short yoke from which the very full gathered skirt hung to the floor. It was so full that with my every turn it whirled and spiraled like the robe of a whirling dervish. But it would have been highly indelicate not to have had such a voluminous disguise to hide my figure. Mother had always said so.

The early part of August, Dr. Hadley had predicted. Though waiting to go down in July was taking chances, it was July fifteenth when we drove to the little mining town I had seen only a few times. Telluride was enjoying its short summer.

Knowing this weather would not last long, the townsmen were taking advantage of it wandering among trees, perhaps taking trips down the river, fishing in a not-too-distant lake, or just lounging in the sunshine.

Now Bridal Veil Falls, stern and forbidding in winter, was leaping down joyously to join the San Miguel River. For the few hours the sun's rays touched the waters, they gleamed with the changing hues of opals.

My new abode stood at the very foot of the Tomboy trail. Every morning trucks and mules passed by heavily loaded, mounting the winding, twisting, turning, snake-like trail that clung to the mountainside rising steeply, higher and higher.

Mr. and Mrs. Walter Warner, recently married and waiting for a shack at the Liberty Bell where he was employed, rented the second bedroom. We shared the small parlor, bathroom, and kitchen.

Amy Warner was a charming girl with wavy black hair, sparkling brown eyes that half closed when she smiled, a small mouth, and quiet voice. Walter had a small moustache and goatee, a rare adornment among miners. His conversation was punctuated with a boisterous laugh and his manner was greatly self-confident.

At the mine faithful Fred Diener kept a horse always ready for George when he would receive my call that I needed him. During all this waiting time my devoted husband rode the trail every other day, rain or shine, reaching Telluride near five o'clock. By four-thirty the next morning he would be up and soon on the horse Rodgers had tied to the fence. By seven he was at work again.

August opened with pleasant weather but toward the end of the month, heavy rains set in: unbroken sheets pouring down in torrents, flooding the canyons, hissing like snakes as the water swished around the little house. Day after day, Amy and I sat in the small dark parlor glad of each other's company. She would be embroidering linens, humming softly, sometimes singing words that I could barely hear through the terrific pounding of the rain. I used to smile as I listened to her favorite song:

> *It is not raining rain to me*
> *It's raining violets.*

That year the mountain peaks ripped the heavily laden clouds wide open and a lake of water fell; seemingly dripping but buoyant, the clouds floated by. One noon, the sky became black as ebony. Lightning flashed and thunder roared. The heavens tore open. I was terrified. Crash! A blinding flash! Cannons thundering! The swish and roar of water, feet deep passing the house. Would George ever get to see our baby?

Rocks, tree branches, and mud from the slopes littered the ground. What was happening at the mine? When the storm passed

I saw from the windows a strange sight, three Indian travois familiar to me only in pictures and tales of the early days—three miners, each leading a horse dragging a litter. On each side of a horse a long pole was strapped, the ends of the poles trailing on the ground. Each pair of poles braced with cross bars and on each frame was lashed a blanket-wrapped body. During the noonday storm, a bolt of lightning had struck a rail of the track running into the tunnel of the Liberty Bell Mine and, traveling along the metal tracks, killed instantly three men working underground. The litters had been improvised at the mine and the bodies dragged four miles down the tortuous narrow trail as there were no wagon roads from the mine to Telluride.

August was passing and still I waited with little to fill the time except writing to my anxious relatives who had sent handmade and knitted baby clothes with much advice about never failing to keep bellyband, stockings, and bootees on the baby until it was months old. I enjoyed sorting them to thank the right donor: flannel bellybands, diapers, long flannel petticoats, dresses three times the length of an infant, tiny knit stockings and shoes, bonnets, jackets, embroidered and beribboned. How could I learn to take care of a precious living baby when learning to cook had been such a test and trial?

Beth and Jim came to see me as they were leaving, and most reluctantly we parted, uncertain about ever meeting again.

Walking near the gate one evening, Amy slipped and fell badly spraining her ankle, forcing her to use crutches. In spite of this she begged: "Harriet, promise you will call me, night or day, if you need help." I promised, glad to have someone nearby in an emergency.

September came. When it was not raining I tramped up and down the trails near the house. George's birthday fell on the second of the month and I wanted to give him a living present. But not until the morning of the ninth, at four-thirty, did I knock on Amy's door excitedly calling, "I need you in a hurry."

She hobbled into my room, more nervous than I, asking feebly, "What shall I do?"

"Please phone Miss Perril to come at once. Then phone George at the mine." I lay down again as strange things were happening to me. Amy made the calls and hovered over me like a mother hen with one chick. Margaret came quickly and almost immediately I heard Amy say weakly, "Miss Perril . . ." There was a crash. I jumped up, shaking violently. Face down across a chair lay Amy, a crutch firmly wedged under each arm. She's dying, I thought, and I'm the cause. I ran and put my arms around her and started to lift her. Quietly but firmly, Margaret said, "Don't do that. Go get her husband."

I knocked on his door calling, "Mr. Werner, come quick. Your wife has fainted." He dashed in, grabbed her as he would a sack of flour and hauled her to her bed. Margaret took my grip and in the early morning light we walked to the hospital.

My private room, at the left of the entrance hall, had a second door opening into a room in the rear. Across the hall on the right was a third room. Behind it was the nurses' dining room and behind that, the kitchen. At the top of a long flight of stairs were two small wards, the much-used operating room between them directly over the front entrance. With meager facilities Dr. Hadley and Dr. Taylor were doing splendid work.

By seven that morning, George was with me. Constantly beside me holding my hand, my beloved with his gentle calmness shared the ordeal of the next five hours.

Shortly before noon, Harriet Anna Backus arrived, the first baby born in the Miners' Hospital at Telluride, Colorado.

All that day rain fell in torrents, pounding on the little hospital, darkening the room. Lights were necessary. A cloudburst had broken the Trout Lake Dam of the Telluride Power Company, completely wiping out the town of Placerville except for two buildings. Between Ridgway and Telluride thirty miles of tracks were washed out, cutting off all telephone and telegraph communication from the north, leaving our walled-in gulch isolated.

As soon as possible, news of Harriet's arrival was telephoned over the range to Ouray and from there relayed to California and Washington state. Thus our families were informed all was well.

A week later George left on a mining examination trip for Dave Herron, so arrangements were made for the baby and me to remain in the hospital until he returned. Margaret slept in the room with us, Harriet snug in a clothes basket nearby.

For two weeks the baby hiccoughed *every* night. At two each morning Margaret would sit in front of the warm kitchen range holding Harriet near its open door in hopes that heat would relieve the attacks. During this time the five thousand people of Telluride were worrying about food. With the railroad gone and the roads washed out not even wagons could be used. Mules were the only possible transportation saviors of the situation. They could bring in enough necessary rations, it was hoped, to ease the pangs of hunger. What food the stores had was rapidly disappearing with no means of replacing it. It would be two months before the railroad tracks could be restored. So French Alec with his mule string was taken from his Tomboy trail and sent to Ridgway for supplies, and all of Telluride eagerly awaited his return.

Ten days later Telluride rejoiced when the mules entered the canyon. The first load of food . . . hurrah! Telluride, saved by the mules! For some the joy lasted but for others it burst like a balloon. Each mule carried fifteen cases of beer, and that was all.

In a short time, beautifully colored posters copied from original paintings advertising *Anheuser-Busch* were erected throughout the country. The title read, "The Relief Train," and pictured a string of mules carrying cases of beer over a trail with a background of superb mountain scenery. Was the mule skinner our French Alec? Perhaps!

Tiptoeing into my room and speaking so softly I could hardly hear her, Amy came to apologize for "failing me in my hour of need," as she said. Laughing, I assured her she had been wonderful until the nurse arrived.

One year later she was awaiting her baby in a cabin at the Liberty Bell. More inaccessible than the Tomboy, it was located on the face of the spectacular, castellated, thirteen-thousand-foot-high Santa Sophia Ridge with only a narrow trail between the mine and Telluride.

Amy and Dr. Hadley had set a time for her safe trip to Telluride, but the baby was in a hurry. She woke one night with forewarning signs and moaning, "Oh, what shall I do?" Walter telephoned Dr. Hadley. "Bring her down at once," he ordered.

It was two o'clock in the morning. Walter helped her mount a horse. Carrying a lantern, he led the animal down the long, twisting trail. Soon, jolted beyond endurance, Amy begged him to stop. A short rest . . . then a little farther . . . rest again. After

Harriet Anna's birth certificate. She is the first baby born in the Miners' Hospital.

two agonizing hours on the trail she arrived at the hospital only minutes before their daughter was born.

I waited anxiously to hear from George. The trip he was taking would be difficult. When one morning Margaret came in waving a letter as if it were a trophy, I cheered up. It read like the diary of his grandfather written in 1849: "Dearest Wife and Baby. I arrived here at Durango this afternoon at four. We had a very rough trip yesterday. Left Telluride at six-thirty a.m. and made it to Trout Lake by two in the afternoon. From Lizard Lake to Rico the road is more than rough. The load was quite heavy, a ton and a half, and we had four horses. Twice the wagon went into the mud up to the front axle and we had to unload the whole works to get out. Once we had to carry six sacks up a steep pitch so the team could pull over it. One of us had to walk ahead to look at the road as it was soon too dark to see. Ran into a boulder and broke the brake beam which took an hour to fix. Finally reached Rico at two in the morning. Nothing to eat since we left Trout Lake . . ." I read and re-read every word. I longed for his return. Yet, my sojourn in the hospital was not monotonous, to say the least.

One of the patients was Shorty Holler, a young miner whom

we had known at the mine. His nickname befitted his stature but his humor and good nature were anything but short. He had fallen several hundred feet down a mine shaft. Projecting timbers had broken his fall and probably saved his life, but he was injured internally and one leg was horribly smashed. Shorty was the delight of the nurses, for never once did he moan, complain, or utter a disagreeable word.

Directly over my room was another miner, brought in when our baby was two weeks old. He had fallen and broken his leg, but his every breath was a groan, day and night. It was futile for the nurses to remind him that others near him were sick and suffering and that his wailings were heard by every inmate. We heard them as though the ceiling was made of paper.

One day when Dr. Hadley was changing the dressings on Shorty's mangled leg the entire hospital was startled to hear Shorty moaning piteously, crying loudly, screaming until Dr. Hadley begged him to calm down.

It worked. The whining and groaning above us ceased.

Margaret carried Harriet upstairs and visited every bed to display our six-pounder to the miners who were all interested in the first baby born in their hospital.

At three o'clock next morning I woke at the sound of men hurrying past my door and struggling up the stairs with a burden. In a few minutes I couldn't shut out the sounds of suffering from the operating room. I lay there, knowing the two doctors were trying to save a life. The patient had been shot in the abdomen in a saloon brawl. His intestines had been so perforated that complete anesthesia was inadvisable. As the mercy of a "local" wore off, he screamed in agony until another injection brought relief. After two hours there was enduring silence. Death had come.

A few nights later, scuffling past our door was repeated. For hours we heard the sounds of the man's suffering; his pleading words: "Please don't. I can't stand it. Let me die."

He had tried to kill himself. Several years before, he had been caught in a mountain blizzard. When rescued, his feet were frozen and had to be amputated. Handicapped and having no relatives, he wandered like a derelict seeking such work as he was able to do, finally being hired as dishwasher in a saloon in Telluride. Constantly brooding about his very real hardships, he suddenly gave way to such frenzied despair that he seized a sharp butcher knife from the greasy dishwater and plunged it into his abdomen. Because of the extent and location, alcohol was poured on his wounds. His screams kept us awake most of the night but toward dawn his wish to die was granted.

Not all the emergencies at the hospital ended in tragedy.

In the middle of one sunny afternoon I was alone with Harriet when there came sounds of some disturbance; many feet rushing downstairs, outcries of the nurses usually so quiet. The door of my room suddenly burst open. Margaret dashed in from the hall, turned the key in the lock, then ran to the other door and locked it. Panting for breath, she leaned against the wall just as someone smashed against the door, then padded feet hurried away from our door and down the hall. The screen door banged at the main entrance. The echo of running feet was followed by peals of laughter from the nurses.

A long-time citizen of good family and highly respectable when sober had succumbed to one of his periodical bouts with John Barleycorn, resulting in delirium tremens. Taken to the hospital, he had been placed in what was thought to be safe control, but working himself free, he sprang from his bed and ran from his room clad only in a hospital cutty sark. A nurse had grabbed for him, missed, and shouted for help as he dashed down the long flight of stairs followed by two nurses, both reaching for him. Margaret had appeared suddenly and blocked his lunge toward the front door. He swung around her heading for the room behind ours which she locked in his face. With this escape cut off he wheeled again and slipping like an eel past the nurses reached the front door and galloped down to the main street, three blocks from the hospital, the tails of his gown flapping wildly.

Helpless, the nurses sank on the steps convulsed with laughter watching the flight of their patient, knowing how sedate and proper he usually was. Seeing him heading down the main thoroughfare in his scant covering was too much to imagine.

Notified by the hospital the police soon returned him, none the worse for his escape which had given them as well as the nurses a jolly morning.

CHAPTER 16

Through a long month I waited for George. How I missed him! When he returned from his trip, the three of us, accompanied by Margaret, rode in a carriage up the trail to our home. Margaret stayed two nights with us, advising and teaching me how to care for our baby. I was as nervous as the proverbial witch about taking over my responsibility.

After Margaret left, the baby had colic every afternoon and Letta Tuller came after school to help me. Following the colic came a disagreeable experience with pinkeye. How did Harriet get that? How in this isolated spot with its rarified, cold, purified air, so fatal to insects, did the germs of whooping cough and meningitis exist and strike in winter? Next, I caught the infection from the baby and had pinkeye too.

Winter began early this particular year and days of ten to fifteen degrees below zero weather required two stoves burning day and night to combat cold draughts working through those hastily built houses. I knew Harriet should have fresh air but it was difficult for me to carry her over the ever deepening snow, so George often gave her an outing after work. How she got fresh air or could even breathe has been a mystery to me ever since, for I bundled her so in blankets there wasn't a peephole for air to enter.

One crystal clear night the mountains stood three dimensioned in bold relief in moonlight, and stars were so million-multiplied the sky looked colorless due to a shrieking wind clearing every thread of clouds.

Our house, hugging the flat, seemed to brace itself for each expected blast. The stovepipes, tightly wired to the ceiling, shuddered along their lengths until ready to pop from the stoves.

With baby Harriet at Tomboy.

It was nine o'clock and I sat near the fire in my little rocking chair nursing Harriet. George was in the kitchen. Suddenly the lights went off. An instant of total darkness, then a weird, bilious-green light illuminated the entire house, accompanied by a deafening noise like the buzzing of a million swarming bees. I hugged Harriet tightly to me, jumped from the chair, ran toward the kitchen shouting "George!" He was running toward me, and in the next moment of intense gloom we crashed together, the baby between us. Her cry added to my terror. The lights came on and George supported me back to my chair.

"It's all right now, dear," he said. "Don't be frightened."

I cuddled Harriet and tried to soothe her wailing, not daring to nurse her until I calmed down. But in a moment that terrifying buzzing came again and again and again with horrifying regularity, each time followed by a moment of pitch blackness, then that eerie and evil glow beyond description, weird buzzing so loud that it drowned out the roar of the wind.

"What is it?" I screamed. "What is it?" I trembled all over while hugging Harriet closer.

"It's a short circuit in the high tension wires over the house. Why in God's name doesn't that fellow at the junction house pull

George and Harriet at Tomboy.

off the power?" George strode toward the telephone.

"Don't touch that! You might be killed." I screamed to George.

"Well, if that damn fool doesn't know enough to pull off the power, I've got to tell him to." George opened the door to the tiny storm porch directly under a wire but already I was screaming to him: "Don't go out that door, *please!* The wires might fall on you. Don't risk it!"

Seeing how panicky I was, he hesitated.

"Let's get out the side window and run away," I pleaded.

"But we can't take the baby out in this wind and snow." Those were the only really foolish words I *ever* heard my husband say.

"Get a blanket—quick," I shrieked, and opened the window. Straddling the sill, I intended to drop into the snow and take Harriet, already wrapped, from George's outstretched arms. The next impression was when I became vaguely aware of people hovering over me and voices, as in a dream, saying, "It's all right. It's all over now." Then, "Let's take her to the Williams cabin."

Fainting was a new experience for me.

I came to lying on a couch with several men and Mrs. Williams near me.

"Where are George and the baby? Are they all right?" I uttered.

"Sure, they're fine," I was told, and then Don McKeehan explained to the others what had happened.

Three high tension wires, each one carrying ten thousand volts, conducted power from the junction house only a few feet directly above our house, up the steep side of the range behind us, over the summit to the lake nestling in its high crest, and beyond to Ouray nine miles down the other side of the range. The wires were strung in the form of a triangle, one wire forming the apex. The force of the gale had torn the middle wire loose from the pole near our house giving it sufficient slack to swing toward one lower wire, then toward the other. As the loose wire swung near a lower wire the current arced, producing that weird light. The short, within a few feet of our metal stove pipe, had pulled to a standstill two large generating plants in the valley far below. Telluride and all mills and mines within a radius of ten miles were plunged into darkness. Each time the blast slackened the loose wire swung central. Generators again picked up the load and the lights came on. That went on for ten minutes.

"But Don," said one of the men, "you haven't said a word about what *you* did. We can all thank you for saving us." From one and another we heard the rest of the story. When the first flash came, Don, in the boardinghouse, realized something serious was happening. When the second blast lighted the whole Basin he knew somebody must reach the junction house before a terrible catastrophe could occur. There was only one way to get there. Don *ran* through the heavy snow from the boardinghouse to the junction house a half mile uphill at a two-mile elevation! Few could have done it. Fewer hearts could have endured such a strain. But lives and property were at stake and Don knew it.

Reaching the junction houses panting for breath, he shouted to the attendant: "God damn you, pull that power and do it now!"

"I *can't* without orders from the company," was the inconceivable reply.

Cursing and furious, in desperation Don grabbed a chair,

swung it over his head and roared, "Pull that switch or I'll do it for you."

Only then did the operator pull the switch and end ten minutes of hell-flashing menace.

The next day we got the comic reactions—the picture of Harriet Backus astride a window sill with one leg in the snow, staging the first faint recorded in her family.

"Dad ordered us out of the house," said Fanny Turner whose father had taken Jim's position. "We ran as fast as we could. Mother fell headfirst in the snow. Anna remembered her puppy and ran back with father after her, but she pulled the pup from under the bed before he grabbed her."

"Tom had just come from the boardinghouse," said Grace Driscoll. "With the first flash he yelled, 'Get under the beds, all of you.' So the four children and Tom and I lay under the beds through that long ten minutes. I shook so hard I almost shook the bed down."

"You and Anna's pup had the same idea," said Don.

All that night extra guards patrolled the Basin for fear a small fire, driven by that furious wind, might get beyond control.

CHAPTER 17

The winter of 1909 to 1910 piled up an average of eight to ten feet of snow throughout Savage Basin. It was a rugged place to live although we had been happy and certainly never bored by monotony. Being together was all we needed.

We had achieved more than our goal, dear friends, wild adventures, our precious child, and George's valuable experience in varied phases of mining and milling procedures.

Mr. Herron agreed with George that he would be wise to seek wider fields, and a milder climate. Soon we began to pack our portable possessions in boxes for the mule loads. Smaller bundles would go with us in a sled to Telluride. Our household furnishings were sold for fifty dollars and I bade farewell to friends and neighbors. A bride nearby, who had done nothing but weep with loneliness and homesickness, broke down sobbing with envy when I said: "We are leaving here Tuesday and Telluride Wednesday morning and will be in Oakland, California, two days later." Little did I know!

George had made all arrangements. Our boxes and trunk were to go down by the mules. Tuesday the sled was to come for us.

Sunday morning the sky was overcast and sullen, a storm was brewing. There came George hurrying up the hill. I knew his shift was not over.

"What's the matter?" I asked disturbed.

"All reports indicate that we are in for a real storm. I am afraid by Tuesday we might be snowbound and be delayed for days. We must get down tomorrow. I engaged a stateroom out of Grand Junction and I don't want to miss that."

"What about our luggage?" I asked.

The Tomboy Mines Company near Telluride.
None of these buildings, seen 1906–1909, remain.

"It's too late to arrange to have the mules pick it up tomorrow. We'll have to take it on the sled," George decided.

So my precious husband went to work. He packed until four Monday morning, slept for four hours, and went to packing again. It seemed as though the snow was falling more heavily every minute. By four o'clock we were ready when Louie, a millman, came to tell us the sled had reached the mill but could not break through to our house. With Louie's help George loaded our belongings on the sled he had made. Wearing our warmest clothes and with Harriet wrapped deep in blankets, we started for the mill, guessing where the hidden trail was.

Dragging the sled, Louie fell first. Next, George went rolling into a snowbank. Holding Harriet tightly, my feet slipped, and I went deep in the snow, my long skirts bucking my best efforts to stay upright. The blankets and soft snow cradled Harriet gently.

Reaching the mill, I took shelter while the men loaded the bobsled, but the boom, boom of sixty thundering stamps was so deafening I was afraid it might injure Harriet's tiny eardrums. I went outside again and stood while our luggage was put on the sled.

Although the sled had broken through shortly before, the trail was already completely obliterated. The weary horses stood like ghosts, their sagging heads hardly visible.

When finally the sled was loaded, there was no place for us, so, with legs dangling over the side, we sat on boxes, huddled together to keep from slipping off. Falling flakes stung my face, filled my eyes and dropped down my muffled neck as I hugged Harriet close and kept brushing snow from her blankets.

Nick Santee, one of Rodgers' most trusted drivers, checked the load twice before starting the horses. Belly-deep in soft snow, they labored against a head wind. Breath billowed from their nostrils. We had gone only a short distance when we heard, as if muffled in a blanket, a faint tinkling. Something was coming. Nick stopped the horses, handed George the reins, and plowed ahead on foot. Very soon an animated snow-mound approached. It was Nick, bearing word that a mule train was coming up the hill and very close to us.

"You folks will have to walk back while the mules pass the sled. There's too much risk of horses and mules tangling for you to stay here," he said.

We slid off the boxes and shuffled back in the tracks of the sled.

On the narrow snow-heaped trail, a steep snowbank on one side, snow-concealed edge of a drop-into-eternity on the other, the horses waited; Nick holding their bridles tight, as Dave Stringer, the skinner, forced his horse, leading the mules, through deep drifts on the uphill side. We stood flattened against the bank.

Heavily loaded, the mules lunged, rolled and bumped against our restless horses, jerking the ropes that linked them head to tail and snorting aloud in their struggles to plow through the fiercest snowstorm that we had seen since coming to the Tomboy. Praying that no animal would slip as he lumbered past, we leaned far into the drifts until the fifteen mules had gone by.

Back on the boxes, thawing a seat-hold, we perched. Unable to go faster than a walk, the horses crept past the Big Elephant. We could *feel* its menace and gauge its span but could not see the brute through the snow.

"First-baby qualms" assailed me: Dear little Harriet, completely hidden in blankets . . . how did she get air to breathe . . . what would I do when her diaper needed changing or when she must be nursed? The latter emergencies were due any minute.

Slowly we passed Smuggler, that loftiest of post offices. It was getting dark. By the time we rounded the Big Bend the wind abated, but after two hours we were not halfway to Telluride. We had encountered no other living being so far on the treacherous snow-covered trail but the blinding flakes softly and relentlessly buried us.

Taking turns holding the baby, George and I eased our numb hands by making violent gestures pendulum fashion.

We passed the frozen spring in the hairpin-curve and, when we had descended twenty-five hundred feet, we could feel the sled runners dragging on the roadbed. A muffled cry came from the depths of the blankets. The crisis I dreaded had arrived. What was I to do?

Thank goodness the wagon came up to meet us and we slid off the boxes. Louder and louder grew Harriet's demanding wails. Without unwrapping her, which I dared not do, I couldn't nurse her even if modesty would have permitted. She was hungry and very wet but I had to let her scream, like it or not.

By the lights of lanterns the men were transferring our boxes to the wagon and with numbed hands were awkwardly winding chains around the rims of the wheels as a safety measure for icy spots along the way downhill.

Suddenly Harriet's demanding screams softened to baby's chuckling followed by real laughter. Never before had I heard her laugh. In a moment this was repeated. More disturbed by her laughter than her screams, with a quivering voice I said, "Dear, what can be the matter with Harriet?"

"I don't know," George answered, a puzzled tone in his usually calm voice.

Harriet was quiet again but only for a moment. Again came

that strange laugh from deep within the blankets. George stepped near the wagon then turned to me with that lovely smile and said: "In a minute she'll laugh again." As usual he had found the answer—the chains' clinking when being put on the wagon wheels. George was right, for Harriet laughed again.

We were climbing into the wagon when suddenly two men on horses came down the mountain, pulled up short and one glaring directly at me, said curtly, "What the devil are you doing out in this storm with that baby? This is the worst blizzard we've had. I'm Dan Masters, the road overseer, and my men and I have had one *hell* of a time all day."

Taking complete charge of the situation, he ordered, "Pete, give that man your horse and you ride down on the wagon. You," he barked at George, "ride with me. And you," he looked at me, "give *me* that baby."

It was eight o'clock and very dark. Harriet was screaming for food and a diaper change. We were half frozen, dead tired, and gladly obeyed orders. George pulled himself onto the horse. I lifted Harriet to Dan's arms and they disappeared into the night.

For the next hour we made our laborious way down the zigzag road, lower, lower. Nearing the base of the mountain the horses quickened their pace. It had taken five hours to cover a little more than five miles downhill. At nine o'clock Nick stopped in front of Dan Masters' home.

Inside near a roaring fire sat Mrs. Masters cuddling Harriet and crooning a lullaby that had soothed her hunger pangs.

In that year, 1910, Telluride was a lively, picturesque town of five thousand, depending on the mines, revolving around the Rodgers Brothers' stable. By that year over sixty million dollars had been produced within the Telluride district and many millions more were to be forthcoming.

We left it with regret on the little narrow-gauge train and arrived at Grand Junction at six in the evening, on schedule. Our next train was due at two a.m., so we rested in a hotel until time to catch it and went to the station only to wearily wait, wait, wait on a hard bench.

The train arrived at five and we were thankful that a drawing room was ready for us. Talking with other passengers, George heard rumors about serious washouts in Nevada. In Salt Lake

City we learned that the reports were all too true. February, 1910, had been a devastating month in Nevada. Floods had torn out many miles of tracks and caused damage worth millions of dollars. We were advised by railroad officials to remain in Salt Lake City until they notified us further.

Two anxious and boring days dragged on before the notice came. On Friday when we had expected to arrive in Oakland, we boarded a special train pulled by an old wood-burning locomotive and manned by an engineer who never before had "whistled" over that road we were to take through Idaho.

That state also had suffered from floods. In many places the tracks were awash. Across the entire state the roadbed was so spongy that the train crept slowly mile after mile. Beyond Idaho and all the way through Oregon to Portland we rattled, then south. *Ten* days after we left the Tomboy, we arrived in Oakland.

PART II
BRITANNIA BEACH

CHAPTER 18

George and I were happy to see my family again, including Harriet's three little cousins, Norton, Alice, and Martha, born while we were at the Tomboy. Yet, at the end of a month we both felt inwardly the call of the wild. Somehow, after the serenity of our mountains, the city seemed tawdry and confusing. George accepted a temporary job until he could get back to his chosen field.

A telegram from Jim Batcheller delighted us: "Edgar Hadley Batcheller born this morning. All well. Jim." We rejoiced for them.

A few days later came a letter from David Herron asking George to go to northern British Columbia where reports of rich gold strikes were current. If he found the rumors true, Herron and his associates were ready to buy claims that showed worthwhile values, and George would have an interest in any successful venture.

That June, 1910, he left for Seattle where he purchased a prospector's outfit and took ship for Portland Canal, landing at Stewart, near the border of Alaska.

The mineralized district was twenty miles inland, in country so wild that not even pack mules could be used. George shouldered his equipment and set out on foot. After several trips, careful study, deliberation on values and the inaccessible country, he wrote Mr. Herron regretfully advising him not to invest money in that district, a judgment that later proved to be correct.

He returned to the United States and, being anxious to send for Harriet and me, took the first work he could find at a mine in the rich Coeur D'Alene district in Idaho, the Bunker Hill and Sullivan. To his disappointment he was assigned to stacking lumber, a job far beyond his strength. The wages were low, barely enough to support himself. We missed each other sadly and letters between us were filled with yearning to be together.

One day after the foreman had told him he must handle more and heavier lumber, he trudged downhearted back to his lonely room. Two letters were waiting for him, my regular one and the other in Jim's familiar writing. George tore that open eagerly. It read:

"Dear George. I have recently been made superintendent of this large copper mine and need an assayer. I hope you can accept the position. Bert Austin, my mine foreman, gave me your address in Idaho. He says you and he were classmates at the University of California.

"If you accept, I want you to come at once. A house will be ready for you. Beth and little Edgar will arrive tomorrow, so I will be happy, and I am sure Beth and Harriet will enjoy being together again. Good luck to you. Jim"

George was overjoyed. He could hardly wait for morning to quit his job. Amazingly his boss said, "Well, I'm sorry you're leaving. You've got brains. If you ever want to come back, I'll take you on."

"Thanks," said George, "but I *won't* be back."

His telegram, which reached me that morning, said: "Am leaving for British Columbia. Have position with Jim. Writing details. Get ready to come at once." Literally I jumped for joy.

Early in November, thirteen-month-old Harriet and I arrived in Seattle where George met us. What a happy reunion!

That night our steamer crossed Puget Sound. We were up bright and early at Vancouver to board a small vessel for Howe Sound. We had only a few minutes to spare as the Britannia would leave promptly at eight o'clock.

George rushed to collect our baggage while I carried the baby to an adjoining pier. We were the last of ten passengers to board the miniature ferry which pulled away at once. Daily, except Sundays, the *Britannia* plowed its course between the city nestled below snowcapped mountains on the Strait of Georgia and Squamish, a small settlement at the head of Howe Sound, one of the multitudinous inlets indenting that bold northern coast. Neither railroads nor wagon roads nor telephone wires had penetrated the sparsely settled country north of Vancouver.

These waters had been the seaway for heroic ventures, and

BRITANNIA MINING AND SMELTING CO., LIMITED

MINE AND MILL AT
BRITANNIA BEACH, B. C.

SMELTER AT
CROPTON, B. C.

BRITANNIA BEACH, B. C., 10/28/10.

Dear George,

Would you accept position here as assayer, to begin with $125.00 per month, – board $1.00 per day, Hospital $1.50 per month. Nice little house goes with the position. Rent $5.00 per month – Running water in house, – at present Co. does not charge for electric lights.

Of course you understand that there are what may be called mining chances, but I believe unless Copper drops to nothing, this job will last. – Furthermore I believe it will better, and has sufficient prospects to be worth your while to try. – I know from what you have said you do not look at assaying as a permanent professional job & You will have a pretty fair equipment here, – with two pretty well trained Chinamen for sample men, to cut down, dry, and buck samples and do most all of the rough labor. At present there is also a Golden (Colo.) undergrad here as an assistant, – but this arrangement may not be permanent.

Letter to George from Jim Batcheller offering the job in Britannia Beach.

the coast had been discovered long before the Pilgrims landed on Cape Cod. The early explorers viewed these same dense forests, evergreen heights, blue-gray in the distance. Vancouver, the Dutchman and great navigator left his mark and name on this great body of land.

From the city that bears his name, Stanley Park juts far out in the Strait of Georgia, cutting Vancouver Island from the mainland.

These were choppy waters and our little *Britannia* shuddered, heading for Howe Sound, the first great fjord in the coastline. Here the cliff-sheltered deeps were calm and we landed one passenger and a few boxes of freight at a small settlement clearing amidst thick forests. Lacing back and forth between islands and mainland we saw only a few men watching the *Britannia* dock and depart at Gambier, Anvil and Bowen islands now turning purple, afloat on a sea of shining gold.

Harriet slept. George and I sat bewitched by the green wilderness, deep blue waters, azure northern sky. The dense woods of Anvil Island diminished in the distance. A long finger-like peninsula loomed ahead and we steamed around it into a romantic cove and tied up at a pier on Britannia Beach.

There stood Beth and Jim holding up Edgar for us to see. Rushing ashore we exchanged babies, loving and cuddling them.

"Your house is ready for you, but you're coming to our house for dinner. We have so much to talk about," Beth said. "I'll go home and put Edgar down for his nap."

"I've told a man to take your baggage to the house," said Jim. "If you need anything, let me know."

A Japanese deckhand cast off the mooring lines, and the *Britannia* tooted farewell and headed up the Sound. We rounded a corner of the large mill, and after a short walk George unlatched the gate of a picket fence.

"Well, sweetheart, here we are!"

"Good heavens, George!" I stared at a white six-room palace with living room, dining room, bedroom, kitchen, pantry, bathroom, and storeroom, with doors between rooms and electricity throughout. There were simple if not elegant furnishings.

"Wonderful, wonderful!" And to think, only five dollars a month, the same as we paid for that shack at the Tomboy.

Unpacking our luggage which arrived on a hand truck I was

Harriet Anna is on far right in Britannia Beach, 1911.

thrilled to have ample space for everything.

"Look in the backyard," George suggested, the smile in his eyes increasing my curiosity.

"*Chickens!* You know I don't know the first thing about raising chickens." He laughed, being well aware of my ignorance of the life of creatures, domestic or wild.

We started for Beth's after a short time, Harriet in her go-cart which we bought in Oakland. The cart couldn't have been comfortable with its wooden seat, wheels without tires and no springs, but it folded and had been easy to carry.

The only thoroughfare on the beach was nothing but a rutted mud road. Opposite our house were two neat cottages, one occupied by Andy Berquist, in charge of loading barges, the other by Frank Takahashi, foreman of the Japanese barge-crews. Next to the Berquist house was the only store, run by the company at no profit. It carried an assortment of meats, groceries, working clothes, ink, writing tablets, and kitchen necessities. Rod McGinnis, a cheery Scot, was the manager. Irving Levine, the postmaster, was caged in one corner surrounded with pigeonholes.

"An official postmaster for this hamlet!" I exclaimed.

"Remember," said George, "this isn't everything. It's only the beginning of the company. The mine is three miles back in the mountains and over three hundred men work there. But you won't see any of your old friends, the mules, because everything goes by tram."

*An aerial tramway brings ore from the mine down to the mill at Britannia Beach.
(Photo courtesy of Britannia Mine Museum Archives, BMM#11247.)*

Back of the store were two boardinghouses, one for Chinese workers, the other for Japanese. Between our cottage and the cove stood the office building, a boardinghouse for the white crews, a small dance hall and a one-room schoolhouse for the four school-age children.

Strolling to Beth's we could see the crescent-shaped shore of the cove, a mere half mile from tip to tip. Mountains rose abruptly so close to the water that land available for building was little more than two hundred yards at the widest place. We passed the mill, assay office, and power plant, crossed the tracks that ran from in front of the store to the end of the pier, and crossed a bridge just wide enough to negotiate single file. With only a handrail on each side as protection, it swayed, bounced and shook a mere foot above the water. It was the only way to reach the Batcheller's house from which the peninsula jutted out into the Sound.

Dense forests rose like a green wall close to the shore and half-hidden we saw a low, rambling house and heard Beth's familiar, tuneful whistling as she worked around her home.

In the living room, her treasures from the Tomboy greeted us like old friends. Cove waters softly slapped around the pebbles on a beach a stone's throw from their front porch. Using Jim's field glass we could see a small settlement at the head of the Sound.

"Squamish, at the mouth of the Squamish River," Jim said. "The river flows through practically uninhabited land. The *Britannia* plows her way up there and back in an hour. That mountain standing like a sentinel over the settlement is Mount Roderick, one of the many glaciers of British Columbia."

Impenetrable forests ran unbroken from the cove to Squamish and down the opposite shore as far as could be seen, smooth green walls with serrated crests. The only blight marring the scene was the quay and huge ore bunkers close by, a scar on the curve of the charming cove nestling deep in a world of scented cedars, spruce, tall hemlocks, towering Douglas firs.

It was no effort here to breathe, there need be no pitying animals struggling and suffering on snow-deep trails in bitter cold winters, we need not wallow waist-high in snow and plummet into its depths head first.

But there also was little personal challenge at sea level with the comforts of civilization encroaching. Though my thoughts and some of my heart still remained in the highlands, I soon adjusted to the change for I was with my George and little Harriet.

The main event of the day was always the arrival of the little *Britannia* when her welcome whistle sounded as she rounded the point at one o'clock. Four or five of the ladies on the beach were often there with their children to watch the nearing of the boat, the deckhand throwing the hawser around the piling and the purser standing by the open deck with the eagerly awaited mail sack. When the waters were choppy, we enjoyed watching the several attempts to moor the boat. It was so small and often danced around as though refusing to dock.

Occasionally there was a traveler or two from as far away as New York, Florida, or England. Lured by many stories about Howe Sound, they would take the twelve-hour trip to Squamish and return, drinking in the boundless beauty of the scenery.

I never saw the mine—a mountain of copper. Only by a narrow path hacked through three miles of forest up to 5,000 feet elevation could it be reached by foot. Consequently, few miners left the mine, especially in winter. Only because it was necessary for the members of the staff to work both at the mine and mill were they permitted to ride the tram.

The tram, a two-section system of cables, followed the contour of the surrounding hills. One section brought ore from the mine and dumped it into bins at the angle station. From there it was trammed over heights and depths down to the mill on the beach. Ore-loaded buckets coming slowly over the ridge descended into the mill, emptied the buckets, and without stopping began the slow climb back, disappearing from sight. Watching the endless movement was hypnotic, like watching waves flood and ebb on the shore.

Also on the tram were steel slings on which were loaded freight too large for the buckets, timber, pipes, and staff members with only an occasional passenger from the outside.

The Company had been without a doctor for some time, but now a recent medical graduate from Vancouver Island was arriving for his first practice.

The welcome whistle of the *Britannia* sounded, and as usual Harriet and I were on our way to the pier. Of course, Beth and Edgar were there also and Jim was there to greet the doctor.

A tall athletic-looking young man stepped ashore. Jim greeted him in his usual cordial and courteous New England manner.

"Dr. Randall, welcome to Britannia." And turning our direction, he introduced him to us. We were happy to know that now there was a doctor within reach, not only for our babies but for the men at the mine and mill, for there were frequent accidents.

After meeting the manager at the office, Jim suggested that Dr. Randall take a quick look at the mill before he started to the mine where he would make his headquarters.

"I'm going up with you today, Doctor, but first I want to warn you that although we have never had an accident on the tram since I have been here, it is a dangerous ride only if a rider is careless by loosening his grip or raising his head when passing a supporting tower." Jim was still explaining the tram system as he and the doctor entered the mill from where they were to start.

"Let's wait and watch them go," I said to Beth. We stood beside Edgar's baby-buggy and Harriet's go-cart. In a few minutes the sling came out from the mill-shed. Jim was holding onto the hook at one end, Dr. Randall at the other. Their legs dangled from the open side only thirty feet above us.

"Wave to them, Harriet," I said, holding up her little hand.

"Goodbye," we called, and with an answering wave of their free hands they went higher and higher until they were out of sight. We strolled toward the northern tip of the beach, passing four small cottages in which the shift-bosses lived, and out to the point to an attractive vacant two-story house overlooking the Sound, a picket fence surrounding a spacious yard.

The children became restless so we slowly walked back to our house where they could play in the little parlor while Beth and I had tea. How much I did enjoy being with her again. All too soon she was saying, "I'd better go. Jim will be home soon." Her devotion to her husband was sacred. I knew that, for my feeling for my husband was the same.

Preparing to leave, she lifted Edgar from the floor where he had been playing with Harriet. As I looked at his fair hair and blue eyes especially, my thoughts turned to little Billy's deep-brown ones I would always remember.

There was a knock on my door. It was Syd Knight, one of the clerks in the office. Anxiously he asked, "I'm trying to find Mrs. Batcheller. She's not at home and I thought she might be here."

"She is here," I said as Beth hurried to the door, having heard.

"Mr. Batcheller telephoned from the mine that Dr. Randall has been hurt. They are bringing him down now. Mr. Batcheller told us to get the *Cuprum* ready at once, and he wants you to bring his good suit to the pier. He's going to Vancouver and hasn't time to come home first."

"Leave Edgar with me, Beth, and you'll save time," I said and she ran out of the house.

Holding Edgar, my hands trembled for I knew we were close to a tragedy like some at the Tomboy. A half hour later I grew so restless that I put both babies in the buggy and started toward the pier. As I was nearing the mill, a sling appeared overhead with Bert Austin at one end and Jim at the other. Between them, wrapped in blankets, lay a figure.

When I reached the pier, Beth was waiting with a suitcase. The Company's small launch *Cuprum*, meaning capper, with steam up was ready to leave. Jim and Bert Austin hurried from the mill. Japanese workers carried the stretcher. The boat engineer watching from the deck went to the engine room; the pilot was at the wheel. Jim grabbed his suitcase, kissed Beth, and said, "We have to get Dr. Randall to a hospital. I'll be back tomorrow. Bert will tell you what happened."

Within five minutes the *Cuprum* was heading into the Sound.

"How awful," Beth said. "I know Jim is completely broken up." Bert sadly shook his head. "It is awful. Jim said they had reached the halfway station all right and had changed to the second section. The doctor was admiring the scenery and they were only a little way from the mine. Jim thinks the doctor must have raised his head to look at the high peaks across the canyon, just as they reached a tower. It must have been a glancing blow or his head would have been smashed. But it was hit hard enough; he has been unconscious ever since."

After a pause he continued: "The doctor would have fallen if Jim hadn't been quick enough to grab him. I don't know how he managed to hold on to him. It's amazing that he did. We did all we could at the mine but that wasn't very much. No one knew *what* to do. All there is now is to hope for the best. Well, I'm going back to the mine on the next bucket." (His expression was one we were very used to hearing.)

We waited anxiously the next day for the *Britannia*. As soon as Beth saw Jim's face she knew that he brought sad news. The young doctor, so recently starting on his life's work, so soon to be married, had died during the night from a broken skull.

CHAPTER 19

The Company lost no time engaging another doctor, this time an elderly, tall, graying Scot, not long from his Lochs, Braes, and Bonny Highlands. His heavy burr amused the miners. He had been overworked through many years of looking after the health of his countryside and had been persuaded to retire and take it easy. Going to western Canada he couldn't remain idle so accepted the position at the mine which would allow him to relax in beautiful surroundings, yet keep in touch with his profession. He quickly became popular.

We were very comfortable in our new home. George could reach the assay office in three minutes and enjoyed his work. There was no need to order ahead and store food while all we needed was just across the road where prices were a housewife's dream. Beef was twenty-five cents a pound, including T-bone steaks. Other food, just as low-priced. The rule of "first come first served" took me early to the store every morning.

Coal cost six dollars a ton; electricity cost nothing. Water was not only free but abundant and piped to our houses. Beyond bare necessities we had no place to spend money. Our supply of clothing would last a long time. Perhaps now we could save something from George's salary.

He took me through the mill one day after work. His capable Chinese assistant had been there since the mill opened, and I stood near the hot furnace watching him deftly handle the long tongs by which he pulled from the white-hot muffler the *cupels* containing the precious bead obtained from each sample of ore.

"Now they cool," he informed me. "I put beads in cups. Mr. Boss," pointing to George, "he weigh 'em. Wong," and he pointed

137

to another assistant, "he grind 'em samples."

Poor Louie, a week before, Chinese friends had come to see him, and showing them through the mill he neglected watching the fire. The temperature had fallen too low and all the cupels had *frozen*. His remorse was pathetic.

Several flights of stairs led to the ore bins. The Britannia mill recovered the values from the ore as copper concentrates—there was no bullion as at the Tomboy. Brought down in buckets the ore was dumped into the bin which fed a large crusher. After the crushed ore was washed, the *fines* went directly into the mill; chunks over two and a half inches in diameter were carried by a two-foot-wide conveyor belt under low-hanging fluorescent lights, which by weird alchemic power changed their colors. The lovely green characteristic of Britannia's ore turned grayish-white. The copper sulphide turned black.

On one side of the traveling belt Japanese workers deftly picked out the copper which went directly to the concentrate bin. Those on the other side as expertly picked up the bits which went to the waste dump.

The mill sounded busy but not with the deafening roar of a stamp mill. I saw ore passing through trommels, jigs, rolls, and screens until it was reduced to twenty mesh. Some ran over the tables which seemed to have the selective brain of a robot, for the tailings, or waste, were discarded from one side and the valuable concentrates delivered into bins at the ends of the tables, then hauled by electric motor along a trestle to the end of the pier and dumped into the bunkers.

Christmas was nearing and even on the quiet beach we felt the excitement that everywhere stirs emotions at that time of the year.

As on our first Christmas at the Tomboy, the Batchellers invited us to spend the day with them.

"Come early Christmas morning and bring your presents," said Beth. "We'll all open them together and it will be fun to watch Edgar and Harriet."

George and Jim cut two stately fir trees from the forest. Ours graced our dining room. With strings of popped corn and cranberries draped over the branches, the little ornamental angel from George's childhood over the top, candles in their holders, we were ready to light the tree—beautiful!

The day before Christmas Beth and I with our babies strolled to the wharf eagerly waiting for the mail bags. "Here she comes!" Our usual shout.

The sky was dark and the water gray. The *Britannia* was plowing a furrow through choppy seas. She reversed from the pier and repeatedly tried to dock against the haul and shoving of tide and wind. Finally the mail bags were tossed onto the pier, bulging as if Santa Claus had been most generous.

Seeing Beth, the freight clerk called to her, "Is Mr. Batcheller coming here today?"

"No," she answered. "He's at the mine."

"I have something for him," added the clerk.

"I'll take it," Beth offered. But the clerk hesitated, turning the package this way and that. "It's marked 'fragile' and 'personal' but I guess it's all right to leave it with you," he said handing it to her.

In his buggy Edgar was peeking from behind a mound of paper bags and boxes, groceries and goodies for Christmas. Beth moved them about to make room for Jim's package and, looking at the postmark said, "I can't imagine who could be sending us a present from Vancouver." She placed the package in the buggy and shook her head wondering. "I'd better not put it where Edgar can reach it. He might knock it off, and it could be china or glassware."

"Let me carry it," I said. "I'm going to the post office and then I'll bring it to you."

"All right. I want to get this turkey home. Poor Edgar he's weighed down with all these packages." And off she went, pushing the loaded buggy over the tracks and across the bridge.

The package, bound round and round with strong cord, was not heavy but there was no place on Harriet's go-cart to hold it; the cart took both my hands to push it over the frozen, bumpy road. So I crooked my little finger tightly under the cord. A strong wind was blowing and swinging the package back and forth. The word FRAGILE in bold red letters prompted me to dig the weighted finger deeper into my palm.

At the store I placed it on the counter while Syd sorted the mail. Slipping ours into a paper bag, I squeezed it tightly behind Harriet, slid the cord of Jim's package again over my finger, and walked briskly to Beth's—over the tracks and across the bridge which was now bouncing and swaying from side to side. The cord

Harriet (left) in Britannia Beach, 1912.

was cutting deeper into my finger so I pushed the go-cart faster.

Beth's tree was beautifully decorated with bright ornaments, packages tied in green or red paper, and ribbons tucked between the branches. Boxes, big and little, covered the floor around and beneath the green plumes of the stately fir.

"Where shall I put this package, Beth?" I asked.

"On the floor with the others," she said and went on draping the bookcase with scented branches of cedar. Suddenly she sat down and covered her face with her hands. "Oh, Billy, Billy . . ." she murmured, the memory of other Christmas times flooding back. My heart went out to her but I felt there was nothing I could say to comfort her. Perhaps she would prefer to be alone, so I prepared to leave.

As I started for home, the tide was flooding in, water creeping up near Beth's porch. The rickety footbridge swayed violently and the wind blew me against the handrail. I hurried home to prepare for my husband's prodigious appetite and the three young men from the boardinghouse whom George had invited for the evening.

After dinner we lit the candles on the tree and enjoyed the company of our visitors.

On Christmas morning the ground was white with snow and a light covering draped the trees in gauzy whiteness, patterned with clusters of green showing through, and the wind had died down. A beautiful Christmas Day!

We ate a hearty breakfast, fed the chickens, gathered our packages, and set out down the road for Beth's.

Everything seemed deserted except for our Japanese neighbor who was repairing his fence, for this was the only day of the year when the entire operations of the mine and mill stopped. The miners weren't digging, the tram wasn't running, the mill was silent, and no ore barges were loaded. The prevailing quiet was uncanny. There was peace in our world at Britannia Beach and I could say truly "Good will toward all men."

Perhaps, too, it was an uneasy peace. Silence around a mill is disturbing, creating the feeling of a ghost town.

The footbridge over the rocks was slippery. But "Merry Christmas" we shouted, entering the house so decked and festive in holiday finery.

We began opening gifts. One entire sack had come from Beth's relatives in Massachusetts. Harriet ran back and forth, often falling down in her excitement with Edgar creeping his fastest to keep up with her. Mittens, scarves, books, toys were unwrapped and the brightly colored trimmings tossed aside until we were in the middle of chaos.

"Jim, open that package from Vancouver," Beth urged. "I forgot to tell you about it when you came home last night, and I can hardly wait to know who sent it."

Jim cut the cord, took off the wrapping paper and lifted the lid of a box. I saw the startled look and the color drain from his face. He turned to Beth and sharply asked, "Who gave this to you?"

"The freight clerk on the *Britannia*," she replied, surprised at his agitation.

"I have to go to the office, right now. I'll be back soon."

With no explanation Jim pulled on his coat and hat and hurried out with the box, leaving us utterly bewildered.

The remaining gifts were left unopened while we played with the children and waited, perplexed and curious, for Jim's return. We had not long to wait.

Beth met him at the door. "Jim, what in the world is the matter? Wasn't that a present for you?"

"*That* package," he said gravely, "contained four-thousand standard blasting caps. If it had been dropped, none of us would be here now."

Exclamations sputtered from Beth and me. George looked at Jim as if he couldn't believe what he had heard and as if it couldn't have happened. Beth had handled the package of death. Edgar's plump hands had slapped it. I had swung it from my finger against the handle of the go-cart. I recalled how it had touched the bridge railing more than once as the wind blew me against it. I had placed it none too gently on the store counter and under the Christmas tree.

Such things as these caps were *never* handled except by those in authority. No explosives of any kind were allowed aboard the *Britannia*, a freighter—but also a passenger vessel!

The mine, having run short of caps, had sent to Vancouver for an emergency order to be shipped up on the next ore scow. But it had just left when the order was received. It would be a week before the next trip. Contrary to all rules and regulations, and unknown to Jim, the caps had been shipped on the *Britannia*, addressed to him, the superintendent.

Our Christmas joy was considerably quieter and we were most thankful for the gift of gifts to us all, and many more in Britannia Beach . . . life itself.

CHAPTER 20

Although living on the level was much less strenuous and infinitely less costly, I did enjoy the work of housekeeping in a larger house with a yard and chickens. The serenity of Britannia Beach in time could have become somewhat routine if there had not been unexpected events.

We were happy because Beth was expecting another baby, soon enough to limit her roaming the beach with me. Then Edgar was taken sick. I went to ask about him and offer any help possible. Beth looked worried.

"It came on suddenly. I've just taken his temperature and it's quite high. He seemed perfectly well this morning."

My heart skipped a beat and I tried to control my voice as I said, "Oh, it's probably just a cold."

"But he doesn't show any signs of a cold. If he isn't better tomorrow I'll call Dr. Ferguson," Beth decided.

I went home thinking about those heartbreaking days at the Tomboy when her beloved Billy came indoors from play saying, "Mommy, I'm so tired."

Next morning, with Harriet in the go-cart, I hurried to Beth's. It was obvious that Beth had not slept all night and I didn't need to ask how Edgar was.

"Harriet," she said, her voice breaking, "Edgar had three convulsions last night. Jim phoned to the mine for Dr. Ferguson. He's on his way down now."

All I could do to help was prepare and take cooked food to them. Brought down on the tram, wise and attentive Dr. Ferguson was soon with them, pulling Edgar out of one convulsion after another. He tried to reassure Beth; he had cared for many, many

143

babies in Scotland similarly afflicted. At the end of the second day Edgar began to improve. Now Beth and Jim were able to take some rest and Edgar was soon his thriving, happy self again.

Fortunately, most of our emergencies occurred in the lazy spring or warm summer days. At the Tomboy our domestic emergencies had a way of happening in the winter's coldest spells, deepest snows, and when the trails were most perilous.

One afternoon, Margery McCinnis, the storekeeper's wife, and I stood by our gate chatting about babies.

"No baby has been born at Britannia Beach as yet," she said, "but Mrs. Takahashi's baby is due any time now."

Just then I happened to glance across the road toward the steep hill. From the top down to the bottom ran a chute, two hundred feet long, worn smooth and slick by logs felled in the forests above and sent down to be shipped from the Beach. The Company's five cows were grazing a short distance away at the top of the hill.

"Margery," I screamed, "one of those cows is headed straight for the chute!"

"I'll get Rod." And she ran like a streak of lightning. He came on the run but stood helpless just as one bossy stepped into the trough and shot down the chute like a log, landing with a crash across the road from us.

I screamed and waved my arms vainly hoping to scare the next cow away from the chute. But no! The poor dumb thing followed the leader and set her cloven hoofs in the slide and crashed down on top of the first cow. We stood by helpless and rooted to the spot.

I turned away, my stomach heaving as one after the other took the slide. In moments the five cows lay in a heap at the bottom of the chute. Two were killed instantly. Two were so badly injured they had to be shot. The fifth cow apparently was unhurt although badly shaken, so was led away to be shot also. The miners enjoyed fresh beef for some time after this pitiful accident.

Our friends who often went deep-sea fishing shared with us a catch of bluefish. Caught in the cold deeps of the Sound, they were about two feet long and six inches thick with pure white flesh of a delicate flavor. I baked them with the head and tail on and served them whole, plain, or sometimes with strips of bacon inserted in the back, or stuffed for a change in the flavor.

Following instructions I struggled to make a crab trap by attaching a net I made of heavy cord to a large barrel hoop. Then with three cords evenly spaced on the hoop and tied to a long rope, the hoop would stay horizontal when lifted from the water.

Rod McGinnis saved scraps of decayed meat from the store for us amateur fishermen.

After lowering my net and tying the rope to a piling, Harriet and I sat and watched whatever was going on at the pier. Those waters must have been a crab haven, for in a few minutes I could pull up the trap full of large and small crabs with many clinging to the outside. I tossed back the small ones and those that had lost a leg, snapped off in a crab fight or by a large fish, and with my catch hurried home. By then the water I had left on the stove in a large wash-boiler was hot and boiling in a few minutes.

Grasping the crabs by their backs I pulled them from the net, carefully avoiding their saw-edged and wriggling claws. Then with my eyes closed, dropped them into the water to instant death. After twenty minutes they had turned bright red and were ready for eating. Having so many, I could afford to discard the end sections of the smaller legs. The largest one of all went to our little girl, "Ahvia Batchy Bidda, Bidda, Be" the only way she could say "Harriet Backus, Britannia Beach." The crab was one of her favorite play-things as she ran from room to room dragging it by a leg.

We reveled in plain crab, crab cocktails, crab salad, creamed crab, crab Louis, or deviled crab browned to a turn in the shells and served piping hot. Never since, anywhere, have we tasted crab as delicious as those.

During the previous winter gales, the water had whipped over the bridge and up to the Batchellers' front steps shutting Beth off from the rest of the cove for three days at a time, so Mr. Leach suggested they move to the spacious two-story house on the northern tip of the Beach with an enchanting view of the Sound and beyond the reach of storm-blown water. With Japanese workers carrying their possessions, they were quickly settled and comfortable and happy to have the picket fence-enclosed yard.

Following one restless day, Harriet was sick all night, unable to retain any food or water in her stomach. Good Dr. Ferguson had left Britannia Beach and a young medical graduate had taken

Jim and Beth Batcheller's house on Howe Sound.

his place. For some inexplicable reason I hesitated to summon him. I held Harriet in my arms all day and at night George and I took turns. Her fever ran very high and she constantly tried to get out of George's arms to "get away from the black cats on the wall," as she said. Finally, at six in the morning, George telephoned for the doctor and by seven he arrived by tram.

"Oh, that's caused by a tooth," he said casually.

Telling George to hold her firmly, he pulled a knife from his pocket and lanced the gum. Poor Harriet! No diagnosis could have been so far from the truth.

"She must be fed intravenously every three hours, day and night." And with that statement he left and returned to the mine.

"Why, you can't do that!" said George, astounded. "We have no equipment and no one to help."

"You get ready and we'll catch the *Britannia* and take Harriet to Vancouver today," he decided.

Beth had come faithfully to help me and that day watched over Harriet while I got ready to leave. Through uncontrolled tears

I burst out irrationally: "If I lose Harriet, I never want another baby!" I felt I could not endure such a loss.

Beth's eyes flashed, but with dignity and reverence she answered, "If that's the way you feel you would never deserve to have another baby." How right she was! I have never forgotten her words.

When the *Britannia* arrived from Squamish at one o'clock, Jim was on the pier and refused to let us go aboard without his personal check. "In case you need it," he said. It was the second token from Jim, beyond the call of friendship. When George had been hauling lumber in Idaho, Jim had sent a check "just in case" when hearing of the death of my brother-in-law. Truly, Jim exemplified real friendship and integrity—a gentleman of honor.

No boat ever crept so slowly as did the *Britannia* that day. Harriet lay all too quiet in her blankets, watched by one of us every minute. Reaching the hospital six hours later, we called Dr. Robert McKecknie, a Scotch physician, much loved by his patients. With his gentle, skillful care Harriet quickly recovered from a severe case of gastroenteritis.

I stayed beside her constantly except when taking time to get relief from a tooth that had been aching the entire time we had been at Britannia Beach. We returned home after a few days.

The summer was lovely, never really hot but pleasantly warm through the long evenings that remained light until ten o'clock. Wild roses flourished everywhere in the thickets and in the clearings. Garlands of long branches in pink bloom tinted the house walls, draped the fences, and perfumed the breezes.

The sun-steeped fragrance of pine and cedar was in the air, sharpened by the tang of the salt sea. We sat outdoors, peacefully languid, enjoying the opal hues of the sky slowly fading and the first faint glimmer of stars appearing.

Harriet enjoyed it with us. She couldn't go to sleep in daylight. Neither could old Biddy, our tame hen. She often deliberately sought a game with Harriet who ran around holding Biddy's disappearing tail feathers. Biddy was an incessant setter. The flock had showered us with eggs right along. So we allowed Biddy to complete her maternal urgings with a nest of fifteen eggs.

We were all thrilled when one or two fluff-balls at a time developed and all fifteen chicks were hatched. We spent hours watching them poke their heads from Biddy's feathers and suddenly burst out all around her on their own feet.

Then one morning as Harriet and I went out to be "thrilled" again by this scene, not one chick appeared. A few downy feathers sticking to the wire netting around the nest told the sad story. Wharf rats! Brought to the Beach by ore scows, they had dragged the babies one by one from the nest. My interest in raising chickens began to lag.

As at the Tomboy, we had no church, but, of course, there was the schoolhouse. And so when the word came that a "sky pilot" would arrive the following Sunday, the school was ready to become a church.

Notices of the service at three o'clock were posted in the store, the boardinghouse and the mill and all were invited to attend. No sectarian affiliation was mentioned.

When the little launch arrived we greeted a young man, deeply earnest in his chosen career. At least a score of men and women spent the worship hour softened by nostalgic memories and spiritually uplifted. When he left to repeat his visit in Squamish, we sincerely wished him well.

In the passing weeks the woods became dry in the summer sun. One day when George was home for lunch he reported, "We got word that the bush is burning far back inland. They can see the smoke at the mine and they are worried."

"If it is so far away, why should they worry?" I asked.

"Why? Because forest fires are the greatest danger for miles around here. There are huge stands of timber that never have been touched, with carpets of dry evergreen needles. Those trees are full of inflammable sap. And there's no way of fighting the fire in the wilderness. They say the wind is blowing from the east so the blaze could carry this way."

"Well, just let us hope it dies down," I said senselessly. I didn't realize that a tiny fire could start a far-reaching catastrophe—the sun shining on a bit of nettle, a single match, or one cigarette; nor did I realize the rapid spread of flames among dry leaves in mountains like these, the terror with which wild creatures flee in all directions, many of the young unable to outrun the flames.

By eight o'clock, the fire in the eight-thousand-foot mountains had not obligingly ceased as I had suggested it might. Word came from the mine that they were making all possible preparations in case it reached them. They kept in constant touch with the Beach, and we were thankful when we learned that the fire was still quite a ways east of the mine.

Then the wind changed and the racing flames started down the canyon to the south, headed directly toward the Sound, dipping down ravines, spreading up slopes.

The sky was bright with quivering orange and scarlet reflections, the scent of burning cedar and pine heavy in the air. Only a ridge separated our cove from the doomed ravine in which a lumber mill had just been completed. If the fire did not jump that ridge, we were safe.

Mr. Leach was planning for every emergency. Every man was put on the alert. George had told me not to leave the house unless he came for us. An empty barge was at the pier and plans were made to take us all aboard and pull out into the Sound if the fire jumped the ridge.

It was getting dark. I walked out to the gate. The flames were getting close to the peninsula. The blazing sky was terrifying. I turned north toward beautiful Mt. Roderick, the guardian of the Sound. Over its head were black clouds. Oh, if the rain would only come now! Though always fearful of thunderstorms, I waited and watched hoping they were moving south.

Then I saw George coming and I could tell he had good news. "The wind has changed," he said, "blowing the fire south. We think it won't jump our ridge and the danger is over, but that new mill is completely gone. Nothing could have saved it." He stayed just long enough for a cup of coffee and then returned to headquarters.

I put Harriet to bed and went out again. The clouds were almost over us and a few raindrops hit my face. Suddenly the black clouds opened and poured down nature's beneficent rain.

The flames slowly and sullenly lessened until they were gone. Britannia Beach breathed a sigh of relief and peace reigned again.

CHAPTER 21

Nurse Ellen Snyder, who had been with Beth when Edgar was born and who was much loved by the family, arrived from Boston. She welcomed the opportunity to take part again at the birth of a baby to Beth and Jim Batcheller. So with no anxiety Beth and Jim left for Vancouver, knowing Edgar was safe with Ellen. In a week, Campbell Robinson Batcheller was ushered into this world at the Vancouver General Hospital. And on Canadian soil! That staunch Yankee, his mother, insisted that the "stars and stripes" be flown above the bed in which he was born. Ten days later, Beth, anxious to be where "Robin" could share Edgar's nursery, was joyously welcomed home.

A few days later Frank Takahashi's first-born arrived without a doctor's help, and that afternoon the little house was crowded with every Japanese worker on the Beach to celebrate the event loudly—as long as the saki lasted. Mother and baby seemed none the worse for the noise.

A week later Jim received an urgent call from the mine, and again ordered the *Cuprum* to be ready.

"One of the miners yawned and his jaws locked wide open," George said when he came home from the office.

"That makes me shudder," I groaned. "What did the doctor do?"

"He wasn't able to unlock them. The poor devil was beginning to suffer, I guess mentally as well as physically. They brought him down by tram and the *Cuprum* took him to Vancouver."

The following day, the pilot reported they had run into a dense fog blanketing the Sound. The launch had gone aground on a small island and hours went by before they could pull free. The "poor devil" suffered intensely before they could get him to the hospital, ten hours after he had left the mine.

But with a few minutes under an anesthetic, his troubles were ended and he could shut his mouth without apprehension of opening it again, even to speak his regret that Bert Austin was leaving. A feeling everyone shared.

Bert had received an offer from Idaho and decided to accept it. He had been a valuable superintendent and the company was reluctant to let him go.

Winter swooped down—not the usual mild winter, but heavy rains followed by icy blasts off the Squamish Glacier. None of the houses had been built to resist cold as at the Tomboy, but *that* cold had been dry. Down here the cold was damp and penetrating.

Rain continued to fall. Ice filled the road ruts. The temperature dropped. On Sunday the thermometer registered zero and the wind asserted itself vigorously.

We closed off the parlor and dining room and used only the kitchen and bedroom, night and day stoking the kitchen range and bedroom heater.

On Monday a howling gale kept everyone house-bound except the men who *had* to work and they labored against the gale with great effort.

George was home for lunch an hour early.

"They've shut down all the mill operations," he said.

"Shut down the mill? But why?" This hadn't happened in the year we lived at the Beach, except for Christmas Day.

"There's so much ice in Britannia Creek that it has plugged the intake. They can't get enough water to keep the mill going. We can't run the assay office even with our furnace and heating stoves going full blast in that small building. The solutions and water pipes keep freezing. Louie will have to sleep at the assay office to keep the fires going day and night. He's putting the bottles of solutions near the furnace to keep them from freezing."

Louie was faithful and successful at this task, to George's joy.

George carried coal from the shed in the back of the yard, stoked the stoves, and filled the hods. The lethal breath of northern glacier fields and the smaller one above Squamish aided the gale sweeping down and around us.

In the afternoon, wrapped like an Eskimo, George bravely went for the mail and groceries and came home to report.

"Rod says the *Britannia* hasn't come and he doesn't think she'll get here today. It's still zero, and he says the coldest he's ever known it to be here."

"My goodness, fifteen and twenty below at the Tomboy was nothing like this," I said. Of course it was the difference between dry and damp winters and wind from the glaciers.

I pulled three pairs of stockings over Harriet's legs and put on her all the clothes I could fasten, one over the other, finally buttoning a warm kimono over that. At bedtime I took off only her shoes and covered her with extra blankets.

The freezing wind howled. We stayed close to the stove which George filled as fast as the coal burned down. We chinked cracks and crevices around the doors and windows with clothing or rags. As soon as the chickens went to bed, and chickens never break their rules, George hauled a large packing case into their house and put the squawking creatures in it and covered it with wire netting, hoping their own heat would keep them from freezing.

Polar conditions continued throughout the night. We hadn't heard from Beth and, being a little anxious next morning, George thought he should satisfy us both, wondering whether they were well and protected. So with hands cupped over his ears, head down, he bucked the wind.

"They're doing just what we are," he reported, "trying to keep warm. So far, they're fine. The stoves upstairs keep the babies comfortable. But I had to go around to the back door as the waves, that were not supposed to go near the house, were blowing clear over the rocks and dashing against the front fence. Jim is worried about how long we can stand this. He's afraid the Company will run out of coal."

I went to lift the chickens out of the box. To my horror, Biddy our pet was not among the others. I ran to the runway which led into the yard. There she was, huddled in a pile of snow. Her bedraggled feathers, slicked down with snow and ice, gave her beady little eyes the look of one whose trust had been betrayed, whose feelings had been painfully hurt. How it happened, we never knew.

We gathered up our half-frozen feathered friend, took her indoors, wrapped her in a small blanket, and kept her in a box until she warmed up.

By Wednesday there was no relief except a slight easing of the wind. So, warmly clad we took a stroll. Britannia Beach looked deserted, lonely, bleak yet somehow beautiful shrouded in icy snow. Icicles hung from wires and eaves, ornamented the trees and shrubs. Near the mill we stopped and stared. From the trestle between the mill concentrate bins, thick stalactites hung halfway to the ground twenty feet below, many of them eight inches thick.

"Water has been dripping from the wet concentrates in the bins and freezing as it dropped from the trestle," George explained. "That's a tremendous weight, and they'll be dangerous when they begin to melt and drop."

"I want to go home, I'm freezing," I said, shivering. As we passed the store, Jim came running out carrying groceries. "I've been talking things over in the post office," he said. "Evidently the *Britannia* can't get up here and food is getting short. Coal is going like hot cakes. If this lasts many more days, they're going to move us all into the boardinghouse to save fuel until a coal barge can get here."

By Friday morning the wind began to die down and the temperature rose a few degrees. Just before three that afternoon, a worker repairing a broken wire on the pier heard the heartwarming "too-oot" of a whistle and from his high perch on the pole and sighted the *Britannia*, rounding the point. He slid down the pole to spread the glad tidings. Every man, woman, and child muffled to the eyes tore from the stoves and hurried to the wharf.

Rolling in the rough gray waters and bucking the gale, the *Britannia* made headway slowly but surely. She was a weird sight shrouded in ice from the top of her funnel to the waterline. Wherever spray had fallen, it froze and, clinging to the rigging, formed myriad designs of dead-white lace. Ice enclosed each strand of the wire guard rail on the deck, filling in the course mesh until only peepholes patterned the crystal film.

Listing from side to side, pitching forward as if trying to shake off the weight of ice slowing her down, she made the turn toward the pier with difficulty and was unable to pull in close. Time and again the mooring line was thrown and fell short and, heavier with water, was hauled back for another try. Only after a half hour did it fall within reach of the Japanese dockhands trying to seize hold of it.

Sacks containing mail of six days back and all the supplies the boat could stow away were unloaded on the pier. Each day, the *Britannia* had attempted to come up the Sound but had been forced to return to Vancouver.

One week after the onslaught of the storm, Britannia Beach was back to normal. The waves calmed down. The chill left our bones. The mill was running with its assuring din. And a cold record had been set for British Columbia.

Boats fascinate me and, along with welcoming the arrival of the *Britannia*, I was always waiting when the barge *Bangor* or the *Argus* was due, hauled into the cove by a powerful tug and maneuvered under the ore bunkers on the pier. They were the relics of fine vessels now converted to carriers for transporting concentrates from the mill to the smelter in Tacoma. Their uncovered decks were divided into three open bins and loading them was a job for experts. The capacity of each bin had to be estimated accurately, the distribution evenly balanced, and tide conditions considered.

The barges were berthed beside the bunkers, and when the chute gates were opened, ore poured like wheat into the stern bin. When this was partly filled, the Japanese crew moved it with hand winches so the middle hold could be filled with the same tonnage; next the hold in the prow. When loaded to capacity it was pulled to deeper water because at low tide there was insufficient depth between the shore and the bunkers to float a heavily laden barge.

Meanwhile, the tug returned to Vancouver since four days were required to produce enough concentrates to make another load. The tug seemed small to haul such an old scow from the Cove on its slow voyage out of Howe Sound into the Strait of Georgia, down Puget Sound to the American Smelting and Refining Company at Tacoma. To those who find romance in the sea and ships that "go down" in it and who could picture the *Bangor* and *Argus* as the beauties they once were, with tall masts, white canvas wings, flying with the wind, to be pulled now by their noses by these powerful, business-like tugs, seemed humiliating.

Shipwreck, fire, but—most probable of all—old age had befallen them. I thought of them at their launchings with flags and pennants flying, their paint and metalwork gleaming, a gay crowd watching, champagne splashing amid cheers and laughter. Now with their super-structures lopped off, stripped of all beauty and grace, they were degraded to the lowest of all that could happen—bare, ugly, begrimed with ore, gutted, empty hulks.

One evening we saw Frank Takahashi coming home, which meant the *Bangor* was loaded ready for the towing tug. At ten that night we heard someone calling loudly to Frank and Andy Sorenson. George hurried out to learn what was wrong.

"Trouble with the *Bangor*!" the caller said and ran back.

"I'll see if I'm needed," George called to me and followed.

An hour later he returned. "There certainly is trouble," he said. "The seams of the *Bangor* are opening up and water is pouring in. I'm going back. Jim has called out every available man. They are trying to unload as much ore as they can, dumping it on shore."

It was a pleasant night and, wrapping Harriet, I took her with me to watch the men hurrying on and off the barge, busy as ants. Power lines had been strung and the deck was ablaze with light. Before long it was evident that unloading the ore was impossible and, after seeing the men hauling aboard a large pump from a flat-car rolled alongside, Harriet fell asleep and I took her home.

George worked with the others until three o'clock in the morning. The *Bangor* had been properly loaded but by some error it had not been pulled out to water deep enough to float her as the tide ebbed. When her prow began settling on the mud, the weight of three hundred tons of ore had opened her bottom seams and water began rising in the hold.

Mechanics, pipe-fitters, electricians, Japanese workers together installed the pump and had it going as soon as possible, but it made no headway with the rising water which rushed in faster than it could be pumped out. The superintendents decided that the *Bangor* would soon sink and every effort must be made to get her out of the slip. If that were blocked, no other barge could be loaded and the entire mine would have to shut down.

George had been working with the pipe fitters and watching the pump. From the first he felt sure they couldn't save the *Bangor*. The tug that was to have taken her in tow arrived when the tide was rising. The towline was attached but the *Bangor* wouldn't budge. For another hour the pump was kept going, and by then the tide was high enough for the tug to pull her free. The pump and power lines were taken off and she was towed out of the slip and maneuvered into shallow water near the footbridge where the

The Bangor, *almost raised.*

bottom is sandy and smooth and would not damage the hull.

In the morning we went to the pier. From the footbridge I could have thrown a stone to the tilted deck of the poor old *Bangor* sticking up out of the water with the rest of her submerged. At high tide we saw nothing but a little stick two feet high above the water.

A diver came from Vancouver and for the next ten days we watched the events. A tug anchored nearby. Assisted by two men, the diver got into his heavy suit, sitting down while his helpers adjusted the ponderous helmet to which lifelines were attached. Weighted by cumbersome shoes, he went down the ladder, slowly disappearing sometimes for one hour, often two, before he was hauled up looking like a dripping knight in armor.

His examination of the boat showed the necessity of caulking the sprung seams. A pump was installed on deck with a suction hose in the hold and a steam line to the tug, the hatches battened down. Meanwhile, a second tug arrived from Vancouver and everything was in readiness to try to raise the *Bangor.* Twice in every twenty-four hours it had been submerged and twice one plank peered out as if to look for help. Only at low tide could an attempt be made to lift her, for the rising tide to float her, with only six hours to complete the rescue before the tide ebbed.

Low tide occurred at eleven a.m. On the tenth day the water was calm, the weather clear, the pump primed, and the centrifugal began its hum-hum-humming. An eight-inch jet of water rose and fell in an arc disgorging a thousand gallons of water per minute.

The surface of the water showed disturbance, then the railing appeared. Within an hour the *Bangor* was sucked free from the sand and the rising tide supported and aided her ascent. The deck and hull rose, and like a wounded monster, groggy but fighting to survive, she floated at last, lashed firmly to the tug.

The centrifugal pump continued aiding her to discharge the water she had imbibed. We watched until the towing tug pulled her around the point into the Sound. For one hundred miles, from Britannia Beach to Tacoma, the big water-logged *Bangor* trailed behind the little tug with a stream of water coming from the holds. Thirty hours later, the little flotilla arrived at her destination.

By a strange stroke of destiny, while the *Bangor* lay on the bottom of the water, the world price of copper rose. By the time the concentrates she carried reached the smelter, the company had made a profit over and above the cost of the disaster.

Winter passed and spring came in beauty to our home: flowers in the woods, birds gaily singing, warmer, lazier days, peace everywhere.

Then came the bombshell that stunned everyone.

Mr. Leach received a telegram from New York informing him his successor would arrive in ten days! That was all! He had guided the company successfully through the years of low-priced copper. Now that the market price was rising, someone else was to reap the benefits. The miners, millmen, and officials were all indignant, but the only thing we could do to show our admiration for Mr. Leach was to hastily organize a farewell party for him.

Miners who could leave the mine came down the trail joining millmen, officials, and loading crews. All flocked to the hall and presented Mr. Leach and his wife a beautiful silver service and a purse of money.

On the arrival of Mr. Moody, the new manager, and his superintendent, Mr. Leach kindly warned him to beware of Britannia Creek and the frequent big floods caused by cloud bursts far back in the mountains and advised him not to build dwellings in the open parts of the delta. The advice went unheeded and a few years later a disastrous flood destroyed all the houses built in that area.

Changes began to take place almost immediately in the staff. Jim was the first to be told he was no longer needed. George was kept for nearly six months longer, probably because he had been in charge of a new treatment for ore, the flotation system, an English process not tried in the United States; but Herbert Hoover, a mining engineer at that time, was using the flotation process successfully in Australia.

Strange how an event which at the time seems unfortunate proves later to be a valuable experience and leads to far better things. This was the case for George as he worked on this new process while at Britannia.

We sold the few pieces of secondhand furniture we had bought and the chickens, with the promised stipulation that old Biddy would be allowed to live out her natural span of life. And so in June, 1912, we left beautiful Britannia Beach, going directly to Colville, Washington, George's childhood home, to visit his mother.

PART III
THE HEART OF IDAHO

Sketch of Fort Colville by Buchtel & Stolte, Photographers.

CHAPTER 22

George's grandfather, Jacob Stitzel, who as a boy had crossed the plains in 1849, had been appointed United States Land Commissioner for the eastern district of the territory of Washington, holding that position until his death in 1911. He and his family lived near Old Fort Colville, not far from the Canadian line. There his daughter, Kathrine, met and married Lieutenant George Benjamin Backus who, with his classmate Lieutenant Robert Page Powell Wainwright, had graduated from West Point in 1875. Martha Stitzel married Colonel Evan Miles, later Brigadier General, who was involved in battles with the Nez Perce Indians.

Lieutenant Backus was transferred to Fort Walla Walla near the Columbia River. There they were quartered next to the house of his friend, Lieutenant Wainwright and his wife, whom he had married in New York in 1879.

In 1883 under General Nelson A. Miles, commanding the department of the Columbia, the lieutenants were detailed to explore the unmapped territory of Washington to find a way to the Pacific Ocean.

With them were General William Tecumseh Sherman, Colonel George Goethals, later builder of the Panama Canal, and Lieutenant Abercrombie, later a Justice of the Supreme Court of the United States.

While they were in the wilderness, two baby boys were born—one in August, Jonathan Mayhew Wainwright, our hero of Corregidor; and the other in September, George Stitzel Backus, my hero. Though the army soon separated the families, the mothers remained lifelong friends.

Lieutenant Backus died when very young, and Mrs. Backus

with George, returned to Colville to be with her father. Eventually, she married Gilbert Ide, a gentleman highly thought of in the valley. Now, Mother Ide was seeing her first grandchild, and Harriet enjoyed the company of her young uncle and aunts.

Capable, alert, and charming, this lovely lady held us spellbound with recollections of adventure and housekeeping vicissitudes of army wives.

After only two weeks as her guests, she was able to decide, for me, our immediate future. A letter from Bert Austin arrived offering George a job running a mill at Elk City in the heart of the Idaho wilderness.

"I'd like to work with Bert again," said George. "As he says, 'it's only a prospect,' but it might be worthwhile. But it is fifty-five miles from the end of a railroad. Would you be willing to go, dear?"

"I would be glad to go but . . ." I hesitated, "taking the baby to a place like that frightens me a little. Would there be a doctor near?"

"I don't know." George then showed me a dot on a map.

"Looks isolated. We'd have to go in from Stites by stage to Elk City." I asked, "Mother Ide, what do you think?"

"Oh, many mothers have done harder things than that! When your husband was only one year old and a frail baby at that, I took him two hundred miles from a railroad to Old Fort Assiniboin in the wilds of Montana. We traveled in an army truck over almost unbroken roads. Why should you hesitate to take your child fifty-five miles from a railroad?"

That was the deciding question. George accepted Bert's offer. His only instructions were "Come to Elk City." We went.

It was July, intensely hot in that rich wheat country. The early afternoon at Arrow Junction reached one hundred and sixteen degrees. There was no shade. Two-day coaches waited at the junction of the main line and spur. We crowded aboard and found a seat. Across the aisle, behind and facing us sat braves and squaws, no Hiawatha or Minnehaha type Indians but fat, sullen, and smelly ones, wearing hit or miss trousers, faded coveralls, old wool pants too large or too small, assorted sad and gaudy shirts, colored scarfs around sweaty necks, copper-toned faces framed in sleek, long black hair, braids twined with multicolored ribbons, and ten-gallon hats to top it all.

Every car window was opened wide but not the whisper of a breeze entered. Suitcases, boxes, paper bags blocked the aisle, and our knees bumped those of the Indians. My clothing stuck to me. The awful germs we're contacting, I thought!

"George, Harriet can't stay in here!" I complained.

"But where can we go? The other car is just the same." But seeing my unhappy expression and knowing how I felt, he added, "I might take her out on the back platform." This he did and I felt somewhat better.

Toward evening, having left many Indians off for the reservations, we reached the end of the Camas Prairie Railroad, Stites, the seat of the Nez Perce Indian affairs, a few miles from the South Fork of the Clearwater River.

During the 1860s to 1870s Idaho was the scene of considerable strife, and the Nez Perces under Chief Joseph made their last stand against the encroaching whites only a few miles from the settlement. Brigadier General Evans Miles, George's uncle, led his troops in encounters with these tribes, which made this country personally interesting to us.

Escaping with his followers, Chief Joseph led them into Montana where they were defeated. Joseph, sick of warfare and distressed seeing the members of his tribe hungry and exhausted, vowed never to wage war again. The Government located them in Oklahoma but later allowed them to return to their beloved Idaho.

They owned many farms around Stites and rented some of them to white men. Rent money enabled them to ride back and forth on the railroad, a favorite form of entertainment.

One block from the depot stood the only hotel, already condemned by the state, a fact we learned some time later. Anyway, we had no choice. Our forlorn room was up a long flight of well-worn stairs. The head and foot of a rickety bed leaned toward each other as if they could stand up no longer. There were also a ragged rug, washstand with the inevitable bowl and pitcher, and one chair! We were there for the night, regardless, and the temperature was nearing one hundred and ten degrees! It was fortunate we had to open the two windows—they were so dirty we could not have seen through them.

George went downstairs to ask if they had a cot for Harriet and to learn the location of the toilets. The clerk was sorry, they had no cots. They really should have had charts to guide guests to the toilet. The directions were "Go to the end of the hall, turn left, go to the other side of the building, turn right, open the door and you will find a trestle. The toilets are at the end of the trestle."

There they were! Holding Harriet's hand firmly, I navigated that long, high, shaky, narrow trestle to two outhouses high over the gulch, with long enclosed chutes leading down to the ground. Abominable!

Since there was no dining room in the hotel, we were directed to a house down the street. Dirty tablecloth, greasy meat, and soggy potatoes! The usual bill of fare.

With our uncomplaining child in the middle of the straw pallet, George and I clung to the outer edges through the night. At this point I recalled Mother Ide telling me that she had stayed awake all night once in a hotel to keep cockroaches away from one-year-old George. With this in mind I stayed awake too.

Every step, word, or cough in that building sounded as though it were in our room. Drunken roomers reeling down the hall bumped our door. The stifling heat was unbearable and I was more than glad to be up at daybreak.

Again we went down the street to the untidy house for breakfast. I ordered a soft-boiled egg and an orange for Harriet, both having protective coverings; but the egg came *hard* boiled. I was disgusted.

Promptly at six the stage arrived. In the high, uncovered wagon were three seats. The hubs and spokes of the large wheels were worn and cracked showing the effects of years of jolting over wracking roads. The four horses, though fresher than the wagon, had long since passed their best days.

Jimmy Coleman, the driver, tall and dark and in his fifties, was checking the tugs as we came out. "Good morning," he greeted us cordially. "We're going to have a fine day. You folks are evidently going to Elk City." Then picking up our suitcases, he strapped them in the wagon boat. "It'll probably be two weeks before the freighters get your trunks to you." Two weeks!

One of the three men going with us climbed up next to the driver's seat, the other two behind him. Setting my foot on the small step, I scrambled over the wheel onto the back seat. George lifted Harriet up to me and then clambered up beside her.

"All ready?" Jim threw the mail pouches under the front seat, climbed aboard, cracked the long whip over the horses, and we left Stites.

The seat tilted forward. My feet scarcely touched the floorboards. Harriet's feet dangled and we had to hold her to keep her from sliding off. If the stage had springs, we could not feel them. Even that early the day was hot and we shed our coats. We lurched along the narrow, crooked old wagon road filled with ruts, rocks, and stumps at a fairly fast clip through the lowlands of the Clearwater River Basin, and by eight o'clock had covered eight miles.

"D'ya see that hill over yonder?" Jimmie pointed with his whip. "Well, right there the Nez Perce Indians made their last stand in 1877. That Chief Joseph was a slippery eel. He was smart. And right under the noses of our soldiers he led his braves out of a trap into Montana." The very Indians uncle Evan Miles had fought! As I thought of that, my mouth opened to say, "How interesting," when the wagon hit a hole in the road and I was diving head first over the wheel. As George grabbed for me, he knocked Harriet to the floor. Jimmie pulled in the horses while we replaced ourselves.

The other passengers left us at Clearwater where we stayed for a few minutes. It was nine o'clock, hot under the glaring sun standing still but a brief respite from the hard seats. From there the road began to ascend, the horses slowed their pace, and soon we were under the blessed canopy of the branches of big trees.

"We're starting up into the mountain. The Clearwater forks near Kooskia, the other side of Stites, and these mountains are between the Middle and the South Forks. Kooskia means clear. You should hear a Nez Perce say it—Kooskooskee," he drawled softly.

"I've lived around here all my life. Been drivin' this road nigh onto thirty years. There's only one house between here and the Mountain House, where we'll eat. Look way down there . . ." He pointed through the trees. "South Fork."

Far down a ribbon of blue water was on its way to join the mighty Snake River flowing through the deepest gorge in North America. A green arcade of white pine, Engelmann spruce, birch, and stately cedars gave a chilling shade after one hundred and ten degrees at Clearwater, so we put on our coats.

Exactly at noon we reached the Mountain House nestling under tall Ponderosa pines and built when prospectors, seeking gold, had poured through on their way to the Salmon River country. The meal was excellent and well served. The cook, one of the few Chinese still in that part of the country, took great pride in his cooking and serving.

The stages ran strictly on schedule, six o'clock at Stites, the Mountain House at noon, Newsome at six o'clock in the evening. Half a mile from the Mountain House we reached the 6,500-foot summit along a winding, tilting road which made it difficult to stay on our slippery seats. It was warm again and we now shed our coats. Our driver produced a rifle and laid it across his knees.

"Good many bears in these woods," he explained. "I'm always ready. Every once in a while one shows up, though I don't shoot unless they get ornery. Even then I warn 'em and generally they go on their way. But horses are awful scared of bears. You know, my father came west in '60. He was killed by Indians when I was a kid."

I was keenly interested in his talk because my own father often had spoken about his adventures in Idaho. One of his favorite stories had been about the time he and seven others had been searching for gold. Coming to a fork in the trail they disagreed about which path to take and after some debate, half went one way and half the other. Father and his companions reached camp safely. The others were never seen again. It was assumed that they had been the victims of hostile Indians.

Another time, when riding the trail, father came to a small spring. He dismounted and filled his broad-brimmed hat with the clear, cold water. Satisfying his thirst he let the excess water trickle slowly from his hat onto the sand at his feet. To his amazement it uncovered a shining two-and-a-half-dollar gold piece which he carried for years afterward as a good luck talisman.

From Jim I learned that the road we were traveling was the old Indian foot trail widened by the white man's wagon. The Nez Perces, bold and clever warriors, had worn paths along the crests of the ridges so they could look down on enemies below without danger from foes lurking above.

Through the long afternoon the stage climbed the heavily wooded slopes, rocking and creaking. At much too fast a pace for my comfort we bounced downhill and around curves under Alpine and Douglas firs. We followed a brawling stream flowing over a rocky bottom to a clearing in the woods, Newsome. At 5,600 feet elevation it marks the dividing bench between two great slopes, one down to Clearwater Valley, the other to the Salmon River country. Undoubtedly, Newsome looked exactly as it did in 1861: a low log cabin beside the road, three small cabins nearby, across the road a barn with a split-log fenced corral.

We were assigned to a pioneer's dream, a clean, neat log cabin of one room, slab roof, wide floorboards, clay-chinked heavy log walls, and two tiny windows too high for me to look out of.

The main cabin where meals were served had sitting and dining rooms with four small bedrooms in the back.

Dinner was ready in minutes. The rough dining table was covered with oilcloth. Two goblets held wild flowers. Oil lamps in wall brackets lighted the room. We had grouse, thick white breasts piled high on a platter. It was my first taste of that tender and toothsome fowl and I found it delicious along with potatoes, fresh vegetables, jellies, and wild berries in generous amounts.

As soon as we finished this refreshing dinner we went to our cabin. Two-and-one-half-year-old Harriet had endured the twelve-hour journey with never a whimper nor a cry. Her patience was certainly inherited from her father.

The moment she was in bed she was fast asleep.

Weary as we were we sat out in front of the cabin with George's arms around me. Such a lovely night: under a canopy of tall, stately pines and cedars, their branches intertwined, our feet cushioned deep in a bed of fragrant pine needles, the summer night calm and peaceful, the sky bright with twinkling stars, no sound but the mysterious voices of nature whispering in the woods.

It was long before we could break the spell of that sublime night, but we had to be ready early to continue our journey. Reluctantly we entered the cabin for such sleep as comes only in nights like this in the heart of a wilderness.

CHAPTER 23

At five the next morning we were awake. At five-thirty the breakfast bell summoned us to bacon, eggs, fried potatoes, fruit, and coffee. Promptly at six, two stages waited, ours headed for Elk City, the other, Jim's, back to Stites.

We climbed aboard. The driver swaggered up, vaulted over the wheel, and settled himself in the seat. He was a big, husky man with red cheeks and flowing brown moustache, plaid flannel shirt, a bandana around his neck, large brown sombrero tilted rakishly, trousers tucked inside high boots—importance stamped on his face.

"Let's go." He flicked the whip. "I'll bet this is all new country to you folks. I've never seen you before. An' I've been haulin' mail in here since I was young. Best job in the world. Rather do this than be president of the country. Everyone 'round here knows me—Jess McPherson."

"I'm George Backus and this is Mrs. Backus and Harriet. I'll be working for Bert Austin in Elk City."

"Great! Hope you fellers make good in there. Elk City needs somethin' to wake it up," he opined.

It was a beautiful day, the ridges less wild but still covered with Idaho's stately white fir and pines. Nearby babbled Newsome Creek, fed by tiny brooks from surrounding mountains hurrying to meet the south fork of the Clearwater.

Jess dramatically poured forth what he knew about the country he loved and we drank it in for we were interested in history, and his stories were history.

Nature is grand, but swinging, swaying, sliding on the seat, hanging on for myself as well as Harriet, dust-covered and weary, my enthusiasm for scenery and adventure began to lessen after fifty-five miles. But soon, Jess, always the actor, straightened up and, cracking his whip, swung the horses smartly around the corner of a log cabin, pulling up before the Parr Hotel.

ELK CITY! Elk maybe, but City?

Its reason for existing had been the lure of gold. In 1860, after the California gold rush, gold was found along Oro Fino Creek in land watered by the Clearwater River. The frenzied rush began. The Government had signed a treaty with the Nez Perces promising that no white man might settle on their lands in this territory. But the Indian agent might as well have tried to hold back ocean waves as to prevent the whites from pouring over lands where a flake of gold might be found or the rumor of gold be heard.

There had been rumors of gold in the Elk River valley, one hundred miles southeast. Over the mountain trail on which we had rolled and joggled, the adventurers had rushed on foot and on horses. GOLD! Greater than the love of life itself to the bold, the reckless, the rover! They settled in the valley, named the settlement Elk City and worked out from there.

Still deeper in the mountains rose the call "GOLD." Up steep slopes, nine thousand feet high, the hordes swarmed, then down into the beautiful valley of the wild Salmon River. By 1861 an estimated thirty thousand had overrun the terrain.

Heavy winter snows shut them in. Supplies ran low and it was impossible to get relief.

Ledges were opened but there was not enough rich ore for those who had dreamed of fabulous fortunes less laboriously and more quickly obtained.

The great strikes at the Coeur D'Alene in northern Idaho and in Montana far outshone the small and less spectacular gold region of the Clearwater and Salmon valleys. Hearing about the wealth beyond the Bitterroot Mountains to the east, prospectors who had not found their El Dorados, receded in waves. There remained in the settlement only a few who hoped for a return of the tide.

But in the wake of departing white men came thousands of Chinese, patient, hardworking, and successful placer miners to dig out the *fines*, the small bits of gold left after the larger nuggets and coarser high-grade were gone.

During the next twenty-five years, the tales of gold continued to drift out from that almost mythical country. A few more adventurers wandered in, making the Elk Valley their headquarters. Some of these, dazzled by the eternal dream of quick wealth, invested everything they had in Elk City business ventures and were stranded there unable to pay their way out.

In 1912 there were people in Elk Valley who had never seen a chunk of coal, a fruit tree, an electric light, much less an automobile.

The great event of the day was the arrival of the stage with perchance a guest or two for the Parr or the Strong hotel in which was the post office. A balcony along the second story of the Parr hotel shaded the rough board walk. On a bench beside the front door sat three men and a gray-haired woman, silently watching. Across the road, four men slouched against a saloon, staring as Jess pompously helped Harriet and me down from the stage.

With footsteps clicketyclacking on the loose boards, Bert Austin appeared. Our greetings over, he said, "Mrs. Parr has your room ready." He introduced us to the elderly woman sitting on the bench and she nodded condescendingly.

The lobby was bare. George wrote our names in a register which held historic names calling up wild adventures of bygone days. The large, dreary dining room, now almost empty, had been built to accommodate a daily influx of hungry men. The well-patronized bar in a side alcove had its own street entrance.

A long flight of stairs led to our room which contained two beds, the usual dresser, clothes rack and stand with bowl and pitcher, worn carpet, tired curtains, and battered furniture, but it was clean and spacious.

Noon dinner was almost over but we satisfied our appetites. Jess McPherson at a table next to ours gulped his food and from the door waved and said, "Goodbye, I'm starting back to Newsome. See you tomorrow."

In our room, Bert Austin explained his project: "It developed so suddenly that I didn't take time to write you the details. It's a grass-root proposition and may turn out to be something, or it may not. I thought it worthwhile taking a chance. Here's the story. In 1880 Buster Smith discovered small outcroppings in the Valley a mile and a half from here. He built a cabin for an assay office and living quarters combined. For years he puttered along with his prospect until in 1907, I think it was, he was able to interest F. W. Bradley. He is that noted mining engineer from San Francisco, you know. Well, Bradley bought the property and sent J. F. Thorn and me into this wilderness and undeveloped district to build a mill and operate this Buster Mine. Mary and I moved into the Smith cabin. But the mine didn't pan out, so we ceased operations in 1909."

"And that's the mill I'm to run?" asked George.

"Yes. It won't take long to put it in shape. It's about two miles from the prospect I'm going to develop. An old prospector found some good gold samples at grass roots. Al Neddar interested Mrs. Parr and she contacted Bradley. He was too busy in the Coeur D'Alenes so he asked me if I wanted to take a fling at it. It's called the Colonel Sellers. We'll go there tomorrow."

"Is there a place we can move into?" George asked.

"I doubt if there is in town. But the Neddars are living in a cabin next to the mill and we've asked them to move out as soon as possible. Then you can move in."

When night came the street was dark except for light from dingy oil lamps behind dirty windows and the flicker from candles here and there. George turned off our one lamp, and despite the uproar from saloons across the street, we were too exhausted to be kept awake.

On the following days Harriet and I idled around the one street, browsed in the few stores, and spoke with people who seemed glad to see newcomers. Mrs. Parr was the dowager of Elk City. Her attractive daughter managed the hotel while her son-in-law, a heavy and slow-moving man, acted as the bartender. He also ran the drugstore, a small shack hugging the hotel; this he went to when drugs were needed, which was not often. The stock consisted of only common medicines, but they were contained in the elaborate jars and bottles (works of art) left from apothecary days.

Closely flanking each other on the Parr side was a mixture of stores and houses. There were a two-story, barn-like building ready for an occasional get together but seldom used, a cabin graced with green shrubs which made it stand out from the rest, a second hotel containing the post office and one other house.

Across the street was the log cabin around which Jess and the stage made daily dramatic arrivals.

The cabin, a relic of gold rush days, sagged tiredly toward a well with a peaked roof adjoining the next cabin. Crowded close together were Mrs. Purcell's laundry, a small assay office, Ben Scott's grocery, Lapp's General Store, and two saloons at the head of the slope. The thirst of fifty men, women and children within a radius of twenty-five miles could be satisfied at three saloons and the well. In front of the saloons was the inevitable bench for idlers, lazy, shiftless, sitting all day spitting tobacco juice on the walk, waiting for night to fall. Then they shifted into the bar to spend their last nickels, or hope someone would treat them. There they decided the country's destiny and their arguments often led to fighting, ending in the road with the vanquished lying with battered heads and body bruises until the doctor arrived to repair them.

At the upper end of town several frame houses surrounded by gardens looked somewhat cared for and pretentious. This was all of Elk City, except for a cabin, a combination of frame and logs at the foot of the road which looked alive and well-kept. A screen-enclosed back porch opened into a yard where a thrifty flock of Rhode Island Reds gave color and animation to the otherwise lazy scene, their cackling sounding cheerful.

This was the home of Dr. and Mrs. Davis who had arrived some time before we did. He was the only physician within thirty difficult miles but he had far from enough calls to provide a living. Consequently, he had an arrangement by which those who could do so paid a regular monthly fee of two dollars for each adult, one dollar for a child, and in return received all needed medical attention.

Even so, I could not imagine how the Davises managed. His office, a small front room, was spotless, and with limited equipment he performed minor operations. He was one of those countless saints who spend their lives in deeds of mercy for those in the wilderness, unappreciated until they are gone and their goodness is sorely missed. He loved the Elk Valley. Forty-two hundred feet above sea level, an oval bowl seven miles long, a half mile wide, the sides green with small pines, the floor a beautiful meadow.

With so little to do living at the hotel, I decided to try to learn to sew and began looking for a sewing machine. I asked Mrs. Purcell of the laundry if she knew of one I might rent.

"Mrs. Clifton has one," she said. "She lives across the road from the next saloon. But if you go to see her, leave Harriet with me. You wouldn't want a child to go there."

"But why?" I asked.

"Hardly any woman speaks to her, much less goes near her." Mrs. Purcell proceeded to tell me all about Mrs. Clifton.

In the days of gold and high hopes, with her two young boys she had accompanied her husband, a miner, into Elk Valley. She was a loving, devoted mother and wife. When their dreams faded, a struggle for existence began. Unable to find work, the husband deserted the woman, leaving her penniless with her sons to feed. She took in sewing, mending the work clothes of prospectors still in the vicinity. As they drifted away the struggle became harder. She took in washing, but the few people left were like herself without incomes. She was well-spoken, literate, and attractive. Her boys were well-mannered, smart, always clean in their patched clothing, but she and they began to show the effects of hunger. People sympathized, said it was a shame, and tried to be kind in small ways.

The woman would work at anything, even washing glasses or cleaning a saloon. She was offered and accepted a drink by someone. It warmed her blood, eased hunger pangs, and dulled the pressure of her desperation. With a drink she could do with less food, so gave her share to the boys. Plenty of men shared their flask with her, told her how pretty she was and how foolish it was to work so hard for so little when there was an easier way.

Presently her sons were sent to a public institution in a distant city, never again to see their mother or know anything about her. Much of her earnings from the "easier" life went to support and educate them, to give them a better chance. In the oldest profession for women, she sank as low as any who follow the camps. She had been found on early mornings behind the saloons, naked, sleeping off the night's debauch.

Yet remnants of her beauty remained. She had been and was a good cook and housekeeper. Paul Clifton, a middle-aged, steady-going miner came along and saw in her much that he appreciated. They were married and now lived quietly in a well-kept home, ostracized by most of the towns people; but they seemed indifferent about it and content with each other.

I knocked on Mrs. Clifton's door. A deep voice said, "Come in." I could not just enter like that, and knocked again. "Come in!" she said, but I waited until she opened the door.

Snatching a pipe from her mouth, she placed it on a table beside a half-full flask of whiskey. Then with a startled expression on her face, a wave of her hand, and a trace of early training she invited me in.

She appeared old but unwrinkled and had melancholy brown eyes and a natural curl in her tangled gray hair. Enough remained of her faded features for me to see that she had been beautiful, not just pretty.

Her husband was one of the miners working for Bert, so we talked easily about the opening of the Colonel Sellers mining project and about sewing when I asked if she would rent her machine.

"You're welcome to it," she said warmly. "But I don't want to be paid for its use."

"You're very kind," I said firmly, "but I couldn't use it otherwise. Would five dollars a month be all right?"

It was, and once a month, when the rent was due, I had a visit with her and she always prolonged it and asked me to come again.

One morning as Harriet and I wandered along the bank of a quiet stream, we stopped near a lovely weeping willow shading a small square plot of tall weedy grass surrounded with broken remnants of a picket fence. Above the grass three weather-beaten slabs tilted crazily. A bit of history must be hidden here in this sequestered, lonely spot. I wanted to know about it. Those with whom I had become acquainted couldn't tell me, so I accosted a stranger near the post office window, a dark little old man.

"Yes," he said, his eyes softening with memories of the past. "I can tell you about it. In the late '60s and early '70s over four thousand Chinese came here and picked the ground pretty clean of gold. Lots of them died. They were all buried here, but after a while a good many remains were dug up and sent back to China. You know the Chinese believe that they can't rest in death except in the earth of their own country. Nobody knows why those three were overlooked and left there."

He left me thoughtful and pondering on tragedies of those who follow the whisper of "Gold," from foreign lands so far away, risking their souls' repose. I wondered if those three left behind under the willow tree beside the gentle waters in this beautiful quiet valley were not resting just as peacefully as if they had taken the long, hard journey across the ocean.

CHAPTER 24

Bert Austin had pitched a tent for Mary and himself on the bank of Elk Creek two miles from the Colonel Sellers prospect. It was an ideal setup for Bert's business and his health; he was recuperating after a recent escape from death.

On one terrible night the steamer *Columbia*, on which Bert had been a passenger, sank off the northern coast of California. He was sucked down into the water as the boat went under. Miraculously, he struggled to the surface, grabbed a life raft onto which he managed to climb. He pulled others aboard, and after many hours, numbed by the cold waters, they were picked up by a rescue ship. Bert's lungs were not yet healthy and normal. The prescription for his recovery was "outdoors," which his business demanded and he loved.

Their tent was too far for Mary and me to meet often. There was little to discuss with acquaintances, but they did interest me with their stories of the past.

In the cabin with the miniature garden lived Brownie, the last of the professional prostitutes in Elk City. One day when the stage pulled out, Brownie was on it. She was accompanied by a miner who would marry her in Stites and take her to Alaska to begin life anew.

The owner of one of the saloons spent much of the day leaning against the door frame watching the passing scene with one good and one glass eye. He was a big man with thinning dark hair, black moustache, swarthy skin, upturned nose, and an expression of insolent defiance. Everything about him was repulsive. The story was that he had killed a man and had been sentenced to the penitentiary; but he was connected with a family well and favorably known which exerted enough influence to have him released on parole, and Elk Valley was a good place in which to be forgotten.

There were pleasant stories, too. It seemed all wrong for Maynard Tytler to waste his talents, his fine education, his infinite capacities in this primitive spot. Obviously an English gentleman, he was the son of a high-ranking British officer in India where he was born and reared, absorbing oriental as well as occidental culture. He was a graduate chemist but with the means and the world before him he began to rove, perhaps to escape a *curse* laid upon his father and the family. Incidents had occurred which reminded them of the "curse."

The story was told that during the Sepoy rebellion, Maynard's father came into possession of a relic sacred to the Moslems and had taken it to England, and the curse was solemnly pronounced. Years later, under pressure of one sort and another, the article was returned to its shrine. But Maynard, the son, did not seem to outdistance the curse. He married the wrong girl according to his family, and home ties were severed. Marital ties ended. With his ten-year-old son, he came to Elk City and opened a little assay office to evaluate samples brought in by those still following the gold will-o'-the-wisp. With these small fees and remittances from England, they lived frugally in the rear of, what had been in early days, the Bank of Elk City. Maynard Tytler became one of our most interesting friends.

And then, one day, a lady arrived on the stage from Dixie; a lady charming and courageous, Miss Caroline Lockhart. It was her second trip in this wild country. A year before she had come to Elk City and gone over the famous ridge known as the Buffalo Hump gathering material for her successful book *The Man from the Bitter Roots* which joined two other popular books, *Whispering Smith* and *The Lady Doctor.*

I was thrilled to hear of her perilous trips.

"My adventure this year was much more exciting than the one last year. I took this trip down the Salmon River for Capser Whitney's magazine *Outing.* The barge I was on did not capsize, though we had many close squeaks, but one of them, containing machinery, was wrecked," she told me. I was kindled with excitement and wanted to know if many others had taken such a risk.

"As far as I know, I was the only woman to shoot these rapids. People, who should know, say they are the worst in the United States, more dangerous even than those in the Colorado River but not as well known."

I was so keenly interested that I asked more questions, which she very graciously answered. Did she walk up from the river?

"No, I did not walk from the river to Elk City but most of the way I led my horse from the placer mine to Dixie from where I either rode on horseback or took the stage. There was only a trail from Dixie to the river and no wagon could get down as it was very steep, narrow, and dangerous."

Of course, I was particularly interested when I heard mention of a mine. "The placer mine proved an awful flop." (How I hoped that would not be the case with the Colonel Sellers.) "The gold was too fine to save. I rocked myself out a pair of gold cufflinks with an old-fashioned California rocker, while I was there."

I thanked Miss Lockhart most sincerely for answering my questions and wished that I could hear more about her adventures on "the river of no return."

The cabin by the mill was still occupied and I was getting anxious to keep house and do my own cooking again. The Neddars said they would be out in two weeks. Two weeks more of the hotel cooking seemed a long time.

"What do you think of living in a tent until we can have the cabin?" George asked me. "Nan Cane's husband says we can pitch a tent on his property."

"That would suit me fine," I answered, "but what would we do for beds and stove?" I laugh now, so many years later, thinking about housekeeping in that tent loaned to us by the storekeeper.

George located two old bed springs and rumpled mattresses which I sprayed abundantly with insect killer. From some abandoned objects near the mill, George found a tiny, rusty oil stove, large enough for only two pans. That was all the furniture we had; the edge of the beds took the place of chairs.

The nights were cold and housekeeping was awkward to say the least.

Nan Cane was a pretty girl with brown, melancholy eyes, a quick, nervous manner, shy to meet but outgoing when one knew

Our lone cabin outside of Elk City.

her better. I liked her, but I felt, instinctively, an aversion to her husband. I was told others had this same feeling about him.

Bert Cane, who had wandered into Elk City only a few years before, was heavy-set, smooth-mannered, smug, always half smiling, somehow obnoxious. Recently he had been manager of a dance in the town hall and had led the Grand March, the only one wearing a tuxedo. It caused as many sniffs as smirks and smiles. Dame rumor said that he mistreated his wife and that she was afraid of him.

After two weeks of living in the tent, the cabin was ready for us and we moved into our "mansion."

It stood two hundred feet from the mill at the edge of the woods overlooking the valley. Eight steps led to a porch protected by a lean-to. A pair of deer antlers hung beside the door.

The living room extended across the front width of the cabin, behind it a dining space and a bedroom, beyond this the kitchen, while next to it was what had once been the assay office years ago. Fifteen feet from the kitchen door was a log outhouse with no door, trees and shrubs acting as a substitute.

The cabin was sturdy and rustic to a fault. The mud-chinked log walls had no lining. Rough one-by-six-inch boards covered the original flooring and having dried out, left cracks where dirt, food crumbs, pins and what-have-you could collect. I often had to use a screw driver to dig out and clean the spaces.

With no ceilings under the peaked log roof, our feeble lamp and candle lights were lost in the upper gloom at night.

There was no furniture to be bought in Elk City so we were glad to find in the bedroom, two sets of coiled springs set on two-by-four boards for legs. This filled the room. Since this "furniture" could not be moved, it was necessary for me to lie prone on the bare floor to clean underneath. One swinging window with six small panes of glass did not afford much light.

How fortunate we were, for in the living room was a couch made of two wide boards boxed in against the wall, two crude chairs and a pot-bellied stove in the middle of the room. A pipe extending from the stove with numerous elbow attachments resembled a fat snake lengthening upward to reach the roof outlet.

From a pile of trash I found the remains of a table with two good legs, one broken, and one missing. A piece of two-by-four replaced the latter and after hours of hammering and many bruises, I spliced the broken leg. The table stood, uneven but upright. In everything I did, serious little Harriet helped by holding nails, handing me the hammer; in all ways she showed she knew the duties of a mine flunky.

When George brought home three empty powder boxes for chairs, we were set to dine. Two more, one on top of the other and draped with a length of cretonne, made a good linen closet. An old bench in the assay office would seat guests if we should ever have any.

Near the front porch stood a tiny log cabin hardly the size of a child's playhouse, so small that I felt like Alice in Wonderland as I stooped down to get in. It was the home of the dozen white leghorn chickens we had bought from the Neddars.

After the hundreds of employees at the Tomboy and Britannia, Bert's list was amusing. Clever manager that he was, he set up the crew to the best advantage: Art Hillier, superintendent; Joe Clifton and Buddy Ralston, miners; Fred Glade (Nan's father), mechanic and carpenter; Tony, handyman wherever needed; George, mill superintendent; Sandy, his day helper; and two men on the night shift, twelve-hour shifts seven days a week.

To haul the ore from mine to mill, a distance of two miles, Syd Ruark moved from his home in Kooskia with his wagon and two horses. Down the hill from our cabin was a deserted spacious barn which Syd cleaned up for himself and the horses.

Tony kept our cabin supplied with wood, heaping it high by the kitchen door. I had never cooked with wood before, and it took me some time to learn that I must keep the stove well stoked.

Just above the mill stood a large wooden tank holding water pumped uphill a quarter of a mile from Elk Creek. Our pipeline was a yoke fitted to George's shoulders, an oil can dangling at each end. Often four full cans stood on the kitchen bench, a tin dipper handy. Wash days for both bodies and clothes meant extra trips for George to fill a large wooden tub in the old assay office, our washroom.

There was much preliminary work to be done before actual mining and milling could start. Art was digging the shaft at the mine, building a head frame with a bin from which to load the ore, installing a boiler, fired with wood, of course, to drive a small hoist. In the five-by-five-foot shaft a large bucket on the end of a cable was to serve as a cage.

While this was going on, George was reconditioning the old 1880 mill, cleaning out dirt and cobwebs, checking the boiler, pump, shafting, belts, screens, and ten stamps.

Tony came one morning to clean up a pile of rubbish and rotten boards long accumulated under our bedroom window. Harriet and I sat on our steps watching him. With a pick he jerked out a rotted box and out squirmed a nest of snakes, all sizes—big, little, and in between. They disappeared like a flash in all directions. I jumped up, suddenly aware that these snakes had been all around us; perhaps we would meet up with them in the chicken house!

In a short time, ore was coming out of the mine shaft, the mill was running, and we were settled in our routine.

With leagues of wilderness surrounding us, solitude was intense except for the rhythmic sound of the stamps, a welcome voice proclaiming the vein was holding up and the ore was pouring into the mill. Only when it stopped at night would I wake up.

What wonderful dreams! Perhaps a Tomboy, a Camp Bird, or another Comstock was within our reach. In his book *They Built the West* the author Glenn Chesney Quiet wrote: "Gold was discovered at Oro Fino, Elk City and Florence . . . When horses of traders were staked for the night to the bunch grass, they sometimes pulled it loose and wandered away. On this certain morning the owners were surprised to find glittering particles of gold where the roots of grass had been."

It was as simple as that at the Colonel Sellers. However, not only flakes, but also gold-bearing rock had outcropped on the surface. For lack of money, Elk City depended on barter, an exchange of hay for meat, laundry for groceries, eggs for lamp oil or candles, an endless chain from which no one could break away.

And so it was a great day when Bert Austin first paid his employees in cash. Now money began to circulate little by little, here and there.

In September the weather was beautiful. It was time for the annual competition and celebration between Elk City and the little settlement of Dixie, the ending place of mail delivery for many miles around.

Each year the two places fought for superiority in horse racing and baseball. Elk City usually won the horse race, while Dixie seemed to star in baseball.

The day was set. Dixie's team arrived greeted vociferously by Elk City. What did it matter that neither team could muster nine men still able to throw a ball.

Of course, the mill must operate so George could not attend the fun, but Harriet in her cart and I set out for the clearing below the woods.

A strange noise seemed to come from the sky. I looked up and saw for the first time a flight of wild geese. Whirring and honking, they flew high then low, keeping unbroken their perfect wedge-shaped formation.

We joined the scene of onlookers sitting on the grass in the clearing. The game began. Both sides seemed about even, a strike or two, then many balls. Dixie scored. Someone shouted, "Hurrah for Dixie!" Then Bert went up to bat. He had not entirely lost his college ability . . . Ball one! . . . Ball two! . . . Strike! Bert was off like a shot for first base, but he never got there.

The crack of the bat hitting the ball was instantly followed by a tremendous blast from above the woods. In mid-flight, Bert swerved and ran up the hill.

He knew and I knew at that moment that whatever it was, was happening at the mill. There was nothing else near it. And my George was in the mill! I must get there at once. I pushed the go-cart with all my strength, gasping for breath, the half mile up the hill. The trees hid everything. By the time I was halfway up, water came pouring down to meet me, filling the ruts and hollows in the trail, tipping the go-cart and soaking my feet, but I finally made it.

There above the mill, held together by only the lowest iron hoop, lay the water tank, flat on the ground, the staves spread out like the spokes of a wheel. Thirty thousand gallons of water had poured through the mill and the woods.

Operations stopped for a week while carpenters rebuilt the tank and cleaned up the debris and the mill was ready to start again.

Next morning, Joe Clifton reported his house had burned down during the night. That afternoon I went to tell Mrs. Clifton how sorry we all felt their loss. Rumors were that she had run back into the burning house to save photographs of her boys.

"But, just think," she said, "Mrs. Purcell of the laundry has invited us to stay with her until we can find a place."

This unexpected offer of help to these people, so long denied the friendship of neighbors, warmed my heart as it reflected a ray of hope for a happier future for the Cliftons. Surely, others in the settlement would follow this kind of gesture of one person's concern for another in time of need. Perhaps they would forgive and forget the past.

CHAPTER 25

My greatest problem was getting supplies. This meant three trips a week, pushing Harriet's go-cart through the dense woods of pine and Douglas fir, dark even in daytime, then through a wide gate into the clearing where we had tented, and on to Elk City. The road, washed out by many years of rain with no repairing, was steep in places, and between the trees wide enough only for a wagon.

Often I waited an hour for George Esh to return to his meat store. From there I'd go to the post office and then to Ben Scott's grocery. Ben's sister always helped me stow away my bundles, some around Harriet, small ones clutched in her little hands, the overflow in a large flour sack thrown over my shoulder.

Mine was a Herculean task. From the door of the store, shoving the cart with one hand, holding onto the sack with the other, over the rickety planks past the Davis house, along the road I labored. I let Harriet ride as long as I could keep going, shifting the sack from one aching arm to the other, trying to steer the cart between ruts and over bumps, through the field to the gate. There, real effort began and inevitable debate.

"Harriet, I can't push you any farther, you must walk."

"Mommy, I can't walk. I'm tired. I want to ride."

"Yes, you can, a big girl like you." I would say. She was not three years old and was small for her age.

"I *can't* walk, Mommy. Honest."

"Mommy's so tired . . ." I repeated as she walked beside me and I counted every yard we gained until, reluctantly, 1 let her ride again. Not a single trip did I miss hitting a rut, tipping the cart over, packages spilling out, picking up Harriet, stuffing her and the bundles back into the cart. Stopping among the trees

Our daughter Harriet at two and a half years old.

to catch my breath and refresh myself with the fragrance of the woods, this routine was often repeated before I reached the cabin at the top of the long slope.

And now began the events that prompted me to say before we came here, "I'll be glad to go to Elk City, but will there be a doctor there?"

After using a six-foot crosscut saw one morning, George hung it on the wall outside the kitchen door and left for work. Toward noon I stepped to the door to call Harriet who was outside playing. Just as she came toward me I saw the saw falling off the nail on which it hung. I screamed; Harriet turned her head—a move which saved her face, but the brutal teeth of the saw slashed straight across her head, digging holes before it fell with a clatter. Blood gushed profusely. Harriet cried quietly and only for a minute, which was usual when she was hurt, but I was panic-stricken. Wildly blaming myself for bringing her to the wilderness, I rushed to the mill for George.

We hurriedly bandaged her bleeding head, wrapped her warmly in a blanket in the go-cart, and went as fast as we could to Dr. Davis's in Elk City. He was not at home.

The night before, a man who accidentally had shot his partner in the leg had ridden his horse to near exhaustion to make a frantic appeal for Dr. Davis to return with him, forty miles over the mountains to the injured man. Though unused to riding, Dr. Davis went at once.

Mrs. Davis, trained in first aid, cut away Harriet's blood-soaked hair, cleaned and bandaged the wound, and assured us all would be well. How thankful we were when it healed without any trouble!

Not long afterward, about nine o'clock one morning, I heard faltering footsteps on the stairs. When I opened the door, there stood George looking deathly white, leaning against the rail and holding one hand with the other. On the steps was a trail of blood. He had cut his thumb to the bone. I dressed it as well as I could and we hurried to town. Fortunately. Dr. Davis was home this time. He dressed the deeply cut thumb, took a few stitches, and then time and nature took over. This wasn't the end of our emergencies, it seemed.

I was pleased when Mrs. Ruark arrived from Kooskia with her ten-year-old daughter to spend the beautiful autumn months with her husband. Syd had blocked off more of the barn to house his family, and they seemed quite comfortable living under the same roof with their horses.

Mrs. Ruark was young and soft-spoken; Elsie was a quiet gentle little girl with long blond curls. I liked Mrs. Ruark and was glad that Harriet would have a playmate instead of the imaginary companion she had invented who sat at our table and must be served first.

We were able to invite the Ruarks to a luxury dinner; at least it seemed so to us, for Tim, Bert, and George jointly had bought three lambs which Tim pastured on his fields. Every month one was butchered and divided among the three owners.

But when the Ruarks came, our dining room lacked its chief splash of color, the cretonne curtain of my linen cabinet. The night before the dinner, I was reading to George, as usual, when a light in the dining room caught my eye. Jumping from the chair I cried, "George! Quick!" and ran for the kitchen. A lighted candle on top of the cabinet had tipped over and set fire to the cretonne curtain. Arriving simultaneously at the kitchen bench, each of us grabbed a can of water and doused the flames. For years I remembered my terror that night and mourned the loss of wedding gifts, beautifully embroidered table cloths and napkins.

I had been hearing much about huckleberries. The season for them seemed to be the festive time of the year for the settlers. Tony had told me about a good patch not far from the mine.

"If you go there," he said, "be careful. Bears love huckleberries but I don't know if they would come down that far from the upper woods."

The next morning when Elsie came up the hill to play with Harriet, I suggested she run home and ask her mother if she would like to go huckleberrying with me. It wasn't long before they came back, ready for the great adventure. So armed with our large buckets which we hoped to fill, we started out.

We followed the road to the mill, then turned off onto a path leading through a clump of small trees. In a clearing just beyond were the shrubs we had been looking for. A lovely sight, the shrubs, almost completely covered by the beautiful dark blue berries that had just ripened, their fragrance filling the air.

"Delicious, luscious, delectable, appetizing" were some of the words the Elk Cityites applied to them. I must make a pie with these tonight, I thought. How George would love that! In a twinkling the bottom of my bucket was filled.

"You pick some, Harriet. Help me fill the bucket." A few of her little handfuls and she had finished. It would take many to fill my bucket. I stopped suddenly. What was that I heard from the direction of the woods? Just a little breeze, I convinced myself as I continued to pick more berries. Again a rustle at the edge of the clearing. Soon I was not able to keep my mind on the berries and after a few more minutes I was full of apprehension at every rustle of the leaves. I imagined a big black bear behind every tree.

"Let's go home," I said. Mrs. Ruark agreed. We grabbed the children and hurried away. That was the end of our great adventure and berry picking.

A few mornings later, Harriet and I went as usual to the chicken house for eggs. I always felt like Alice in Wonderland stooping low to get into the miniature cabin, lighted by one small window. Harriet had just happily found an egg in one of the nests and put it in the basket when we heard a strange sound. A soft pad-pad-pad, something that seemed to come from the woods below, came nearer and nearer. We listened. I peeked through the dusty window, then from the door. There was nothing to be seen but certainly something alive was coming closer.

If the noise had been loud, I wouldn't have been frightened, but these sounds were stealthy, uncanny, like the furtive steps of sneaking feet. Whether of men or beasts, I couldn't tell. Bears, perhaps, prowling near our cabin. Or men! But if it were men, there would be voices, surely. And why did they sneak up toward our cabin?

My heart was pounding hard. There would be no use calling for help. The millmen couldn't hear any screams above the roar of the stamps. Gingerly I pulled the low door shut and whispered to Harriet, "Don't make a sound! Not a sound!" I crouched down close to her ready to clap my hand over her mouth if necessary.

Now the pad-pad-pad was closer, too close. In a moment the head of a horse emerged from the woods, then his neck and slowly plodding, unshod hooves. On his back sagged an Indian, stolid, silent, his long black braids of hair hanging over his shoulders. Following closely behind the first horse, came another, then another, all looking as though they had come to "the end of the trail." Fifteen braves went slowly by, followed by six squaws slouchingly straddling their horses. Then, six pack animals loaded with supplies. Not one of the band uttered a word or even raised a head as each one rode along, passing the chicken house within five feet, while we crouched near the window watching them.

I couldn't help being frightened. I felt my scalp tingle. Only one generation before, these Idaho tribes were collecting scalps. With no other sound than the pad-pad-pad of shoeless hooves they passed the mill and disappeared into the woods.

After they were out of sight we hurried to the mill. One of the men on duty was an old-timer. Excitedly I told him what had happened and he laughed heartily.

"That happens every year," he said. "They come from fifty miles away and spend three weeks in the real huckleberry country higher up. There they camp and gather their year's supply."

My fears were unfounded, but at the time I knew not what to expect and a woman's instinct usually says it is better to be safe than sorry.

After Harriet was put to bed each night, George rested, if rest he could on the board couch. How much he enjoyed my reading to him; something I happily continued to do in many years to come. We received magazines by mail and were loaned books by the few who had them. Mrs. Glade, whom I had never met as she seldom left her home, sent some by her husband Tim to the mine. From there Syd carried them to the mill on his load of ore and George brought them home. I wanted to return them and to meet Mrs. Glade. To her house and back was a distance of over five miles, and as I had to walk, Mrs. Ruark offered to keep Harriet with her.

Yes, it was a long walk, but I was amply repaid by a fascinating and interesting visit. Mrs. Glade was attractive with graying hair and deep-set eyes, greeting me in a quiet but courteous manner. The house was large, two stories, with attic and basement. The rooms were spacious with pioneer furnishings.

"How attractive and home-like your house is," I began.

"Thank you. It's been our home a long time. You're from Oakland, California, aren't you? My girls speak about you. Nan enjoyed having you tent on their field."

"I enjoyed visiting with her. Is she your eldest?"

"No, Abby Ballington is the oldest. She lives on the other side of Elk City. We have two boys older than the girls. Our youngest son is attending the University of Idaho, working his way," she told me.

"That is fine," I said, pleased to hear that the boys were branching out. "I often chat with your youngest girls as they pass our cabin going home from school. They have a long walk."

"Oh, Sadie and Liz are used to walking. But my two married girls both have horses and ride well. They generally win in the races on the Fourth of July. You and I both have come a long way to here, Mrs. Backus. I was born in San Francisco. We came here right after we were married and my oldest son is now thirty-five. In all that time, I've been home once."

She had married a sailor, young, adventurous, English, who having been lured by the call of "gold" brought his bride to the Elk Valley. He never found gold. They homesteaded, raised vegetables and chickens and kept cows. Hunting was good, wild game plentiful with deer, grouse, pheasants, wild geese, fool-hens, and rabbits. Their first cabin was too small, so Glade built the big house himself.

"At the time we moved here, Indians were troublesome," Mrs. Glade continued. "Often when my husband had to be away from home, I stayed awake nights for fear they would come. My six-year-old boy would stand near the window at one end of the house with his gun while I watched at the other. Those were anxious nights and I was glad when morning came. Six of our children were born in this house. My two oldest girls have been to a city only once. Sadie and Liz have been no farther than Dixie, fifteen miles back in the mountains. But every once in a while there's a celebration and they go to that."

"They dress as well and stylishly as city girls," I said.

"Yes," she smiled. "They pore over the mail order catalogues and try to keep up with the styles. They copy the pictures. Sadie has gone through all the grades here. Liz will go to school a couple more years."

Before I left, Sadie and Liz came home. They were well-mannered, attractive-looking girls with their mother's dark eyes. I wondered if Mrs. Glade hoped for their escape from the drab routine of the life they were living.

When I said goodbye, I looked again into her deep eyes which seemed to tell a story of loneliness and frustration. Perhaps this was true. Only she knew.

CHAPTER 26

Sadie Glade was falling in love with Leslie Turner, a young fellow who had come to work at the mine. For some time I had seen them coming up from the woods together. Both of them graced by the transforming warmth of young love. Each time they stopped when they reached the clearing, and after a little while he returned to town while she went quickly home. We who knew about it understood.

Sadie and Liz Glade were not allowed much freedom. Sadie dared not let him walk her home.

It was seldom that I saw Mary, Bert's lovely wife. She was not very well. Their tent, pitched by Elk Creek, was a half mile straight down the pathless hill from our cabin, but one night they trudged slowly up the long way to have dinner with us.

"Bert," I asked, as we sat on our boxes at the table, "what do you know about Leslie Turner, and what do you think of him?"

"Why, he seems like a very nice young fellow. He graduated from a university and is now out to get experience in mining. I understand he comes from a well-known family in eastern Washington," Bert answered.

"I notice he's seeing Sadie quite often. I hope he's not a trifler. She's a lovely girl and I'd hate to see her hurt," I said.

"Yes, I've noticed his interest in her, too. I think he's sincere," he answered. That made me feel better, for their ways of life had been far apart and I was afraid when he left, it might be a case of "out of sight, out of mind."

The days were short by now and darkness descended early, so soon after dinner Bert lit his lantern and he and Mary started down the hill.

"Sweetheart," I turned to George, "I think you don't feel well tonight," for I noticed he had been more quiet than usual.

"No, I don't," he answered. "I ache all over."

In the morning he was too sick to go to work, but I had a hard time keeping him in bed. I left home long enough to go to Elk City for Dr. Davis who returned at once with me.

"He has the grippe," as we used to say, "his temperature is quite high. Keep giving him this medicine. Send word by the millmen tomorrow. If he isn't better, I'll be here again."

After three days, George went to work, though he was very weak. Four days later his temperature came up quickly to one hundred and three degrees. Several years earlier he had become delirious when running a fever. Suppose he was that sick now; what should I do? I had to do something, but what, for Bert had told me that Dr. Davis had taken a man in serious condition to Spokane for a major operation. A horrible thought, that poor soul jolting over the mountain roads for two days!

Would whiskey make George sleep? He was not used to liquor, so perhaps it would help. Castor oil surely could not hurt him. Rubbing alcohol would make him feel good. I could think of nothing else.

"Dear," I said, "stay in bed and keep warm. I have to get some medicine. Harriet, stay out of Daddy's bedroom and look at your picture books. I'll be back as soon as I can."

Carrying my lantern, I went to the mill and asked the men to please look in on George whenever it was possible and put wood in the stoves. I hurried through the woods and over the fields. Before I reached Elk City it was dark and the saloons were doing well, perhaps better than usual because the now circulating money was having an effect.

Bert bought the whiskey and Mr. Basset opened the drugstore to sell me rubbing alcohol and castor oil. I hurried home, dosed my patient, gave him a good rub, and sat up most of the night. He slept and in the morning his temperature had dropped three degrees.

At noon Bert came to see if we needed help.

"After you started home last night," he said, "I phoned Spokane and located Dr. Davis. I told him what you were doing for George and he said no harm was done, but for me to get these medicines from Mrs. Davis. You must follow the directions strictly. When I called, he was at the hospital preparing his patient for surgery. He had planned to stay a few days for an operation on his own nose, but he canceled his plans immediately and has started back today to look after George."

"Oh, I'm so sorry he did that," I said. "But I'll be more than glad to see him. It'll take three days, won't it?"

"If George isn't better tonight, I'll stay up with him," Bert said. That afternoon the fever was up a point but George felt easier. By midnight he was perspiring freely and his temperature was down slightly. As soon as Dr. Davis reached Elk City, three days later, he walked straight to our cabin for he had feared that George might have pneumonia.

On the stage coming back with Dr. Davis was a retired minister, Dr. Randle of Seattle. He was white haired and eighty-two years old, and he had been left some mining claims in this district which he had come to investigate. There never had been a church in Elk City and he was the first ordained minister to visit there.

Shopping in town a few days later, I heard the stir of gossip about Dr. Randle going into the saloons at night trying to speak to the men about their downward paths and a better way of life. He was laughed at and derided, but, undaunted, he asked permission to hold a service the following Sunday in the old meeting hall. No announcements were made of it but the news traveled miles around by the grapevine.

George worked on Sundays but Harriet and I climbed the long flight of stairs to the second story of the hall. Of the few gathered there, several had walked many miles to attend the service. Old Pa and Ma Burns, still living on their small tract near Dixie where they settled in 1875, had hitched up their old horse, now tied in front of the hall. The quaint wee bonnet and faded coat of Ma Burns looked as if she had worn it since first she came to the valley.

Jack Spengle, in rusty black, aided by his cane tottered to a place beside me on the hard, backless bench. On the very front seat sat Mrs. Clayton. Seldom in town, Mrs. Glade with Liz and Sadie had come. Dr. and Mrs. Davis, Mary Austin, Mrs. Purcell, and a few I did not know were also there.

The service was conducted as nearly as possible like those of city churches. Even without song books, everyone joined in singing the old standby hymns "Rock of Ages" and "Onward Christian Soldiers." I remember that service especially because of a poem Dr. Randle recited so expressively:

There is no unbelief.

Whoever plants a seed beneath the sod
And waits to see it push away the clod

He trusts in God. . . .

Whoever sees 'neath winters fields of snow
The silent harvest of the future grow

God's power must know. . . .

and on for three more beautiful stanzas. After the service I asked him the name and author of the inspiring poem.

"I really don't know," he replied. "Some years ago I was preaching to a group of cowboys down in Texas. After the service one of them came to me and recited that poem. I, too, felt it deeply and asked him for a copy. If you like, when I return to Seattle, I'll make you a copy."

Investigation of Dr. Randle's claims proved them worthless, and, much disappointed, he climbed on the stage and left the valley.

A week later I received the copy of the complete poem. Several years later after a search, I found it in a collection of verses marked anonymous. But finally, in an old book, the name was given: Elizabeth York Case, 1840–1911.

Rains came and winter cold. The hens stopped laying. The woodman came oftener to replenish our woodpile. Mrs. Ruark and Elsie moved back to Kooskia. The sweethearts, Sadie and Leslie, no longer lingered near our cabin although I had glimpses of them in the woods. Coyotes howled, coming down lower into the valleys, a pack of three or four sounding like a hundred with their weird, melancholy, and penetrating calling which chilled me. After snow began to fall, I couldn't take Harriet to the settlement and had to wait until George came home from work to care for her. I usually had dinner cooking by six-thirty and the minute George came up the steps, I swung down the hill, lantern in hand, the empty sack over my arm. It did not take long to fill the sack at the grocery and swing it onto my back.

By this time, the saloons were noisy, the drunks warming up—the only thing I feared. Hurrying through the snowy field with my trusty lantern, I always felt safer when I reached the gate and was in the dark of the woods; here I stumbled in ruts and snow-weighted branches brushed me. The light hung low as I trudged forward, my ears more aware of the rustling of wild things in the thickets, the creaking of swaying limbs, the raindrop sound of falling needles or pats of snow. I didn't loiter.

I began to whistle the call I had known since childhood. If I should hear it in the Caves of Ajunta or on the road to Mandalay, I would know that one of my family was near. And when through the night and the woods would come George's answering whistle, I felt almost home.

By then he had bathed, carried wood from the high pile, stoked the fires, taken care of Harriet, and continued cooking the dinner. He knew how long it should take me to reach Elk City and return. When I got beyond the trees, I could always see my beloved lode-star on the porch, waving a lantern to welcome me. The cabin was always warm and cheerful. Dinner would be ready and three hungry, happy people sat on powder boxes and feasted, more eagerly because it would then be after eight o'clock.

Thanksgiving and Christmas were approaching. No one in the valley raised turkeys, so George sent to Stites for a pair of live birds. They arrived in such a shallow crate they could not stand erect and had been so badly shaken in such cramped space that one bird could not straighten its legs. It looked too sick to eat. The other, in better condition, began to revive as soon as it was out of the crate. After a few days, seeing the crippled bird unable to move about, George killed it and burned the body in the mill firebox.

One day George and Bert took me down the mine shaft which I had been waiting to see. Harriet stayed with the hoistman on the surface and we three stepped over the rim of the four-foot-high, steel bucket. There was just enough room for our three pairs of feet as we faced each other closely and tightly grasped the cable from which the bucket was suspended.

"Stand up straight, Harriet," said Bert, "but lean a little forward toward the cable. Remember, the mine timbers are only ten inches back of you."

We slowly descended to the fifty-foot level. When the bucket settled at the unloading platform, we stepped down and walked through two drifts which had been opened to the right and left of the shaft.

After the Tomboy, this seemed like a model mine scaled down to miniature size. Still, it might prove a bonanza for its financiers and Elk City. The vein was of considerable width, values were good, and, so far, the mill was recovering more than enough gold to pay for the work of development.

"Values are holding up," Bert said, "and George is making good recovery in the mill. We'll go down another fifty feet; then we'll drift again. If the vein doesn't pinch out we may have something big here. It remains to be seen."

We rode home on the loaded ore wagon, two miles over deep ruts under a dark sky, and by the time we reached the cabin, it was snowing. In this valley, snow was never deep enough to make a smooth trail, and no ordinary sled could be pulled over the ditches in the road, so George made an extraordinary one by mounting a wooden box on a single runner. Theoretically, it should have worked. But even empty, it was unwieldy. One of us pulled by a rope tied to the front end of the runner, while the other tried to balance and push from the rear by gripping an upright handle. If one stumbled, over went the contraption, Harriet and all. I much preferred the two-runner box at Britannia Beach with its large red Sal Hepatica label on both sides.

We were cozier here than in our former houses. Unlike the dampness of the Beach, the air was dry in Elk Valley and we were nestled deep inside protecting mountains.

We did not miss having turkey on Thanksgiving. Instead, we had a platter heaped with tender, tasty roast pheasants. The stoves crackled with fir and pine chunks and heat radiated from them in visible waves. True, if we stepped outside, our faces stiffened in the cold. There was one other drawback—the outhouse.

In summer, as George said, the ventilation without a door was excellent. In winter, snow, ice, and winds held rendezvous there and ventilation was all *too* excellent.

"How cold do you think it is today?" asked George, coming home for lunch.

"Below zero, I should think," was my guess.

"You're right! It is *thirty-five* below. I've been standing at the plates all morning, holding the steam hose over the vanners to keep the moving water from freezing."

Three days of this temperature kept the day and night shifts busy shoving wood into the furnace to keep up enough steam.

It was not just the cold weather that put an end to the meeting in the woods of Sadie and young Turner. He was leaving for his home in Washington. I was fond of Sadie and wondered if he would return to her.

Christmas was upon us. Gaily wrapped packages arrived from my dear mother and father, sisters, and brother, besides many from our friends. I knew the family worried about us in this remote spot. Little did they realize how happy we were together in our log cabin in the midst of beautiful woods and valleys.

George cut a tree in the woods. With the wonderful fragrance of fresh pine and with green-and-red-colored wrappings on the gifts under the tree, we thought of the Batchellers' home in Britannia on that Christmas Day when Jim had opened the box of deadly percussion caps.

How good it was to receive greetings from Jim, Beth, Kate, Alex—these dear friends who in later years we were blessed to see many times.

George killed and I stuffed our well-fed turkey that had been wandering around for a month, and again we were thankful for our many blessings.

The old year went and New Year's Day of 1913 arrived. We still had high hopes for the Colonel Sellers Mine and looked eagerly for Maynard Tytler's assay report. The shaft was down eighty feet and all was well. Eighty-five, ninety, ninety-five feet. From the one-hundred-foot level. Bert sent samples to be assayed.

Next day when Clayton brought the daily report to the mill, Bert opened it and stared at the paper in his hands. Finally he said, "Look at this," handing it to George whose unbelieving eyes read, "Gold content .00."

For minutes neither man spoke. Then Bert said, "Perhaps the

vein has slipped. We'll drift out from the shaft." And he left on the ore wagon for the mine.

New drifts were cut out from the shaft. Ironically, the pattern formed a question mark as they searched, desperately hoping to pick up the values again. But the golden bubble had burst!

For one hundred feet straight down from the grass roots, nature had trickled the shining ore, but it was only a teaser.

Poor Elk City! The hopes of her citizens had soared as high in them as in us. We could follow the gleam of gold in other places, but *they* could not leave this valley where they had been stranded by past "strikes." The roots of poverty go deep and are tenacious, not to be uprooted without money—of which they had none.

The history of all quartz discoveries in this district had come to the same dolorous ending. But perhaps next spring, or the next, or the next . . . at the end of the rainbow. . . .

CHAPTER 27

We were far from another mining district and the expense of moving and relocating loomed large, but just at this time George received a pleasant surprise.

Congress had recently passed a bill awarding retroactive longevity payments to West Point graduates. As the only child of Lieutenant Backus, long deceased, George received a welcome check from the United States Government. At *such* an opportune moment!

George had not forgotten David Herron's standing offer to invest in a prospect of promising value. Tales of gold continually spread from the Buffalo Hump country, a somewhat mysterious and potentially rich district forty miles farther in.

Art Hillier, foreman of the ill-fated Colonel Sellers, a miner with intimate knowledge of the surrounding terrain, had often spoken of claims that he and others owned by the great Salmon River; and about eighteen and twenty-dollar ore, which is good ore, indeed. But miners, like fishermen, can tell tall tales. The only way to learn the truth is to investigate.

It would be three months before the snow melted enough for the Buffalo Hump to be passable. Except in midsummer, any travel beyond Dixie or Oro Grande required snowshoes in such trackless country, the trip rarely being attempted before May. Those living in the Salmon River valley were always snowed in for the winter.

We discussed the problem together, as we always did. Could we afford the waiting time? The Government check was still in our hands. Suppose we did not risk the chance? Perhaps next year the big strike might be made! We would never return. Yes! We decided to wait.

We left our cabin near the mill and moved into the one at the end of the street around which Jess made his last turn as he daily entered Elk City with the stage.

One tiny room was divided by semi-partitions into three. The kitchen had room for only a two-burner oil stove, a small table and the usual box-supported tin basin.

While waiting to close the affairs of the Colonel Sellers, Bert bought an interest in the only meat market within a radius of twenty miles, donned a white apron, took his station behind the counter and became a highly popular butcher. We feasted on T-bone steaks at twenty-five cents apiece. None of his other customers would eat beef tongue, so he gave them to us. I budgeted closely: twelve dollars a month for rent, twenty-five dollars for food and everything else. Our meals were simply—simple. Our suppers were bread and milk for Harriet and George; I preferred crackers and milk.

Poor little Harriet! She was the only small child in the settlement. The idlers on the street began giving her cheap candies until I forbade her accepting it, but when they introduced her to gum, I had to compromise.

Whenever Harriet saw Mrs. Kinkaid at her well, turning the crank, the long rope winding around the windlass and pulling up a bucket of clear, cool water, she became thirsty and must have a drink. Milk was difficult to obtain and I was pleased when a family with a cow moved across the road. I sent Harriet to ask if they would sell milk to us. Our three-year-old returned saying, "No, we can't have milk now because the cow is dry. But Mommy, pretty soon she will be all wet, then we can have some."

Now we were near Dr. and Mrs. Davis and were soon invited to dinner, where we enjoyed chicken and other delicious dishes. Coming home, Harriet asked, "Mommy, what does Dr. Davis say when he bends his head and says, 'Wah, wah, wah' to the chicken?"

These thrilling incidents, with visits from Maynard Tytler and his stories of Turkey and other faraway lands, and neighborly chit-chat were all that filled our days as we waited for the snowpack to break.

It was quite a morsel of gossip when the word flew that Leslie Turner was coming back for Sadie Glade. Everyone in town would be waiting when the stage arrived, eyes and ears agog to watch the reunion of the sweethearts.

"All the world loves a lover" and my lover and I knew the bliss of being alone after a separation, and the sadness of goodbyes.

"Dear, can't we do something to save those young people from Elk City's curious eyes?" I asked George who shared my feelings. Together we made a plan. The next time I saw Sadie in the grocery store, I quietly said to her, "Sadie, we have heard that Leslie will be back soon. We are very happy about it, but we know everyone around here will be watching for the stage and we felt that you would rather meet him alone."

"Oh, I would, Mrs. Backus. I want to meet the stage when he comes, but I know how it will be and I've almost decided not to go." Her lovely eyes were soft and shining but expressed her dilemma.

"Well, perhaps we can help you. Come to town early that day and straight to the back of our cabin. Leave the rest to us. When do you expect Leslie?"

"Day after tomorrow. And I surely thank you for helping me. I'll be at your place early."

On the great day Sadie slipped in through our back door at eleven o'clock. From one o'clock on, George and I took turns standing in back of the cabin out of sight of the street, watching for the first glimpse of the stage as it emerged from the woods.

"Here it comes," I whispered after nearly two hours of tenseness. George was ready. Sloshing through the mud, he strode up the road holding up his hand to signal Jess to stop. Jess pulled in the horses so abruptly his three passengers almost slid off the seats.

"What's the trouble?" asked Jess.

"I must see Lee right away," George answered. Leslie jumped off the stage.

"There's someone in our cabin waiting for you." George shoved him in the back door, then came around to the front where Harriet and I were waiting. Casually we walked to the hotel where two men, strangers, stepped off the stage. Elk City's crowd of thirteen people were staring at them. Then came the whispered remarks. "Where's Turner?" "I bet he's not coming back." "Sadie isn't here today." "I guess it's all off."

Sadie and Leslie had wanted to be married away from Elk City, but her father objected. The only person in that area authorized to perform a marriage ceremony was her brother-in-law, Cane, who had the title Justice of the Peace, to our disgust. The young couple had no choice. A week later Mr. and Mrs. Leslie Turner left for a world Sadie had never known, followed by the sincere good wishes of everyone in the valley.

When weather conditions warranted the trip over the Hump, George and Art prepared their packs, some food, one change of clothing, and snowshoes.

My beloved husband begged me not to worry, saying they could not return before three weeks at the earliest, and I knew I could receive no word during this period.

"Remember, Kiddy," he said, "it all depends upon the conditions we meet. If the snow is soft, snowshoeing will be difficult. There will be icy places that will slow us down, too."

The days dragged by. It was difficult not to worry as I mentally wandered with George into the dangerous Salmon River country.

Suddenly, the entire valley was shocked by a senseless tragedy. One night, Bert Cane walked into the hotel lobby and calmly announced: "You'd better send somebody to my house. I've just shot Nick and my wife. Nan may not be dead yet."

Three men ran to Cane's house in the field and found his statement true. A young man lay dead on the floor. Nan Cane was dying.

Cane had returned unexpectedly from a business trip and had found Nick Conger visiting Nan. Nick, a young man who had lived in Elk City for years, had known Nan all her life. No one knew if there had been anything between Nan and Nick beyond friendship, but Bert Cane was convinced otherwise. He was not the type of husband to be trusting and with his suspicious nature and cold heart nothing would settle his mind but to end their relationship with horrible finality.

It was told later that Cane, after shooting his wife, disrobed her and left her in disarray to make the scene obviously compromising. This was never proven, but everyone who knew Bert Cane was well aware of his character, and this was the type of action he was most capable of.

There was no doubt that if Nan and Nick had been more than friends, she would have been understood in seeking tenderness and love from another man since her husband was brutal and inconsiderate.

To me, he was repulsive. My original dislike of him became absolute abhorrence after this terrible happening. Cane! . . .

Three weeks passed. Then each day Harriet and I went to the hotel at the time Esh was due from Oro Grande, hoping George would be arriving home. Each day, a disappointment. Finally we saw the sled. The man I had been waiting for was on it. I was happy again.

George immediately left his samples with Mr. Tytler to be assayed the next day, and then we went home.

That evening after I put Harriet to bed, George shared his trip with me, for he knew his interests were mine, always.

"The first part was pretty rugged. The road was uphill and the snow was not packed. The horse had to struggle mighty hard, so finally Art and I walked for three miles up from the three-thousand-foot level. Then, Esh put snowshoes on the horse."

"Snowshoes on a horse?" I said. "You're fooling, aren't you? How do they do that?"

"The shoes are round blocks of wood about two inches thick and fifteen inches across," he told me.

"But how do they keep them on?"

"Well, the lugs of the iron shoes fit into holes in the blocks and a clamp holds them in place. It was then much easier for the horse, and we rode the rest of the way reaching Oro Grande about six. It took us all day to cover twelve miles.

"One store, run by Don Morris, the innkeeper, contained everything to be bought by the half-dozen inhabitants—foods and household goods besides the post office. Several cabins there were almost hidden by the pines and firs.

"Moose, elk, deer, mountain goats, black and brown bears, all are known to abound in those woods, while lakes literally teemed with fish in that spot. It's called 'the Gateway to the Buffalo Hump country.' "

After a good night's sleep, George and Art, on snowshoes, were on their way by six in the morning. The snow was deep and unbroken by any trail; their packs grew heavier hour by hour. George had begun to realize that building a road over this range would be a major project. Beside the fifty-five miles from Stites, there would have to be thirty-five or more miles to get over the

Hump and down to the Salmon River valley.

With his keen sense of direction, Art found the way among the white firs and lodgepole pines, straight to the cabin of his friend Pete the Trapper. Pete was out on his trapline, but they took possession of his cabin which, according to the wilderness code, was unlocked.

It was understood by the unwritten law of the trappers, hunters, or other travelers that a caller should use his own supplies if possible but if necessary he used the trapper's. One should leave something in place of it. If he had no food, money should be left. If he spent the night, he should wash his dishes, clean the cabin, and leave plenty of firewood by the stove.

"We built a fire and were warm in a short time. The only food of Pete's we ate was a few eggs. The trappers, Art told me, set their traps a day's trip apart. I surely would not want to follow that business. If the trap does not kill the animal at once, sometimes it gnaws off its own foot, leg, or tail. If it gets free, it probably dies by inches, slowly and painfully."

"That is horrible," I said. From that time on the thought of it sickened me.

After a refreshing sleep on mattresses made of boughs from the trees, they made an early breakfast, left some money for Pete and started out on their webs. In two miles they reached a wide slope heading almost due south to the Salmon River, but it was so steep they followed the hogback to where the snow was almost gone and then went down into the valley and tied their webs to a tree. By afternoon they reached the home of Hillier's friends, Sam Easton and Tucky Sinclair. The two men lived there all year round near the river in a two-story, well-built house surrounded by trees.

Co-owner of the claims with Hillier, Jim Stevens was staying there during the annual assessment work.

"Sam and Tucky," George continued, "had just come back with trout for dinner. You should have seen those trout! Two or three feet long, right out of the icy cold rapids that tumble down just upstream from the house. They're both fine cooks and what a dinner *that* was! They pack in everything they don't raise. Don't have much meat, but plenty of chickens, rabbits, salmon, and trout. Raise all their own vegetables. Bake swell bread, pies, cakes, even apple dumplings. We lived like kings and ate like pigs. According to them the winters there are mild. All night I could hear the splash of water swirling over the rocks.

"Art's claims are on a steep slope above the Salmon, half a mile from the house. He's located several but this was the only one he's done development work on. There were three assessment holes, open cuts, running into the vein. They caved in during the winter, so we had to clean them out to get samples across the outcrop of the vein. We checked corners and survey lines so I could make a map. After dinner each night, we bucked down the samples small enough to be carried out. I marked each one and tied it in one of those little bags you made. Then for a couple of hours I listened to the fellows tell stories about the unconquerable wilderness, about the turbulent river that old timers claimed cut the world in two. Nowadays they call it The River of No Return.

"The only human being nearby is famous China Mary. You know, the one we heard about when we came to Elk City. One day we stopped at her place five miles down the river. It was a neat, clean little house with all kinds of flowers around it and fruit trees and a vegetable garden. The stories you hear about her are true. She's a landmark in the valley—famous. She went there forty years ago with the placer miners and married a white prospector. They built this cabin along the river and she keeps it like a new pin. He died a couple of years ago, but she always gets a meal for anyone passing by. She's highly thought of."

Bert had told George about his friend, Mr. Painter, who lived near the river. Yes, Sam and Tucky knew him too but they did not see him often as he lived a long distance upstream.

"Strange fellow," said Sam, "seems to have lots of money. From the books he has he must have been a college man. Came from Philadelphia four years ago and says he intends to stay."

"Didn't Bert tell you he had some love affair that didn't turn out and he wanted to just bury himself down there?" I asked.

"Yes, Bert didn't know anything more about it. Painter said he wouldn't drink any whiskey from Elk City. He either sent to Philadelphia for it or made it himself. Tuckey said this fellow bought a place called 'Aitkine Bar,' a river bar, you know, and he has a fine house and two guest houses, loves music, good books, and pictures, keeps a Chinese cook and second boy, and dresses in a tuxedo every night for dinner."

George was silent for a minute then said, "Boy, I'd hate to live alone like that."

George and Art spent ten days at the claims and three days more at some long-abandoned claims worked during the gold rush of the sixties and seventies. They had everything needed for a report and started home, a hard climb, in rain.

Art led straight to the tree where they had left the snowshoes. They found Pete at his cabin and enjoyed a stew of jerked venison with him for supper. It took all day to reach Oro Grande where the sled picked them up. There they learned about the death of Nan Cane and Nick.

"I'm glad I've seen that country," George went on, "and while Art's claim appears to be good, I feel not much can be done until a railroad runs nearer."

I was fascinated by all that George had told me and very proud of him.

Exhausted that night, George slept soundly. I tossed and half-dreamed, not about the danger of exploring old mines with rotted timbers and snowshoeing unmarked trails, but about what I had heard of the mighty Salmon River: rushing through tumultuous stretches of rapids, turning and twisting in whirlpools, arching over rocks and lashing madly the abrupt lava walls towering nine thousand feet high, then plunging down through gorges. I half-dreamed about Caroline Lockhart on a barge in midstream, daring that challenging ride down the "River of No Return," and I woke as from a nightmare—thankful that George had returned to me safely.

He was satisfied, yet disappointed, to report to David Herron, that while Art Hillier's claim produced ore averaging twenty dollars a ton, the vein was narrow, limiting the exposed ore, and the difficulties of transportation were almost insurmountable.

George could not recommend the investment necessary to open the Salmon River property. Mr. Herron and his associates accepted without reservation the report.

"I think the best thing for us to do now," George said, "is to head for Butte where there are large mines. I can get some kind of a job there while I'm looking for something better."

And so we gathered our belongings, saying goodbye to those

who with little hope for the future stayed on in the valley, and were ready to board the stage, a little wistfully, for after all, romance can dwell as well in a log cabin as in a palace.

CHAPTER 28

In June, 1913, we left Elk City. The sun was bright but the road was slushy and we had snow and ice-covered mountains to cross. Our chief concern was keeping Harriet warm. She wore a dark-blue wool dress, a Christmas present, overalls pulled on top of the dress, a wool knit cap covering her ears, rubbers on her shoes, mittens, and finally a warm coat.

At half past twelve, Jess stowed our baggage in the boot and swung Harriet onto the seat. Seth Livingstone, a salesman from Spokane, made a fourth passenger. We were on our way out of the protected valley with the temperature dropping rapidly, snow banking the road, and ice in the deep ruts.

Down went a front wheel. As it rose, the rear wheel plunged into the slush. I clutched Harriet tighter and braced myself against the arm of the seat. Down went George's side. I shot up into the air.

"Jess," I called, "I want to walk. I can't stand any more of this."

"Wa-all," he drawled, "it is kind o' bumpy." He stopped the horses and we four passengers trailed along the sloppy, slippery road. When it leveled out we rode again to the rim of the bowl and looked long at the valley we would never see again.

Descending through the woods alongside a swiftly moving stream, I cried, "Oh, look there!" In the icy water lay two dead horses.

"We lose horses every winter," Jess explained. "Maybe these two slipped on the ice and broke their legs. Maybe they just plain died from exhaustion. Remember, Ma'am, the mail must go through. We have to get it to Dixie, Elk City, and Oro Grande. Sometimes I can get only a few miles out with the sled, and then I

Leaving Elk City in 1913.

have to go the rest of the way on horseback. There's a couple more dead horses farther on."

We left the stream to ascend the second and higher ridge in air rapidly growing colder.

"Last year there wasn't a bit of snow at this time," said Jess, "but we had some hellish trips this winter. There's at least three feet of ice and snow even now and there'll be more higher up."

As we hit frozen ruts the horses slipped and we slid, lurched, and bumped each other, Jess's "damns, hells, and God's" coming back to us through the cold air. Again he agreed that it would be better if we walked. Harriet held George's hand tightly. I plodded behind. There, a few feet from the road, lay another dead horse, partly covered with snow.

On the wagon again we covered four miles in three hours. Along the right where the soft snow covered the ice the horses had better footing, but in the deeper snow they struggled to drag the stage. Again I cried out, "Look!"

By a stately Douglas fir, under its snow-weighted branches,

were the head and beautifully arched neck of a horse. A little below appeared its knee, curved like that of a stepping pacer starting a race. The rest of the horse was hidden in snow. I needed only a little imagination to picture the tragedy. Urged on by his driver, the horse had evidently struggled valiantly through the drifting snow. But the winds blew harder and the heavily falling snow piled higher. He lost the trail. His exhausted legs plunging in a last desperate effort hit the tree, and floundering, the horse ceased to struggle. Snowfall after snowfall covered him and only now in summer had the white blanket shrunk enough to disclose his head, his neck and one lifted knee, still erect, still frozen stiff. I felt heartsick and saddened for a long time afterwards.

After suffering seven hours, we reached the log cabin at Newsome—cold, stiff, weary, and hungry. A roaring fire and hot meal worked their welcome magic and our sleep was deep. At six the next morning, Jimmie Coleman, our driver of a year before, waited with a platform-covered bobsled with one seat which Harriet and I shared with Jimmie. Our baggage was roped to the floorboards. On our trunks sat George and Livingstone, their feet wedged between pieces of baggage, nothing to hold on to.

The sun was shining, the sky clear. The sled slid easily between the pines, firs, and larches. Exactly a year before, there had been no snow and the sun was hot.

"It's unusual for the snow to last this long," Jimmy volunteered when I mentioned seeing four dead horses en route. "I hate to lose a horse. These four I'm driving know the road so well they could take you without me. We call the two-wheel fellows 'snow-horses,' especially George," and he pointed to the wheel horse on the left. "I've driven him over this road for years and he behaves like a trooper in an emergency."

"Maybe because of his name," I ventured, facetiously.

Gliding smoothly we followed the high trail where banks dropped steeply to one or the other side or down from the crest on both sides. Melting snow trickled from the road. On a level stretch with the horses at a fast trot, I was looking down the slope dropping from the edge of the road when George, the trooper, lurched; his hoof had broken through the softening ice. The sled shuddered. I felt it tilting over the brink. It isn't possible to relate consecutively what followed.

I thought of Harriet and whirling on the seat, I slid towards the road, yelling, "Jimmie, throw Harriet to me!"

Before he could grab her, my feet hit the snow and I went sliding down like a toboggan, bolt upright until I stopped astraddle the trunk of a small tree. Terrified, I looked up. Thank God, the sled was still on the road although tipping precariously.

George, the snow-horse, was sprawled out on his side just above me, with his neck clamped as in a vise between two small trees.

Thrown off the trunk when it happened, my George, horrified to see me skidding down the bank, jumped from the teetering sled, grabbed Harriet, and rushed her back a safe distance, then hurried down to help me. By then I had pulled myself away from the tree but had fallen into the snow just as George reached me. My hero had retrieved me when Jimmie called, "Backus," calmly but firmly, "trample down the snow as hard and firm as you can around the horse. Livingston," Jimmie called authoritatively, "hold the bridle of the lead horses tight and don't let them move."

My concern was for Harriet as I clambered up avoiding the outstretched hoofs of the helpless horse.

Jimmie was patting the horse's head and talking reassuringly: "Quiet, George, quiet. Steady, steady, old boy, quiet . . ." As soon as I reached the road, Jimmie called again to Livingston: "Let Mrs. Backus hold the horses now. You bring me the axe from the back of the sled."

I was really trembling as I grasped the bridles of the lead horses as firmly as I could. Harriet, a seasoned trooper herself, stood obediently a short way back of the sled.

While Livingston and George vigorously trampled down the snow for the moment the horse would attempt to get up, Jimmie began chopping one of the trees that held the animal's neck. Each blow was close to him but George made no move. One hard twist could have broken the horse's neck. "Steady, boy, steady . . ." Only after the tree trunk broke away did the animal move. Then, "Up boy . . ." and he struggled to his feet, the packed snow providing a firm foundation.

Jimmie led the horse up to the road to his place in the team, tied the broken tug with a piece of rope he always carried, as though nothing had happened. George trotted gaily on. Truly a valiant animal!

We were late reaching the Mountain House. As a year before, a delicious dinner was waiting for us. Jimmie hurried through the meal in order to change the horses from the sled to the stage for we would soon drop down and be out of the snow.

In a few minutes he was calling us. After some miles of slushy roads, we steadied down, and by the time we reached Clearwater, all traces of winter were gone. Flowers were in bloom and birds were singing.

"See that bird sitting on the log? He's what we call a fool hen," said Jimmie, pulling in the horses. "I'll have one for dinner tonight."

"How can you catch him?" I asked, hoping desperately that the bird would fly away.

"It's easy," he said. "They're the craziest birds on the wing. That's why they're called fool hens. They just *let* you catch 'em."

When the horses stopped, Jimmie left the wagon and walked straight to the log. To my amazement, he stepped close to the bird, grabbed it, and unceremoniously wrung its neck. Throwing it into the wagon he said, "Wonderful eating! Something like a grouse, but they're so *damned* stupid!"

Nearing Stites, the horses quickened their pace. The road was level and I was feeling "all is well" when we came to an abrupt turn in the open road. Swinging sharply to the left, the wagon wheels cramped, forcing the front wheel high in the air. In a flash, Jimmie jumped from the seat, stood on the hub of the wheel, and by his weight alone kept us from tipping over.

And so we were in Stites again to spend another night in a condemned hotel. In the morning, along with many Indians, we boarded the train on our way to Butte, Montana.

On our arrival in Butte we went in search of a place to live in that barren city where all vegetation had been killed by fumes from early smelters. We found that houses and rooms for rent were shabby, dirty, and too expensive for us.

After much prospecting for accommodations, we moved into an old house near the center of the city. Our apartment consisted of a small living room containing a couch-bed and a trundle bed for Harriet, a table and four chairs, and a dark kitchen in which an old stove constantly leaked gas. The bathroom adjoining our apartment we shared with the other roomers.

We put Harriet to bed in the kitchen but would move her into the living room as soon as we were ready to retire later in the evening.

George was able to get work immediately for Butte was a busy city with many rich mines running constantly. His work was sampling, at three dollars a day, but if the price of copper went up, he would get a fifty-cent raise. I was not happy at the thought of the long uphill walk George had to take every day and working eight hours underground in the High Ore Mine.

Oh, the longing for the San Juans, clean and pure! Oh, for Britannia Beach with its beautiful green forests overlooking the Sound! Oh, Elk City, its lush valley, gentle river . . .

We tightened our budget. Rent was thirty-five dollars a month. Fruit and vegetables grown far away were high priced. Milk, thin and with an unpleasant taste, was expensive. Picture shows cost fifteen cents for adults, ten cents for children. We allowed for one every two weeks. Luxuries were out of the question. I wondered how long we could go on.

One day, recalling better times, I thought of the sampler George had used in the assay office at Britannia, an improvement on the original. I had always thought that George should have been rewarded for it, and now we needed extra dollars. Looking through his papers, I found a catalogue issued by Braun, Knecht, and Heiman who manufactured the sampler in Los Angeles.

Unknown to George, I wrote a letter saying that I, as an assayer, had used their sampler at the Britannia Mining and Smelting Company and had found it very satisfactory for small samples but unable to handle large ones. I had changed it in such a way that I could use it on samples of all sizes. Would they be interested in the change I had made? I signed my husband's name and mailed the letter.

Back came a courteous letter. They were interested, and if I would send a drawing and description of my idea and they considered it had merit, they were sure we could come to some agreement.

Right there I knew I had hit a snag. I could neither describe it nor make a drawing.

"George," I said one evening, "will you please make me a drawing of that sampler you fixed at the Britannia?"

"What on earth do you want *that* for?"

"To make us some money," I said confidently. His smile was benign, slightly commiserating.

"You can't do anything with that. The machine is patented."

"Don't worry. I've received an encouraging letter. Read this."

The drawing with his description, signed by George, was sent immediately. George gladly accepted their offer and back came a check for one hundred dollars. We were rich! Hurrah!

Ringling Brothers Circus was coming to Butte, August fourth. All my young life my father had gathered our friends and taken us all to every circus that came to town. I loved them and now we could afford to go.

When the day came, it was bright and intensely hot. Harriet and I went by streetcar to the grounds near Columbia Gardens, an attractive public park and playground. By one-thirty we were seated halfway up the bleachers and there were few vacant seats in the big tent holding four thousand perspiring spectators.

By twenty minutes before two, the sunshine between the animal tent and the Big Top was gone, replaced by deep shadow. The narrow space above the seats which had been sunny was black, and the scallops of the tent top were flapping noisily. The interior was dim, and suddenly there came a crash of thunder followed by another and another, until it was continuous.

Rain poured heavily and almost as noisily as the rolls of thunder. Crash . . . bang! The rain was driven in under the tent top, flooding the ground. Spectators started to move up from the lower seats and people at the top tried to move down to find dry seating. Water ran like a river between the two tents. Realizing the futility of trying to change positions, the people returned to their seats but a restlessness prevailed. My fear of the storm mounted uncontrollably within me. What if four thousand people panicked! We were doomed. My instinct to protect Harriet fought with the overwhelming fear that this was the end of us and this fear would be transferred from mother to daughter.

We could hear nothing above the din and roar of the storm above and about us, but men were hauling bales of hay from the animal tents and spreading it over the rings. Then the band marched out, taking positions in the three rings, but we could not hear any music because of the storm. Women trapeze artists, carried in on the shoulders of men, climbed high and began their performance to distract the attention of the crowd, terrified by the storm.

At five minutes before two, the storm ended as suddenly as it had begun. My fears likewise. And the sun shone brilliantly again. After the show was over we walked through the animal tent to see the elephants. Their legs were chained to heavy stakes as they swayed back and forth restlessly.

"Don't you usually show these big fellows at the matinee?" I asked of the keeper.

"Generally, we do, Ma'am, but elephants are deadly afraid of storms if they're under the tents. This was one of the damnedest storms I've ever seen. We were afraid they'd stampede, so we took them out and chained them on the hillside. After it was over, we brought them in, but all twenty-eight of them were so nervous we didn't dare show them."

All afternoon I had worried about George, and we hurried home, meeting him near our rooms.

"Oh, where were you during the storm?" I cried. "I was so anxious about you." Having gone through an emotional strain, my eyes were on the verge of tears at this point.

"Don't think I wasn't worried about you and Harriet! Just after one o'clock, when I was waiting to go underground I saw a black cloud over the mountains. I went down to the twenty-third level to take a sample. About a quarter of two I started up and after we got to the thousand-foot level sparks flew from the guides as the skip was hoisted. Lightning was striking the gallows frame and running down the guide rails. I realized it was a bad storm and all I could think of was you and Harriet."

This particular cloudburst inflicted heavy damage on Butte. The greater part of Columbia Gardens was destroyed, and it was months before it was restored.

As suddenly as the cloudburst had struck came our release. A telegram for George arrived from San Francisco: "As we have received no answer to our letter mailed three weeks ago, we assume you are not interested in our offer of position to operate flotation mill in Colorado."

It was signed by a name well-known in mining circles. Apparently, George's success in similar work at Britannia Beach had brought the offer.

With apprehension that it might be too late George hurried to send a telegram explaining that he had never received the letter but would be happy to accept if the offer was still open.

Days went by. My heart began to sink lower and lower. Are there any other two words expressing such despair as "Too late!"? Then a wire came. "Offer still open. If you accept, come at once to San Francisco for a month's instruction."

Joy and elation reigned within our squalid room. We would stay in Oakland, during that month of instruction with my parents whom I had not seen in three years. So excited and happy, I had difficulty preparing dinner. It finally was on the table and Harriet was in her high-chair. George sat down. My mind, miles away on the future, was suddenly jerked back to reality when George calmly asked: "What's *this* for?"

I had securely tied Harriet's bib around George's neck.

Two days later we were ready to leave Butte. "I'll call a taxi," George said.

"We have plenty of time and the streetcar goes right to the depot," said his budget-minded wife.

We carried three suitcases three blocks and waited on a corner. After twenty minutes I was churning inside, still waiting. Where was the streetcar? "We'll miss that train!" I complained.

"We should have taken a taxi. I'll call the first one that comes this way," said George.

None came so he telephoned from the nearest store, urging a taxi to hurry. After what seemed an hour, we and our belongings were stowed in a taxi, and I was pleading to the driver, "Please hurry, please! Whatever happened to the streetcars?"

"They had a breakdown and we've been deluged with calls, Ma'am."

I held myself rigid as the taxi careened around corners recklessly and the tires screeched at its sudden stop. A long freight train on a switch track fifty yards from the station blocked the crossing. We had just five minutes to catch the train.

"Let's get out and run," I fairly screamed. George threw the fare to the driver, grabbed the suitcases, and, holding Harriet's hand, I followed as we tore past one freight car after another until we found a conductor.

"We *have* to get through this train, we don't have time to go around it," George said in a tone of authority he rarely used. The doors were opened just enough to let us through. The bell on the engine of our train was clanging. In flying leaps we reached the steps of the last coach just as the wheels began to turn.

Gasping, I plunked myself down on the first vacant seat and shut my eyes. How we made it in time we never understood. Now to relax, we thought. But the nagging cough which had been bothering Harriet for days, began again. She coughed until she was breathless.

"That old cough will go away when we get to Oakland," I assured her. "Grandma will give you some medicine that will stop it."

Oakland, California. Home once again! But Grandma's medicine brought no relief for Harriet's cough. She had carried that distressing disease, whooping cough, to her three little cousins who with their parents were living with Grandma. Four little youngsters coughing at once took away part of the pleasure of being with my family again.

I was unhappy at the thought that soon George must go to his new location alone, for we did not dare take Harriet to a high altitude until she had entirely recovered. At the end of a month, George left Oakland and I waited until all four children were well. Most of my time at home was spent caring for the little ones and helping my mother.

The longing to be home again soon changed to the stronger urge to be at my husband's side. This I eagerly awaited while my days were filled with routine chores.

PART IV
LEADVILLE, CITY IN THE CLOUDS

A distant view of Mount Massive.

CHAPTER 29

On the cornerstone of the old courthouse in Leadville, Colorado, is carved, "Elevation, ten thousand, two hundred feet."

The plateau which it dots is flanked on the east by the Mosquito Range, a series of peaks eleven to thirteen thousand feet high. Ten miles straight across the mesa is the Sawatch, or Saguache Range, a chain of gigantic pinnacles, some more than fourteen thousand feet high: Mount Massive, Mount Elbert (the highest in Colorado), La Plata, Harvard, Yale, and Princeton, mighty and magnificent beyond description. Along the foot of these titans flows the Arkansas River on its two-thousand-mile turbulent race to join the old Mississippi in Arkansas.

As soon as George arrived in the famous town of Leadville, he began to look for a house to rent, as he wanted Harriet and me to join him as soon as possible. Within a few days he found a house at 617 Leiter Street and rented it from the owner, Mrs. Brittain, who lived in a large house on the same spacious lot.

Happy were we to be together again by Thanksgiving, 1913.

From a picket fence a walk led to high steps of the small frame house. The door opened onto a small front room, two bedrooms, bathroom, and a tiny sitting room. From there, stairs led down to the kitchen and dining room on the ground floor. The house was plainly but sufficiently furnished—twenty-eight dollars a month.

Mrs. Brittain, whose father had been the first postmaster of Leadville, was very pleasant and concerned about our being comfortably settled.

"Has the house been vacant long?" I asked.

"No," she said, "just two days. A woman and her daughter lived here a short time. They skipped out last Thursday at

The first house in Leadville in which we lived. Baby Doe and Silver Dollar Tabor moved out of this house because they could not pay the rent.

midnight owing the rent. They were Baby Doe and Silver Dollar. Of course, you've heard of them."

I didn't admit that I had never heard those names before. The next day I went to the library to read the history of Leadville and from that time on and from many sources I learned the dramatic history of that most famous mining town.

One of the last links between the early campsites and the modern town, the structures of Leadville still standing are saturated with history, memories of human drama, romance, pathos, and tragedy. Perched between the pinnacles of the Great Divide, its meteoric rise to fame, its sordid and gaudy heyday, its pathetic fall is a chronicle rife with stories more incredible than fiction. Tons of the stuff fortunes, fabulous beyond belief, were made of, came from the nearby depths: lead, zinc, manganese, silver, gold, and by-products. There may still be some undiscovered and unnamed treasures here.

Wealth gathered in Leadville importantly affected the whole world. Nearly one hundred years after the startling first discovery of valuable metals in this plateau, books and plays are written, moving pictures and light musical comedies entertain us with characterizations and stories about the men and women who flocked to Leadville. They fought to fulfill a dream, some succeeding, some failing and perishing body and soul in the frenzied battle for honest or ill-gotten wealth.

In 1860, following the bursting of the Pike's Peak bubble, prospectors found gold along the Arkansas River near Mount Massive. An excited miner shouted, "This is California," meaning gold, gold, and more gold, and so it was called California Gulch.

Almost overnight, ten thousand men were digging frantically in the new El Dorado. Tents, huts, cabins mushroomed into the greatest camp in Colorado. But the placer miners were constantly hindered by heavy sand that clogged their sluice boxes.

After taking out more than a million dollars in gold, all the while cursing the difficult delaying sands, the prospectors deserted the town they had founded and roamed farther in search of "easier pickin's."

In 1876 Uncle Billy Stevens took the time and trouble to test the heavy sands. The result electrified the country and led to the development of the greatest mineral deposits ever known. These sands carried almost sixty-five percent lead and ten percent silver. In a short time fortunes were made that have financed industry throughout the world.

In 1878 a group of prominent men took on the responsibility of a town council, of sorts, and named it in honor of lead which had made it possible, called the main street Harrison, after the smelter treating the ores, and the first bank, the name of another ore—Carbonate. A year later, arriving at the rate of one thousand a month, forty thousand men and women were jammed together in a town that now seriously needed rules for law and order to control the greedy, ruthless, lawless mob.

Clyde B. Davis, in his book *The Arkansas*, wrote: "Meanwhile, Leadville was growing in population and wickedness. It is probable that no community in America has ever seen at the same time such lavish, medieval orgies and such extremes of poverty and privation. There have been other tough towns in America, but certainly nowhere as licentious and crime more uncontrolled."

One hundred and thirty saloons thrived mightily. Gambling

went on day and night. Every man wore a gun and murder was common. Fortunes made in the morning were lost before dawn of the next day. Many fortunes were made before picks opened the ground. Hundreds of women filled the brothels. Tiger's Alley and Stillborn Alley along State Street were notorious from the east to the west coast. They called the ugly, shack-cluttered place "The Marvel of the Ages," and in all that was evil, sordid, lawless, sensual, it was.

It was not long before a group of men and women held religious services, hoping to draw in some of the sinful citizens. It is said that one old miner, working his claim on Sunday morning, heard the church bells ringing and stopped digging. Leaning on his pick handle he exclaimed, "I'll be damned if Jesus Christ hasn't come to Leadville, too."

Uncle Billy Stevens, who had blasted Leadville to fame, took a partner, A. B. Wood. Wood sold out to L. Z. Leiter of Chicago and the Iron Mine was under the partnership of Stevens and Leiter. They made money fast and bought and subdivided a large tract of land in the western part of the townsite.

Leiter returned to Chicago with his millions and provided the means for his son's attempt to corner the wheat market in 1897 and 1898. Instead, *he* was cornered to the tune of ten million. But Leiter's daughter, Daisy, married Lord Curzon and became Vicereine of India when Curzon was Viceroy.

Thomas Walsh prospected around Leadville with no success. He tried running a hotel with the same result, so he wandered to the San Juans to woo Lady Luck and the jade smiled on him. The Camp Bird Mine, which we had visited, made millions for him.

A man called Haw Tabor had been lucky, and Marshall Field of Chicago sent him five hundred dollars to invest. Within a year the five hundred ballooned into seven hundred thousand dollars.

David H. Moffat made a fortune at Leadville, part of which he invested in banks but the greater part in railroads out of Denver, eighty miles east of Leadville. He started building several roads, ran into difficulties with Harriman, lost his banks, then his railroads, and, broken-hearted, died. But his dream of a tunnel through the Rockies materialized in the Moffat Tunnel.

Samuel Newhouse, a tunnel builder, pyramided his fortune in Leadville and put some of it into the Flat Iron Building in New

York City. And a man came there who had failed as a merchant in the East and bought two or three small claims. He ran into a vein of pay-dirt and took out millions. With his sons and luck at Leadville, Meyer Guggenheim founded smelters in Colorado and Mexico under the name American Smelting and Refining Company.

But perhaps the best known, a legend in his day, with his name woven into the history of Leadville, was H. A. W. Tabor, better known as Haw Tabor.

He and his wife Augusta left New England in 1859. For years she followed him from one place to another as he prospected, wildly chasing the dream of wealth. To feed her family, Augusta took boarders, made and sold cakes and mince pies from a wagon beside the road. In Leadville, while running a store and acting as postmaster, Tabor grubstaked two miners with food and supplies worth sixty-four dollars and seventy-five cents. The miners struck pay-dirt and the Little Pittsburg Mine was developed. It paid Tabor over a million dollars. He acquired prospect after prospect and couldn't lose. The Chrysolite Mine developed into a bonanza. He paid little more than a hundred thousand dollars for the Matchless and in time it repaid him more than that every month. He had acquired the Midas touch. Where other men failed to find a vein, Tabor's men would dig deeper and produce millions.

A heavily built, pop-eyed man with drooping black moustache, Tabor was a loud-mouthed backslapper, and all his wealth did nothing to refine this ambitious man. As his ambitions grew, Leadville grew around him. He became mayor of the town. He supplied the money to establish police and fire departments. At a cost of ten thousand dollars he organized a Light Cavalry Corps of fifty men. Annually he gave an equal amount to schools and churches. He built the Tabor Opera House which still stands on Harrison Avenue and many other civic improvements. Genial, easy to approach, he was popular with miners, many of whom he grubstaked, and with gamblers and prostitutes.

When Leadville seemed too small for his expanding ambitions he ran as candidate for lieutenant governor of the state and won. He bought an elaborate house in Denver and spent a fortune improving it. He owned mines and banks and was dabbling in railroads. Tabor was riding high, wide, and handsome, and Augusta, who didn't like the swath he was loudly cutting, had difficulty keeping up with him and keeping him within marital bounds.

A sparkling blonde, Elizabeth McCourt, the wife of a miner, was much in the public eye and attracted Haw Tabor. She was dazzled by his wealth. He finagled a divorce for himself and his "Baby Doe," as she was called.

In Denver, he built entire business blocks, one of which included the Tabor Grand Opera House, fitted with knobs of silver and gold, and huge chandeliers dripping crystal pendants. The gala, grand opening was never to be forgotten.

Tabor bought forests of mahogany in South America, purchased mines sight unseen whenever they were offered for sale. He boasted that he was worth one hundred million and would soon be worth more. He bought a position as United States Senator to fill a vacancy for one month, and in Washington, set the stage for his wedding in March of 1883 with Baby Doe.

Horace Austin Warner Tabor was on top of his world and at the elaborate, lavish display that President Arthur and many senators attended, he bedazzled the Capitol city. Baby Doe sparkled with enough diamonds to stock an early Tiffany's.

When each of two daughters arrived, he spent fortunes on them. The second daughter was named Rose Mary Echo "Silver Dollar" Tabor.

But the rocket soaring to its zenith was soon on its downward curve. A strike in the Leadville mines, the failure of one large investment after another, the revelations of goldbricks he had acquired involved him so deeply he scarcely knew when he started slipping.

Congress had passed a law that shoved Tabor over the brink. During the panic of 1893, the Sherman Silver Act, establishing silver coinage, was repealed. The price of silver dropped from a dollar and twenty-nine cents to fifty cents an ounce and Tabor was penniless. Baby Doe pawned her jewels. In 1899 he was digging with pick and shovel to support his family when a few political friends obtained for him the position of postmaster of Denver. But Haw Tabor died soon after. His last admonition to Baby Doe was to hold on, at any cost, to the Matchless Mine, the only thing left.

Without a guaranteed silver market, the great boom in Leadville collapsed like a punctured balloon. The population dwindled to thirty thousand, then twenty. By the beginning of the century, it was fewer than ten thousand. Values dropped. Corner lots that earlier had sold for ten thousand were worthless. Yet, those remaining in Leadville were a steadier class of people who established homes, enforced the laws, and boosted civic pride.

Baby Doe Tabor and her younger daughter, Silver Dollar, returned to Leadville. Through affluence and poverty Baby Doe remained faithful to Tabor, and now she was living from hand to mouth aided by his friends whom once he had assisted.

When taxes on the Matchless Mine were in danger of falling delinquent, someone paid them and Baby Doe was able to hold on to the mine which never again was worked. No longer able to pay rent, she moved into the shaft house off the mine. Dressed like a miner and armed with a gun she remained on guard in fear of claim-jumpers or other menaces.

In 1935, seventeen years after we left Leadville, Baby Doe Tabor was found there, dead from cold and hunger, still faithfully guarding Haw's last possession.

Heigh-ho! Now George, Harriet, and little Harriet Backus were living in a house on property blocked out by Leiter, father of Lady Curzon, once Vicereine of India, in a house just vacated by the destitute widow of the fabulous Haw Tabor and their daughter Silver Dollar—whose christening robe had cost five hundred dollars.

I must come back from the thoughts of those dazzling days to the less spectacular years from 1913 to 1918. Yes, much less spectacular, filled with hopes and disappointments, but much, much happiness.

While shopping along Harrison Avenue one day with Mrs. Brittain, I saw a girl riding a beautiful cream-colored horse.

"Who is that girl on that beautiful horse?" I asked.

"Oh, that is Silver Dollar. The horse belongs to an old friend of her father. She rides it quite often," Mrs. Brittain divulged.

Not long after my one and only glance of Silver Dollar, she and her mother left Leadville. Later, the news came back that Silver Dollar had been found dead in the red-light district of Chicago. A life begun amidst wealth and beauty ended in disgrace and filth.

It was several years later that her mother, Baby Doe, made her final trip to Leadville, there to die in deprivation.

CHAPTER 30

Many mines were closed down, the high-grade ore having been dug out. Only a few were still operating. The Leadville District Mill, which George was reopening, had been idle for many years until Otis King, O. A. as he still is called, was attracted by the refractory ores around Leadville. He proceeded to arouse the interest of three prominent men: Wilson Pingrey, a banker in Iowa, Louis Noble, a well-known mining engineer of Denver, and W. B. McDonald, manager of the local American Smelting and Refining plant. King captured their interest in the idea of using the new process, the one with which Herbert Hoover was making a notable success in Australia at the time. So, they formed the Pingrey Mines Company and leased the idle mill.

The building stood on a slope a mile and a half from Leadville and was served by spur railroad tracks from the smelter, a half mile beyond. Tests indicated that the process could produce marketable concentrates with reasonable profits. The company then contracted to buy selected low-grade sulphite ores from mines which had been closed and from old tailing dumps.

From the beginning, the work was difficult. The ores were so low-grade that every step in the treatment had to be extremely efficient in order to recover values.

George's hours at work had no limit. The mill ran three shifts and he tried to follow every step of every operation. On many days I packed two meals, often enough for three meals. He left the house on foot, before seven in the morning and came home when he could. We had a telephone only because he might be called at any hour, day or night, when anything went wrong, or when questions came up about the process which was new to the men.

Often, at two, three, or four in the morning the telephone woke us. If the question called for more than advice, George dressed and started on the mile-and-a-half walk to the mill.

That winter was severe. From December to March the temperature was below zero most of the time. Changes in the air were sudden and sharp, causing violent storms as winds slashed at the mountains. We felt the cold more than at the Tomboy even though Leadville was a thousand feet lower. Between the mighty ranges of the Sawatch and Mosquito mountains, the gales swept unimpeded in the utmost fury of biting cold.

Still, the house was comfortable and though George's much-too-long and broken hours spoiled the evening leisure we had enjoyed previously, things ran smoothly until Harriet became ill with one of her frequent stomach upsets.

From the telephone directory, I picked the name Dr. Jeannotte, called, and asked if he could come at once. In a short time he had climbed the hill and under his care Harriet quickly recovered. Dr. Jeannotte proved to be our friend, guide, and philosopher. He was a French Canadian from the Province of Quebec, well along in years, with gray hair, brown eyes, and red cheeks. As a young man he had tuberculosis and had come to the Rocky Mountains where, if the heart could stand the altitude, lung conditions improved.

Before long, I had become acquainted with many people, some old-timers with their memories of Tabor, Brown of the Little Johnny, and others who had made their fortunes from the mines.

The wives of the men connected with Guggenheim's smelter were most cordial and I soon began to feel at home. There were church gatherings, a moving picture house, and occasional entertainment at the Opera House. There were sidewalks, and streets were named and the houses numbered. Some of the stores delivered orders. Leadville had many of the advantages of a city when compared with most of the places we had lived previously.

The famous opera house is of historical interest to a large and active national organization today. Charles Algernon Sydney Vivian, a young Englishman visiting this country in 1867, gathered a few congenial friends together and formed a group calling themselves "The Jolly Corks," later to become The Benevolent Protective Order of Elks. In 1879 Vivian came to Leadville and renovated a building for a theater, hoping to produce drama and classics at a time when entertainment, of necessity, catered only to the rough element who smoked and drank throughout the all-night performances. Vivian failed in this but continued his work with small theatrical groups until he died on March 20, 1880, in an old dwelling house on East Second Street.

In 1900, the, B.P.O.E. bought the Tabor Opera House and renamed it "the Elk's Opera House."

On Sunday afternoons, if George was home from work early enough, we went for a walk down 7th Street to Harrison Avenue and south to the Elk's Opera House and back. In later years on many Sunday afternoons, one of us would say, "Let's take a walk to the Opera House," and we would revisit in our minds that brief stroll in Leadville: the picket fences around little houses in various stages of disrepair, gutters carrying away snow-water, fringes of dreary dumps, mounds of discarded ore and waste rock, unused trestles, broken gallus frames, and old shaft houses. Then on through Stumptown, Bucktown, Chicken Hill, and Shanty Town to the mill and beyond to the mountains—majestic beyond all telling, grand, snowy and sublime!

Toward the end of April, the weather was warmer; melting snows turned the roads into sticky mushy mud. By the end of June, the mud had dried in deep ruts. Often we walked through clouds as they rolled along the streets—a strange experience. This, the highest incorporated city in the country actually, "The Cloud City."

The frequent thunderstorms terrified me. Sometimes I ran with Harriet to Mrs. Brittain's house. We would sit in the big dining room while lightning blazed with the brilliance of sunshine and each bolt filled the air with charges of electricity that ran down the stovepipe and crackled on the stove while peals of thunder rocked the house. Then the storm would pass over, hurling all its power and armament against Mount Massive's hoary head. Only the foot of the peak was visible; the top would be engulfed in pitch-black clouds ripped open by slash after slash of lightning. It was too far away for us to hear the roar of battle, but when it was over, there stood the giant in all its beauty, victorious.

As the days went by, the results of mill operations constantly varied from disappointment to satisfaction. Besides variations in the kinds of ore, the character of the same lot might vary with each carload, thus necessitating a change in the grinding from coarse to fine, or reverse, and in the kind and amount of reagents to be used. There was a constant struggle to solve each problem, but the mill was making a profit.

The mill was old and had been idle so long that many repairs were constantly being made, and George was always warning his men to be careful and avoid accidents. Men who were eager to work found George to be a kind and fair boss.

Our second Christmas and New Year's in Leadville were happy days.

Soon there were signs of spring. One morning a knock on the front door surprised me. When I opened it, my heart began to thump. W. B. McDonald stood there, a serious look on his face. He was a man who made few contacts with anyone except those to whom he gave orders.

"Mrs. Backus," he spoke quietly, slowly, "George has met with an accident."

"Serious?" I choked on the word.

"Not vital, but he's very uncomfortable. He's in the hospital and he wants to see you. His jaw is broken and the doctors are working on him. I've just come from there and I'll go back this afternoon. Go to him as soon as you can."

I sent Harriet at once to Maude Stevenson, a friend whose husband was a chemist at the smelter. I knew she would take care of her until I returned.

Inwardly trembling but determined to copy the calmness my beloved always showed I climbed the stairs of the small hospital to his room. Sitting up in bed, he was waiting.

"My goodness, dear," I tried to hide my emotions with a breezy greeting, "what have you been doing to yourself?"

His eyes smiled, but the rest of his face was hidden. Just then Mr. McDonald walked in with a nurse.

"Take that pencil and paper away from him and don't let him have them again," he said, then turning to me. "He's worrying about the payroll. He wants to make it out so the men won't have to wait for their wages, but I'll attend to that. I've arranged to send him to the hospital in Pueblo, one of the finest in the state. You go with him. The train leaves at nine-thirty. You will be met at the station about three tomorrow morning." I knew Mr. McDonald was always obeyed.

Downstairs I learned what had happened. The two mill-men who brought George to the hospital had given the doctor the details. Once in a while a rock, too large to go through the crushing roll, would block the feed to the mill. When this occurred, a millman took a square-headed bar and cracked the chunk so it would pass through. Warning the men of the danger of this, George ordered them to shut down the rolls before breaking the rock. But this particular morning, in the middle of an urgent and important test, a piece of rock had plugged the rolls. Not wanting to delay the test by shutting down the plant, George himself picked up the bar and hit the rock. The end caught in the rolls, the bar straightened up and bashed against his jaw with terrific force. Somehow, he had managed to reach the foreman's office, then sagged to the floor. Jess Theobald, a shift boss, stepped in to leave a report on the desk and immediately rang the emergency gong. A roustabout came running and, seeing blood spurting from George's mouth, grabbed a begrimed towel and wrapped it around George's face. As they were telephoning for a wagon, McDonald arrived to make one of his frequent inspections. He ordered two men to take George to the hospital; he would be there later.

Dr. Blake at the hospital said George's jaw was badly broken, three long breaks on the right side and one all the way around his jaw. They had tried to set the jaw several times but were unable to align all the teeth. McDonald had refused to let them try again.

Maude brought Harriet to see George and she watched, without comment, as he took nourishment through a tube. At parting, she said, "Goodbye, Daddy. I'll write you a letter and you'll soon be well."

I hurried home to pack my clothes and to take Harriet to Maude's. When I saw George again, I hardly knew him. His face was badly swollen. A fresh bandage had been wound around his chin and over his head to support the jaw. He put on his overcoat and his famous old hat, a dicer. We were driven to the train. He went to bed without undressing, but slept fitfully. I cat-napped. At three in the morning we reached Pueblo. Now George's face was swollen beyond all recognition and the skin was purple up to his eyes. Blood had seeped from both sides of his mouth and soaked the bandage. He looked so pathetic I wanted to cry. But when he put the dicer on top of his bandaged head, he looked so comical I had difficulty trying to control both sobs and laughter.

An ambulance awaited us and took us to the hospital—built by John D. Rockefeller to care for employees of his nearby industries, coal mines, and steel plants under the name Colorado Fuel and Iron Company; and the Minnequa Hospital had the finest modern equipment for every emergency. Dr. Corwin, head physician, was then in Europe and Dr. Senger was in charge.

George was put to bed at once. I was allowed to stay with him. Since the accident happened there had not been a single sound of complaint from George and I marveled at his stoicism.

At nine in the morning he was taken to a room down the hall and after a long time he returned, with a nurse beside him, walking slowly. I gasped at the change. The bandage was gone and there was no sign of swelling. His face looked pinched and thin, and instead of purple his skin was a sickly yellow.

"Dearest, what did they do to you?" I whispered, my voice choking.

Dr. Senger had wired the jaws together and George, himself, had helped by pushing up his own chin. I think I suffered more than he did as I sat beside his bed. At noon he began to mumble and point to his mouth. I called a nurse. The wire no longer held the jaws in position. A piece of broken bone had slipped from the wires allowing other fractured pieces to slip out of place. Dr. Senger said they must wait a couple of days to let the swelling subside before resetting the bones.

I found a room to rent a block from the hospital. On Friday morning, the jaw was reset. At six that evening the wires again slipped and were entirely out of alignment and his jaw sagged to one side.

"We'll wait until Monday and give him a general anesthetic," said Dr. Senger.

Early on Monday they used heavier wires and encased George's chin in a cup made of fibre-board supported by a bandage over his head. After the operation, Dr. Senger came to speak to me with one of his fingers bandaged. I asked about it persistently and finally he said, "George bit my finger. Of course, he knew nothing about it." I was concerned because his skilled fingers were badly needed in his work. Thank heaven, the wires held this time and George took nourishment through a tube. At the end of the week I went home.

After three weeks, George returned home, very thin. He wanted to go to work but McDonald refused to allow him to go to the mill.

George used the tube to eat and lived on strained soups and partially melted ice cream.

Two weeks went by before I said one morning, "Dear, you don't look well. Your lips are dry and your eyes are . . . well, not right." Then in a subdued voice he admitted, "I haven't felt well for a couple of days but I thought it was because my face gets so tired. I didn't want to say anything about it."

I telephoned Dr. Senger and told him George had a fever.

"Get him here at once," he said.

George insisted on going alone. Next day, Dr. Senger telephoned me saying: "Infection has set in. We watched for it from the first but his blood was in such excellent condition his system was able to fight any trouble up to now. He's weak and hasn't the resistance he should have, but we'll get it under control. Don't worry."

Poor George! Three openings were made under his jaw and drainage tubes inserted. Dr. Senger's finger had only recently healed from George's bite.

At the end of a month my dear one returned home, fully recovered but weighing only a hundred and fifteen pounds. The company decided this was the time for George to have a vacation, long overdue, so we left for Oakland to visit my family. In a few weeks, George regained his strength and we returned to our home in the high country.

CHAPTER 31

Harriet started to school and, wanting to keep in touch with the teaching profession, I registered with the school department as a substitute teacher. Almost immediately they asked me to take a class for the full term, but I declined because it would keep me away from home too much.

My first call as a substitute was in Stringtown, a long row of little houses on both sides of the road leading from Leadville straight to the smelter. Most of the laborers living there had come from Austria, Hungary, and other middle European countries. Arriving at Leadville, these immigrants signed up with an Austrian named Zeitz who obtained work for them in the mines. When George needed a laborer he called Zeitz and a man, perhaps newly arrived and unable to speak English, would report at once.

Children from these families were interesting, alert, and well disciplined. After ten years away from teaching, I enjoyed facing thirty to thirty-five youngsters looking to me for guidance through the mysterious three R's.

A week later a call came from the Little Johnny School. I walked east up Fifth Street, past the old stores and houses to the street end, followed a narrow road around mounds of tailings until, breathing hard, I reached the one-room schoolhouse with its bell tower piercing the clouds.

Close by was the Little Johnny Mine which had made its discoverer, John Campion, a multi-millionaire. David H. Moffat was in partnership with Campion, and there was a third part-owner, J. J. Brown, who made millions from it. His wife became famous as a heroine in the great tragedy, the sinking of the *Titanic* in 1912. A light opera and a movie were produced about her, entitled *The Unsinkable Mollie Brown.*

Here I was, avidly interested in the colorful character who had made fascinating history of the West, teaching in a school surrounded by mines which had produced the foundations for immense fortunes.

I was teaching here one day when the clouds were so low they settled on the roof; and they were *dark clouds* this day. Then came the first peal of thunder. The storm was right over our heads! I must never let the children see my fear, I vowed. The lightning flashed through the windows on both sides of the room, the thunder deafening. The children sat as though nothing were going on. I suggested it was time for a song and asked them to sing one which their regular teacher had taught them. They gaily began singing. "A little louder, please," I said. Little did they know that their young voices were helping me in my hour of fear. In truth they were teaching me one of the R's—the respect for their stalwartness.

Summer came, but in name only for even on the Fourth of July, snow was falling. Harriet and I went to see Maude Stevenson in her sprawling old house and snow slapped our faces all the way. Her young son, Harry, and his playmate were out in the storm excitedly jumping around something they were working with.

"They've made a small, muzzle-loading cannon to celebrate the day," Maude explained. "I don't like the idea, but I made them promise to be careful."

The house, a one-story mansion in its day, was interesting as the old storm-windows, relics of its one-time luxury were still intact.

"Look here," Maude drew my attention to one which was scratched with names in all directions. "We don't intend to remove these storm windows, either. You must have the light favorable and stand in just the right place to read these scrawls. I asked Mrs. Stickley about them; she's an old-timer here. She said one could read the social history of Leadville on these windowpanes."

"These two," she pointed to the scratches, "were married. This one was shot in some love affair. *That* horrible scribble belonged to a man who got rich quick. *This* one skipped out of town in a hurry."

"I suppose these names were cut with diamonds that dripped from the women when this house was built," I said.

"Probably. A sort of guest book . . ." She was interrupted by

Harriet (right) posing with a friend in Leadville, 1914.

a loud BANG from the yard. We rushed to the door. Harry lay on the snow, his hands over his eyes. The boys had loaded the cannon with powder and wadded paper, and Harry had touched it off. The burning powder had backfired and caught him in the face, full force.

One of the neighbors had an automobile that was the talk of Leadville, a Stanley Steamer, and in it Harry was rushed to the hospital and given first aid.

"Get him to Denver as fast as you can," said Dr. Strong. "The powder is embedded in both eyes as well as the entire face. Keep on treating him with this solution until he is in the hands of the best oculist in Denver."

I helped Maude get ready for the heartbreaking journey just as she had helped me when George was hurt. It was months before Harry was home again, his eyesight saved only by prompt and special treatment, unavailable in Leadville.

When school opened again in the fall, we were expecting our second baby, and hoping for a son. Called to substitute, I taught school occasionally and also a Sunday School class in a large building dating back to early Leadville.

Our experiences at the Tomboy, Britannia Beach, and Elk City had confirmed more than ever our convictions that the denomination of a church made little difference and help was needed here. The Sunday School class took me back to the Tomboy and Grace Driscoll in the little schoolhouse leading her small group, singing "Jesus bids us shine with a clear, bright light . . ."

Harriet enjoyed school. George was busier than ever helping to install an Oliver Filter for de-watering concentrates in the mill, a valuable machine filling a widespread need in the milling industry. An engineer arrived from the Oliver Company in Oakland, California, to direct the installation until the machine was operating.

After a sufficient time to test the filter, George was still not entirely satisfied with the results.

"It's really a fine machine," he said to me, "and I am sure it will be a great success; but I'm not entirely happy about its construction for our problems. I'd like to make some changes which I think will improve operations."

And so, George and his capable mechanic, Otto Johnson, took the filter apart and rebuilt it, using a more rugged construction which gave the results he had hoped for. Little did he imagine how happily his work on this machine would affect us for the next thirty-five years.

We were comfortable on Leiter Street but found a house about a block away more suitable for us as the rooms were all on one floor. We moved as soon as we could so as to have everything ready when our hoped-for boy would arrive. The house had a small but convenient porch and a yard containing two attractive trees.

For the first time we used hard coal in the large heater. Banking the fire at night, we were overjoyed to wake up in the early mornings to a warm house when outside the temperature would be far below zero. Day after day Harriet, warmly wrapped, coasted down Seventh Street on a "Red Flier" that Santa Claus brought at Christmas time. She would come home with hands and feet nipped by Jack Frost, tears frozen on her cheeks, but the minute she was warmed she was gone again. That hill was a children's playground in winter, and often I saw Harriet being pulled uphill with the rope of her coaster looped to the rear of a sled delivering groceries.

George and I treasured the thought that when our children were older they could say they had been born in two of the world's most famous mining camps, Telluride and Leadville. But one day my feet slipped on the icy walk and I fell headlong. I was horrified! What had I done to our baby? I went directly to Dr. Jeannotte's office.

"Don't worry," he said with his comforting smile. "That often happens in winter. You'll be all right." But my fear continued.

The month of May arrived and the days began to drag. "Any day now," we thought, for three weeks.

"If you want a boy," said Dr. Jeannotte, "you'd better hurry. Every baby I've welcomed this month has been a boy. But if you wait too long, the style may change."

It was not until the evening of June thirteenth that I said to George, "Call Dr. Jeannotte." He did, but that blessed man could not put his foot to the floor because of an acute attack of rheumatism.

O. A. King always insisted that in an emergency we call upon him for transportation because he owned one of the few automobiles in Leadville. George called him and we bounced over the rough road in his small, topless car to the hospital.

A young doctor, recently graduated, took Dr. Jeannotte's place; and again for the next few hours, my beloved stood holding my hand. Happy indeed were we when George Fish Backus arrived to join Harriet, a devoted sister. Unlike my nervous care of Harriet in below-zero weather, George was soon taking his naps on the porch no matter what the thermometer read. He thrived and with such a happy disposition, we nicknamed him "Sunshine," a name which stayed until he was old enough to object. What a pleasure he has been!

A house on the next block was for sale, one which probably would have sold for ten thousand dollars in the heyday of Leadville. With the small amount of insurance George received after his accident, we decided to buy the house for the total sum of five hundred dollars. We felt proud to own a house in one of the select districts of Leadville.

It resembled the only sort of house I was ever able to draw, a rectangle bisected from one side to the other with a peaked roof. Up two steps we entered a three-by-four-foot hall. To the right was a sitting room with a small bay window. A wall halfway across divided it from the dining room. I wouldn't dignify the cooking area by the name of kitchen. It was a miserable little lean-to over a four-by-six-foot cellar, entered by a door in the floor. At the head of the stairs was a front and back bedroom lighted by a window at each end of the house. The only source of running water was in the lean-to and we had to return to a Chick Sales.

But the house stood proudly on Capitol Hill, among houses equally old and weathered, in which millionaires had dwelt in the famous old Stevens and Leiter addition. Best of all, it was *ours*!

The thermometer was hugging freezing point when we moved in. During the winter, the winds blew savagely. The old house shook and swayed. Often a storm in the night sent me downstairs to sleep on the couch. And these gales usually lasted three days. Many times the lights were out for hours and we used candles which we always kept on hand.

It wasn't long before the crumbling lean-to became intolerable and George decided to replace it. We were young and no undertaking seemed too formidable. The mill had been running without a hitch and occasionally George was home before six o'clock; time enough, he said, to build me a real kitchen.

He moved the range into the dining room where, fortunately, it could be piped into the chimney in the middle of the house. The lean-to came down in no time at all. Every minute not spent eating, sleeping, or at the mill, George worked renewing boards which lined the cellar, laying flooring for the new addition he had planned—a real kitchen, also a large pantry and complete bathroom!

George worked against time because the addition must be enclosed before snow began to fall, leaving inside work to be done later. The walls were up and only to help with the eaves did he require a carpenter.

Five families in the block owned a small private sewer system and we were finally allowed to buy in on it. George ran a pipe from the house to the cesspool, our community disposal plant. This bathroom, with its fixtures and the sewer pipe, cost twice as much as we paid for the house and lot. Extravagantly, George had satisfied my longing of ten years for a bathtub in which I could lie full length and relax in all the water I wanted.

By October the costly addition to our mansion was enclosed against the weather. The range was in the kitchen, wide shelves in the pantry were stocked with supplies, the bathroom filled me with bliss, and George began sealing the interior with tongue and groove. I could do this part of the job and worked on it until all was finished.

During this time, while our country was at peace, Europe was being torn apart by fanatical leaders. Leadville began to feel the effects of the roar of cannons in rising values of metals and renewed interest in her products. O. A. asked George if he could handle more tonnage. George said he could and soon the mill was running at full capacity.

"George, this is what warms the cockles of a man's heart," said O. A. as George was instructing his men about loading a car of lead. "Boy, you've made good!"

Mr. King was called by one tycoon in the mining industry "the damnedest little fighter I ever ran up against." He did not give the impression that he was a fighter. He was short in stature, pleasant in manner, kind, a devoted husband and father, sincere friend, the soul of integrity. Neither he nor anyone else could have foreseen the reason why he earned that sobriquet. But important events were forming which, viewed in retrospect, could have changed the fortunes of many of us.

Meanwhile, King had become interested in the stories of Charles Senter, a roving veteran of the Civil and Indian wars, who had been placer mining in a gulch thirteen miles from Leadville and had staked out some claims.

When King asked Senter what kind of claims they were, the answer was, "I don't know just what the ore is. It's up on Bartlett Mountain and some old-timers call it 'Molly-be-damned.' "

O. A. King, farsighted and ready to take a chance, asked Senter to give him an option on his claims. Senter had no money and lost no time in signing the papers for which King paid him a very substantial sum of money.

Samples of the ore were sent to New York. It was a new metal to most of the local assayers and their opinions differed greatly. The assayers in New York reported that the ore was an excellent source of low grade molybdenum sulphite, valuable for strengthening steel. Their report caused excitement in the rare metal world although the market was small and no satisfactory process for concentrating it had as yet been worked out.

It was 1917 and the United States had entered the war. Rapidly the price of metals rose. Would this turn of events increase the demand for molybdenum?

While King was trying to find a market and financial backing to develop the mountain, which was almost solid molybdenum ore (his alert mind could see almost untold wealth), he was also hunting for ores suitable for treatment at the mill which he desperately wanted to keep running.

Why not have George Backus try to concentrate molybdenum? This idea took root in O. A.'s active mind. It might refine the stubborn stuff from the Bartlett Peak. If a market were found, he would be able to go ahead. Eventually, a firm in Liverpool offered King thirty-five hundred dollars a ton for the pure concentrate. In their opinion, one ton would supply the world market for a year.

The ore must be brought down the precipitous peak to the station from where the C & S Railroad could carry it to Leadville. But how was it to be done?

At the base of the peak was a wayside switch, called Climax, on which trains shunted their helper engines when they reached the pass. Passing this Bartlett Peak the Colorado and Southern ran a narrow-gauge line between Denver and Leadville over miles of the most difficult hauling in Colorado. Throughout eight months of snow, the railroad, like the Denver and Rio Grande, was piloted by snowplows and struggled through drifts often high above the tops of the cars, bucking the death-dealing blizzards. There were times when even with the aid of snowplows this line was idle for days, even a week, the trains unable to break through.

No trail had been made to the open cuts which were two miles from Climax, and June of 1917 displayed snow on the mountain still twelve feet deep. There were no means of getting the ore down except on the backs of little burros.

From Alma, a town a few miles away, King obtained forty

burros whose owner took them up the slope and loaded each one with three hundred pounds of ore. In the lead was Prunes, a pioneer among his kind around the vicinity, hero of many difficult and dangerous packing adventures, and locally as famous as many outstanding *human* pioneers.

Prunes picked his careful way calmly down the hazardous face of the Peak and guided the string of burros safely to the railroad. Trip after trip was made until three cars, waiting on the siding at Fremont Pass, were loaded, ready to be hauled to the mill.

Prunes was then fifty years old. Fifteen years later, at the age of sixty-five, he was laid to rest at the crossroads of the main street of Fairplay. All the stores and places of business were closed during the services befitting a faithful, hardworking little creature whose life had been spent assisting his human friends. A headstone marks his grave.

On the ore brought down by the burros, George made a test run and secured about seventy-five percent recovery, an exceptionally high return considering the low values in the feed.

O. A. King, years later, wrote a fascinating book, *Gray Gold*, giving detailed accounts of his struggle to develop the fabulous mountain of ore.

A condensation which the *Denver Post* published of the book, stated: "George S. Backus combined the British flotation process with some ideas of his own. He worked out the formula for a flotation process that is used to this day for the separation of molybdenum."

With the results George had produced, King enthusiastically and with astonishing stamina went ahead with his plans. The obstacles for actual mining operations into this giant, sky-high Peak were staggering. There were living quarters to be built, means of transporting the ore to the railroad. These alone seemed an insurmountable problem. But with the pertinacity for which he became famous and encouraged by the returns of George's first run, he sold three and a half tons of concentrates for $2,550 a ton.

Near the switch-house he built a bunkhouse for his men and a cookhouse in which to feed them, with a room for George and himself, if they were detained overnight.

King's troubles, however, were just beginning. The sale of three tons of molybdenum concentrates saturated the market in

America. As stories of the successful milling were published, they attracted much attention, especially that of a German company in New York. Germany knew very well the value of molybdenum and needed it for her war manufacturing.

O. A.'s claims extended over only part of the mountain. On every other available inch of the slopes and even down into surrounding gulches, claims were rapidly being staked out by other men. Trouble soon started.

One day, with the weather at ten below zero, King climbed to one of his chief claims on snowshoes and to his surprise found his location stakes removed and new ones in their places. That meant just one thing—claim-jumpers! Those words were frightening at this time and place for the womenfolk of miners and mine officials. Men were killed for much less than defending their property from such thieves.

I was very worried when, next day, King returned to Leadville and with George and two miners boarded the train for Climax to plot assessment work. They were to return to Leadville that night at six o'clock if the C & S train were on time, which it seldom was.

Nine o'clock came and George was not home. I called Sally Becker, one of our three friendly telephone operators, who were always interested and helpful in reporting train movements.

"Sally, do you know anything about the C & S?" I asked.

"The last word we had at six tonight was that the train was thirty miles the other side of Climax. It's been late all along the line."

During heavy snows the trains from Denver were generally late, sometimes for hours, sometimes days. Resembling giant polar bears, the engines made spectacular arrivals behind one or two snowplows, cutting a narrow way through drifts and piling snow on the already high snow walls on both sides of the hidden tracks.

I was worried for I knew the gulches between Climax and Leadville were choked with snow, and if the road were impassable for trains, the men might try to come the rest of the way on snowshoes. I couldn't stop thinking of the night, a month before, when George had been in Climax and walked into the house about six o'clock, bedraggled and bleary-eyed. I had jumped when I saw him, he looked so near collapse from exhaustion.

"How did you get here?" I had said. "The train isn't in yet."

"Well, some fellows from Kokomo came into camp at noon

The Leadville District Mill, which my husband managed for five years and in which he ran the first ton of molybdenum from Climax's Bartlett Mountain.

and said the train was stalled by a rock slide thirty miles back and it wouldn't get through for a couple of days, so I started hiking home."

"George Backus," I had shouted, "how awful! That's thirteen miles through deep snow . . . and alone!"

"Well, I wanted to get home," he had said, "and I didn't realize what a trip it would be. The fellows said I was crazy to try it, but I came right down the Canyon which saved a little of the distance. Anyway, I'm here."

I had scolded my slender, tousle-haired, blond husband (whom I adored) as I never had done before, hoping he would never do such a thing again. My voice had grown louder and I talked faster, enumerating the risks he had taken. I reminded him of the time O. A. King had been coming from Denver in a furious storm. Near the top of the Divide a huge snowslide hurtled down the mountain and rolled the entire train over and over down the mountain slope. Miraculously no one was killed, but there are few such fortunate endings to a snowslide.

Now, again, George was late. I waited, tense with fear. At eleven o'clock he arrived and told me about a different but no less deadly peril he had encountered. Time after time claim-jumpers had interfered with them and tried to drive the Pingrey workers off their diggings. Threats and verbal battles never ceased. Men also had approached the aged Senter from whom King bought the claims and tried to buy out his interest, but he remained loyal to his contract. As King was to learn later, the gigantic German Gesellschaft Company in New York, with headquarters in Frankfort, Germany, were instigating the trouble. They had tentacles all over the world and owned a majority of stock in innumerable corporations, smelters in many places, vested interests in gold and copper, silver and zinc mines, and controlled the Ohio and Colorado Smelter at Salida. They were trying to corner molybdenum, especially this mountain of it. If the concentrates were not shipped to Germany, they meant to make certain the ore would not be available to America. Their many agents using American names, reported to Max Schott who was head agent of German Gesellschaft in New York. Their hired thugs stopped at nothing. King was defending his claim in court, but the law moves slowly and King's opponents took advantage of delay.

Every night George related instances of their persecution in which he, King, and the men had been involved. They had thrown King bodily down the mountainside and only the deep snow had saved his life. Time after time they grouped themselves where the men were digging and prevented further work or the loading of the already loose ore. Even old Senter carried a gun and was prepared to use it, but King relied on going unarmed as a safety measure.

On this morning O. A., George, and two men left the train at Climax, lashed on snowshoes, and climbed the first slope of the mountain. Two rough-looking strangers met them and, recognizing King, accosted him.

"Get the hell out of here, King," one yelled. "This ain't your property. Your claims are dead."

"This certainly is my property," King replied calmly. "You're the one to get out of here."

"You G—damned trespassers. Take your men and git or we'll make you." The speaker pulled out a long, wicked-looking knife and started toward King.

With a quick lunge King struck the knife from the man's hand, toppled him into the snow, and jumped on him. The second brute lifted and swung his pick at King's head. George and one of the miners jumped and knocked the would-be killer down, rolling him over and over. Getting to their feet, the pair took time to curse and threaten, then disappeared around a cliff.

It was one of many similar incidents, increasing in violence, besides the fight King waged in the courts to protect his claims. O. A. was bucking a colossus, almost alone. The small companies knew that some big concern with unlimited finances was staking claims and doing everything short of downright slaughter to hinder the work of the Pingrey Mines Company and bring suit after suit in the names of various claimants.

Even the United States Government seemed unsuspecting that back of it all was the German Gesellschaft Company. And whatever suspicions the officials of small companies might entertain, they had no means of proving anything, and Gesellschaft was bleeding them of their finances with every suit in their legal fight to defend their claims.

The hired claim-jumpers and thugs did not stop with accosting only the men but carried the threats to families as well. These were certainly trying times for the miners and their families.

It seemed to me that George was always away, leaving early in the morning and coming home "when he could." The Leadville mill often closed down for a few days. He was spending more and more time at Climax where the danger was greater. The weather was unusually severe. For days the thermometer registered from twenty to twenty-three below zero.

On one of these dark and bitterly cold days, when a gale was raging, I waited dinner for George. At seven o'clock I fed Harriet and little George and put them to bed. The storm increased in violence and snow was piled high against the windows. I put more blankets over the children because the bedrooms were so cold they might as well have been outdoors. I fed coal into the stoves and sat down with a book. I read while I waited; yet, I could not make sense out of a single page.

At the Tomboy I had spent as many nights alone and waiting but never with the uneasy feeling that gripped me these nights in Leadville. I feared for the children, for one thing. I had never used a gun, but I could certainly swing a hammer, so under my pillow was kept a vicious looking but useful carpenter's tool. If defense were ever needed I could rely on my quick temper to give me strength to use it. Beware intruder!

At nine o'clock I called Sally to ask about the train. "We have no idea when it can get in, Mrs. Backus. The snow is very deep, even out of Denver. When we get news I'll keep you posted." It was good to hear a friendly voice, especially when after a short time, she called me back.

"We've received a report from Breckenridge. The train just left there. I'll call you when it reaches Kokomo, if you want me to."

"Oh, please do, Sally. I won't go to bed," I told her.

I opened the book again. The wind howled and the house shuddered. I went upstairs to be sure the children were covered. At twelve the telephone rang.

"They're leaving Kokomo now, Mrs. Backus, and ought to reach Climax at one o'clock. Of course, we can't hear from them after that," Sally reported.

"Thank you, Sally, you're such a comfort in a time like this."

The front gate had blown open and was banging back and forth. I wrapped myself in my coat, tied a scarf around my head, put on overshoes, and ventured out to the gate to lock it. Back again by the stove, I took up the book. Then the lights went out. It could be a long time before they were on again because in such storms breaks in the power lines often occurred miles away and it took hours for the repair crews to reach the trouble.

So I lit the candles and bending low over the book continued to wait, wait, wait . . . until four in the morning when George dragged himself up the steps to the door I held open. Such was life in Leadville!

CHAPTER 32

We had a comfortable house, our love and interest in two sweet children, and always the happiness of just being together. George liked his work, even with its perils, and his future looked particularly bright if the plans of O. A. King worked out successfully.

But rival companies now were working claims they had acquired and the Climax Molybdenum Company was causing the most disruption and trouble for the Pingrey Company. The rival company workers outnumbered the Pingrey men three to one, and it seemed as if all of them were as competent trouble makers as they were miners.

Lawsuits brought against King in the Denver courts were decided in his favor, but it made little difference to the constant harassment of Pingrey miners who now had to fight as well as work.

Water was another bitterly disputed factor. To defend his water rights, along with all the other things, money that should have been invested in the Pingrey Mines Company was being poured out for more lawsuits which had little effect in protecting these rights, or their men from personal abuse and threats on their lives.

Every night when George came home I heard of new offenses, more interference, and brawls. Not even the merry jingling of sleigh bells in the streets, the joyous prattle of Baby George and Harriet's delight and progress in school, my Sunday School class, or Red Cross work could dispel the shadowy forebodings always at the back of my mind. I feared for George's life.

In the old days, claim-jumping brought swift retribution, but Leadville was not the lawless mining town it had once been. Yet, fear prevailed now. King himself worried about the strain on his wife, Marietta, as much as she worried concerning his safety.

The price of molybdenum increased enough for O. A. to interest a group of leading financiers such as Charles MacNeill, the copper king of Utah; multimillionaire Spencer Penrose, the mining and oil Croaesus; Oliver Shoup, and A. B. Carlton of Cripple Creek. In December of 1917, these financial titans, with O. A., rode into Leadville on a special train called the *Hundred Million Dollar Special*, this amount representing the combined capital of the group of passengers.

Next morning the little C & S train took them to Climax to inspect King's claims. Before the day was over, MacNeill, who began as a $75-a-month clerk before a mountain of almost solid low-grade copper had made his fortune, gave an enthusiastic opinion about Bartlett Peak: "Boys, she's just as big as Utah Copper!"

They paid King $125,000 down on their agreement to buy his claims for $300,000. King was to remain as executive for the new company and George was to be superintendent of operations if the plans worked out by King materialized.

These were successful and important business men; their influence would smooth away the difficulties. Moreover, the Federal Government had been convinced of the danger of Gesellschaft, and that company, well aware of the anti-German sentiment that was increasing, changed its name to The American Metals Company. This change of name did save them from governmental action, and the shares owned by enemy stockholders were turned over to the United States, which appointed five stockholders— Henry Morganthau, Andrew Mellon, George McEneny, Louis C. Clark and E. C. Converse. This action by the Government did not stop the Climax Company from instigating endless legal proceedings and making more trouble. Its workers, a rough class, had started out with orders to be tough, and they continued as they had begun.

The critical trouble went deeper. There was little, if any market for molybdenum. The War Minerals Board saw no future and no current need for it although the Liberty Motor, developed during the war, was made of molybdenum steel. Henry Ford was obtaining small amounts of it from Canada and using it sparingly in the axles of his cars because of the high price. He predicted its use if the price was much lower, but said that would probably be twenty years hence and he was not interested in investing. Years

Our two Colorado children—Harriet, born in Telluride in 1909, and George, born in Leadville in 1916.

later Ford tried to buy the Climax Company, but he had waited too long. The opinion he expressed was enough to discourage King's backers. They could not wait twenty years to develop a market and dropped the agreement.

O. A. made endless attempts to interest other financiers, without success. The Oracle had spoken! King had won the suits brought against him by the Climax Company but it cost him dearly. Just when there was peace between the Pingrey and Climax companies, King had no recourse but to sell out to them.

In the spring of 1918 the first cases of epidemic flu hit Leadville. Because of the very high altitude the danger was extreme. We avoided all groups and gatherings and anxiously watched the children. Death lists in the daily papers lengthened alarmingly and the citizens all knew we were facing a crisis.

A pregnant woman had little chance to pull through an attack, and I was pregnant, and the thought that our children might be left motherless appalled me. I must stay well!

Dr. Jeannotte was trying desperately to save his lovely niece, Theresa, who was fast slipping away. As a last hope, he gave her a serum that so far had not been proven. She rallied and recovered.

Within a few days the daily mortality list had risen from a normal three or four to fourteen—then sixteen. Dr. Sidney Blake, so badly needed, died of the plague. The two hospitals were filled to overflowing. Nurses worked almost around the clock. I was sick but reluctant to ask Dr. Jeannotte to come to see me, so I talked to him over the telephone. He would try to see me within a few days, he said. Now the death list had reached eighteen daily and two more doctors were dead!

Maude Stevenson, whose lungs were not strong, declared that she was needed and against the pleading of her husband, went into stricken homes to care for the sick.

Leadville desperately needed help. Denver, with difficulty, spared one doctor and a few nurses to help. Women from the notorious State Street "houses" showed innate nobility in the crisis and went wherever they were needed to nurse the sick.

My baby was stirring within me. I felt cold and my head ached. The beginning of the flu, I was sure. I telephoned Dr. Jeannotte again and exhausted by endless days and sleepless nights of work, he came.

"I can't promise anything from this serum," he said, "but it just might prevent the flu. I won't spread the doses as usually advised. I'll give you all three at once."

The disease, greatly aggravated by the altitude, was taking a dreadful toll. When the daily list of dead reached twenty-three, Leadville was unable to bury the victims fast enough. In the bleak cemetery on an unsheltered stretch of the plateau, more and more lay unburied, the snow their shrouds. I knew of one mother who had lain unconscious beside her dying daughter and later could never find where the child had been laid to rest.

The end of the war was in sight. The price of all metals was dropping. The supply of ore suitable for milling was dwindling rapidly, and George foresaw the permanent closing of the mill.

King's plans were meeting endless obstacles. The de-watering process and work going on in Leadville had not been successful and the operating company pulled out, leaving the mines to fill again.

The tragic months of the flu epidemic and the disappointing turn of events at Climax made me anxious to leave Leadville. I felt that our chances to escape the insidious disease and to safely have our baby would be greatly increased if we lived in a lower altitude.

George had gained valuable experience during the five years with O. A. King and the Pingrey company. His work was good and what he had done had been praised by King in mining circles.

When George received a letter from San Francisco, asking if he would complete some important work that had been left undone by a young man who was called into the service, he decided to accept the offer.

Early in November we left Leadville, thankful we were alive. I looked from the train window to the snow mound on the hill slope and remembered many whom we had known.

At Malta, the railroad junction, we went aboard a train of the main line of the Denver and Rio Grande. As we crossed Tennessee Pass, I felt a sense of relief, for during the last weeks and months "the sorrow of others had cast their shadows over me."

In California we were with my mother and others of my family, but I greatly missed my father, whose passing two years before was brought close to me by his accustomed chair and intimate possessions. Yet, it was good to pick up the threads of our lives with those we had known in school days.

With my children George and Harriet in Oakland, CA.

In January, 1919, our baby daughter, Mary Kathrine, was born; but to our great and lasting sorrow, she lived only two days. The memory of her remains vivid although we knew her for such a brief time.

For a long time I felt the pressure of living in the city, and I longed for the rugged, adventurous, yet infinitely more peaceful, primitive years of living in the high mountains.

George had time to look around and one day dropped in at the office of Edwin Letts Oliver, the inventor of the filter that George and Otto Johnson had rebuilt for the mill in Leadville. Already George was looking for leads to another job.

"Mr. Oliver," he said, "I am about to finish some special work here and then I expect to return to milling. I know you are well acquainted with mining companies and I thought perhaps you might know of some openings where I would fit in."

"Well, mining is very slow just now," Mr. Oliver said. "But, I've been thinking. You know my machine. How would you like to work for me?"

This spontaneous and unexpected offer was the beginning of thirty-five years of happy association. Without missing a day between positions, George joined the Oliver Filter Company; and under the friendship and leadership of Mr. Oliver, George helped develop the business, now a part of the Dorr-Oliver World Wide Company.

Whenever possible, I accompanied George on his business trips, as our being together was our greatest happiness. His work took us into most states of the Union, Canada, the Hawaiian Islands, and Australia.

We enjoyed traveling by automobile, streamliners, luxurious ocean liners, and airplanes. But the old creaking wagons, the sliding sleds, and the back of old Chief are among the most cherished memories of the woman who long ago had been a Tomboy Bride.

A happy Tomboy Bride and her husband.

EPILOGUE

The Tomboy Mine, the precious gold exhausted, was shut down in 1925. All the buildings torn down. A million-dollar highway now takes the place of the old mule trail over the pass in the mighty San Juans.

Britannia, that great copper producer, shut down permanently in 1934.

Elk City, Idaho, has wakened somewhat because a road was built making the little town more accessible to the outside world.

Leadville lives on because of Bartlett Mountain and the Climax, the largest mine development in the United States, source of valuable molybdenum. In 1943 during the Second World War, it was a contributing factor to the success of the Allies. By 1956 the Climax was producing thirty thousand tons a day, $25,000,000 worth a year. It has been estimated that one thousand dollars invested in the Climax during the troubled times of the Pingrey operations would today be worth five million.

In 1964 newspapers reported a record blast, the biggest ever staged in this country when the Climax Molybdenum Company broke loose over one million tons of molybdenum ore and dropped it six hundred feet to their mine known as the Glory Hole at Climax. Nearly half a million pounds of explosives were used, and black dust was hurled fifteen hundred feet high against the face of the twelve-thousand-foot height of Bartlett Peak.

When O. A. King was asked by a Climax company official how he obtained the seventy-two percent return from the ore in the early days, his answer was that it was due entirely to the experiments and work of George Backus.

And so far as we know, the flotation process, along with some

259

of his own formulas and ideas for the separation of molybdenum, is still a basic part of processing the "gray gold" into its fabulous future.

Throughout our high school and college days and fifty-seven happy years together, George and I shared a life of many blessings.

In July 1964, with my arms around him, my beloved went peacefully to eternal sleep.

AFTERWORD

I grew up listening to my grandmother's stories about her adventures
with my grandfather. I also heard them from my mother, Harriet
Anna Backus Walton, who typed several early drafts of Tomboy
Bride on a manual typewriter before the first edition was self-
published fifty years ago.

My grandparents didn't shy away from adventure, that's for
sure! After living in mining camps and towns for thirteen years,
George and Harriet began a new phase of their life, raising their
family in Oakland and traveling for George's business—together.

The new era was launched when George met with Edwin
Letts Oliver shortly after leaving Leadville. "Oliver Filter"
became a very familiar term during my growing-up years in
Oakland, since George's thirty-four years with the Oliver Filter
(later Dorr-Oliver) Company provided the couple with many
more opportunities for travel and storytelling. The biggest story is
told in the huge scrapbook Harriet created that begins:

> *"On Board S.S. Lurline Los Angeles, Cal. June 8, 1939. At*
> *long last we have started our adventure after a send-off that quite*
> *thrilled me to the bone..."*

Their voyage on the S.S. Lurline took them to Australia for
the Oliver Filter Company, from 1939 to 1940, just before WWII
erupted in the Pacific. This was a rich source of many more stories
about their travels and the fascinating people she met and the
many more friends she made along the way.

The Backus home at 355 Adams Street was family central for
many years. I have very fond memories there, including the huge

holiday dinners, and of my grandma and her love of peanut butter and thick lambchops, and playing Canasta with her.

Hattie was a remarkable person in many ways. She was to me a study in fascinating contrasts. Her life was centered around her husband, and the devotion to him that she describes in the book was just as clear to their grandchildren. Yet she was at the same time fearlessly independent and strong on her own. She had Victorian-era conservative morals, but she was also an adventurous young woman, a combination of old fashioned and modern. She was fiercely strong and domineering in some situations, generous and compassionate in others.

She was sixty-two when I was born, so I knew her as the grandma who hosted large family gatherings and took loving care of my grandfather as his Parkinson's disease progressed. I didn't witness the previous side of her that considered living in a tent in Idaho to "suit her fine," and I didn't appreciate until later that raised as a city girl she braved temperatures down to thirty degrees below, rode horseback over terrifying mountain trails, and didn't seem to mind snowshoeing and falling headfirst into deep snowdrifts.

Duane Smith, a professor of history at Fort Lewis College, interviewed her numerous times for his book *A Visit with the Tomboy Bride*. He told me that, as any good scholar would, he checked up on his sources to ascertain their veracity. He never found Hattie's stories inaccurate, confirming what her family had suspected for a long time: she had a nearly perfect memory and retained an amazing amount of detail, especially about her friends. She loved to talk about the old days, so the family knew the stories long before the book was published.

She'd even tell her stories when the audience wasn't listening.

I remember my grandmother as being in charge of the family—a matriarch in many senses of the word. She had no tolerance for alcohol or tobacco and would not allow the use of either in her home. She regularly had twenty or more people over for holiday dinners and loved to host such occasions.

She stayed active all her life, studying Spanish and reading Reader's Digest in Spanish so she could keep current. She wasn't interested in sports—except for "her" baseball team, the San Francisco Giants and her favorite player Willie Mays.

George S. Backus, baby Robert Walton, and Harriet Fish Backus at 355 Adams Street, Oakland, California in 1948.

Her patriotism was legion. She was so proud of the men in her family who served their country in the military for many generations (George was in ROTC through college but never served on active duty). My mother told me that her mother lost her third child not only due to life at high altitude and exposure to the 1918 flu epidemic, but also because she was so steadfast in rationing food during the WWI that she suffered from poor nutrition. During and after the WWII, she volunteered thousands of hours for the USO and the Ground Air Watch (in which the air force trained citizens to spot enemy versus friendly airplanes).

Near the end of the Idaho section of this book, she described herself as "budget-minded" when she recommended they walk and take the streetcar rather than taking an expensive taxi. Their real mettle came out, however, after the stock market crashed in 1929. Like many others at that time, they had purchased stock "on the margin." When the value of their shares in Oliver Filter Company plummeted, they faced a difficult situation because they owed such a large amount of money to his employer. According to my mother, many employees declared bankruptcy because they were unable to pay the large amount they owed, but not Hattie and George. It took them twenty years of installment payments, but they paid it all back.

When it came to religion, she and George were very open minded and tolerant. As she said in the book, the denomination of a church made little difference to them. She attended the Unitarian Church in Oakland for many years and was extremely proud of the fact that her church welcomed people of all faiths to come worship there.

Hattie was eighty-four when *Tomboy Bride* was first published, fulfilling her long-time dream. She received praise and correspondence about the book from all over the world and was thrilled to communicate with old friends and people she never met. The correspondence hasn't ended, and her family continues to hear from people charmed by the story and the woman.

Harriet Anna Fish Backus, the Tomboy Bride, passed on at the age of ninety-two in 1977, in the town where she was born. Her son George passed in 1989, survived by his daughters Kathy (and her daughters Kristen and Kerry), and Susan (and her daughters Elizabeth and Sarah). My mother, Hattie's daughter Harriet Anna Backus Walton, passed on in 2001 also at the age of ninety-two, in Portland, Oregon, near me and my wife Kristi (and our two sons Courtney and Seth).

Robert G. Walton, Grandson of Harriet Fish Backus

TIMELINE

Year	Event
1880	Tomboy Mine officially opens.
1883	George Stitzel Backus is born in Fort Walla Walla, Washington.
1885	Harriet Anna Fish is born in Oakland, California.
1894	Tomboy Mine starts producing gold ore.
1900	George moves to Oakland to attend high school and meets Harriet Fish.
1906	George graduates from UC Berkeley and is hired by Japan Flora Mine in Colorado. Harriet and George marry in Denver and move to the Savage Basin at 11,500 feet.
1909	Harriet Anna Backus is born in the Miner's Hospital in Telluride.
1910	The Backus family moves to Britannia Beach, British Columbia.
1912	The family moves to Elk City, Idaho.
1913	The family moves to Leadville, Colorado.
1916	George Fish Backus is born in Leadville, Colorado.
1917	USA declares war on Germany and enters World War I.
1919	The family moves back to Oakland, California.
1919	George is hired by Oliver Filter Company.
1925	Tomboy Mine closes.
1929	The stock market crashes, signaling the beginning of the Great Depression.
1947	Grandchildren Katherine Elizabeth Backus and Robert G. Walton are born.
1952	Granddaughter Susan Kimberly Backus is born.
1953	George retires from Oliver Filter after 37 years.
1964	George Stitzel Backus passes in Oakland.
1977	Harriet Fish Backus passes in Oakland.

BOOK CLUB DISCUSSION QUESTIONS
by Isabel Marlens

1. Harriet lived in a time of distinct, codified gender roles. As a mother and housewife, she always knew exactly what was expected of her. From all accounts she was confident, happy, secure, and she drew great satisfaction from her relationship with her husband. Today, a woman is encouraged to choose the way of life most appealing to her. Is it possible that having too many choices might sometimes lead to confusion, unhappiness, and dissatisfaction rather than proving a means to prevent them?

2. What are the most important factors that determine whether people are happy or unhappy? Socioeconomic position? Physical location? Personal relationships? Innate temperament? In Elk City, Harriet meets Mrs. Glade, a woman whose eyes "seemed to tell a story of loneliness and frustration." Meanwhile, Harriet, living a similar (if slightly less stagnant) life herself, declares that she is entirely content. What kind of person does it take to be happy in Harriet's position? Do you feel that you would be?

3. While living in Elk City, Harriet meets Mrs. Clifton, a woman who sank into prostitution when she was abandoned by her husband with two young children and no means of making a meaningful income. Her sons are then sent to a public institution in a far-off city. Do you feel it would have been better for the children if she had continued to work at menial jobs and kept the family together, albeit in dire poverty? Or were her sons better off with their mother able to pay for their education and necessities, even if it meant they never saw her again?

4. Of Mrs. Clifton's pre-prostitution poverty Harriet remarks: "People sympathized, said it was a shame, and tried to be kind in small ways." But there was no social structure in place to prevent her fall. What does it say about a community/society that it allows such things to happen? Should institutions exist that provide women with better options? Or should it be the duty of friends and neighbors to help out those in need? Under what circumstances might the same thing happen today?

5. How did it change Telluride society in Harriet's day that, rather than just breaking up the unions, the union men were driven out of town entirely? How would Tomboy have been different in Harriet's time if the strikers had remained as prominent and celebrated members of the community? Would Telluride be different today if their children and grandchildren were here now?

6. In Harriet's time, the idea was beginning to arise that certain working conditions might be unethical. This idea led to the institution of standards for the humane treatment of laborers still in place today. What similarly significant cultural and ethical shifts might be taking place in our time?

7. While living in Britannia Beach, Harriet's daughter nearly dies from a serious case of gastroenteritis. Her close friend Beth had recently lost her own child. Beth and Harriet lived at a time when, for every 1,000 live births, six to nine women in the United States died of pregnancy-related complications, and approximately 100 infants died before they reached the end of their first year. People were legitimately fearful that a slight winter cold might turn lethal; any ailment that would today call for a course of antibiotics was then genuinely life threatening. How do you feel this constant specter of death might affect your approach to life? To loss? To grieving? Are we more willing to express emotion today because we're "safer" with more medical knowledge and support?

8. Harriet had the dedication and confidence to write a memoir of her personal life—and most would agree that it was worth the

effort. Was it the remote and unusual places she lived that make her account so captivating? Was it her personality and approach to life? Was it the language she uses to describe everyday events? Do you feel that anyone could write a memoir and find a way to make it interesting, or need one's life be marked by extraordinary events?

9. It took Harriet some time before she was able to cook successfully at 11,500 feet. Share your most notable high-altitude cooking failure!